D1018375

The Arrogance of Power

THE

ARROGANCE

OF

POWER

by

J. William Fulbright

CHAIRMAN
SENATE FOREIGN RELATIONS COMMITTEE
THE UNITED STATES SENATE

Random House

New York

ACKNOWLEDGMENTS

To MANY of my colleagues in the Senate and members of the staff of the Committee on Foreign Relations, I am grateful for their patience and understanding during innumerable discussions of the ideas contained in this book. To the authors and journalists who have written with precision and with objectivity about the issues and the events discussed herein, I am deeply indebted. I have also learned a great deal from the expert witnesses; members of the Administration; the scholars; the former military leaders and diplomats who have testified before the Committee on Foreign Relations. From all, I have received facts and opinions for which I am grateful, without, of course, holding any of them responsible for my own conclusions contained herein.

To the Johns Hopkins School of Advanced International Studies and its distinguished Dean, Dr. Francis Wilcox, I am indebted for having been given the privilege of delivering the Christian A. Herter Lectures, which constitute a portion of this book.

I am especially indebted to Dr. Seth Tillman for his friendship, wise counsel, and assistance in the writing of this book.

Finally, a word of appreciation to Peggy Brown for the long hours of typing and retyping and editing of the Lectures and the notes which resulted in this manuscript.

PREFACE

IN 1964 THE FACULTY of the Johns Hopkins School of Advanced International Studies established the Christian A. Herter Lecture Series with the idea in mind that our lecture platform here in Washington might be used by highly qualified individuals to present different points of view about our foreign policy and to examine in depth some of the basic issues that face the United States in a rapidly changing world.

For the 1966 series the faculty extended an invitation to the distinguished Chairman of the Senate Foreign Relations Committee, Senator J. William Fulbright, to speak on those aspects of American policy which he considered most important and which the American people ought to be thinking about. He chose as his topic "The Arrogance of Power," and he proceeded to deliver three lectures: The Higher Patriotism, The Revolution Abroad, and The Arrogance of Power.

This book is an outgrowth of those lectures. The basic theme remains the same but the original lectures have been expanded, a number of new topics have been developed, and much new material has been added.

It is not my purpose in these pages to review Senator Fulbright's book but I cannot resist the temptation to say a few words about it. His thesis can be simply put. He rightly points out that many great empires in the past have collapsed because their leaders did not have the wisdom and the good judgment to use their power wisely and well. For the most part the United States has made good use of its many blessings both on the domestic front and in connection with our foreign policy. We have now reached that historical point, however, "at which a great nation is in danger of losing its perspective on what exactly is within the realm of its power and what is beyond it." In past centuries other great and powerful nations that have reached this critical juncture, "have aspired to too much, and by overextension of effort have declined and then fallen." It is this tragic fate, this fall from the pinnacle of power, that the writer hopes we can avoid.

In this respect the book is much less a criticism of the past than it is an expression of genuine concern about the future. It is not a denunciation of yesterday as much as it is a prescription of hope for tomorrow. It is not an angry protest as much as it is a sober warning that we must do our utmost to avoid the many pitfalls that have beset powerful nations in the past if we are to retain our position as a truly great power.

After examining some of our major foreign policies, and particularly our relations with revolutionary movements in Latin America and Asia, the author comes to the conclusion that there are two Americas. One is the America of Abraham Lincoln and Adlai Stevenson; the other is the America of Theodore Roosevelt and the modern superpatriots. Or to put it another way, two strands have coexisted in American history: "a dominant strand of democratic humanism and a lesser but durable strand of intolerant puritanism." The great challenge that faces us now, he believes, is to make certain "that the major strand in our heritage, the strand of humanism, tolerance, and accommodation, remains the dominant one." The America of Lincoln must prevail.

What are the chances this will happen? Senator Fulbright believes the current trend is toward "a more strident and aggressive American policy"; that is, in the direction of a policy closer to the spirit of Theodore Roosevelt than of Abraham Lincoln. To be sure, we are still trying to build bridges to the communist world and our foreign-aid program is helping to develop a higher standard of living in many lands. But military activities in Asia have proven to be a serious handicap. As a result there has been less emphasis on détente and economic development and more on military power; less emphasis on social change and more on the politics of war. These developments, he believes, have impaired America's image abroad. We must, therefore, dedicate ourselves anew to an "idea that mankind can hold to," if we wish to play a truly effective role in helping to shape the spirit of the age in which we live.

In the course of his analysis the author puts forth various suggestions about the direction our foreign policy should take. Space precludes any comment on these suggestions here. I do recall, however, Lord Acton's maxim that "power tends to corrupt; absolute power corrupts absolutely." This book is about the wise use of national power. In a nuclear age, in which the intelligent and responsible use of power is of urgent concern to all of us, I can think of no more compelling subject than this one.

There are a number of reasons I remain optimistic about the future of America. The first has to do with the great traditions of the American people. It is obviously true that, as a nation, we have made a good many mistakes in the past, some of which in retrospect we would like to disown. But on the whole, in our dealings with other nations, we have been noted for our generosity and our devotion to the great humanitarian principles of freedom and justice and human betterment.

In the second place, the growing importance of world opinion will have its inevitable impact upon the conduct of the powerful nations. It can still be argued that there is no power above the sovereign state—especially if it is equipped with nuclear weapons. It is also true that our position of power and influence in the world is dependent upon the friendly support of a good many small nations. To keep this support we shall be compelled in the future—much more than in the past—to make a good case for our policies before the bar of world opinion.

Still a third reason—and by no means the least—stems from the fact that in a free society like ours congressional leaders like Senator Fulbright can speak out in dissent on major policy issues. It is not often that the Chairman of the Foreign Relations Committee has openly and vigorously opposed his President on a really important foreign policy question. Indeed, if my memory serves me right, with the exception of Senator Fulbright, it has not been done since the end of World War II. But the fact that it *can* be done constitutes the best possible guarantee that what the Senator fears *might* happen to our country will never take place.

Senator Fulbright's rich background of experience in foreign policy can be matched by very few men in public life today. His long service with the House Committee on Foreign Affairs and the Senate Committee on Foreign Relations spans the terms of office of five presidents (Roosevelt, Truman, Eisenhower, Kennedy, and Johnson) and eight Secretaries of State (Hull, Stettinius, Byrnes, Marshall, Acheson, Dulles, Herter, and Rusk). He has thus had something to do with almost every important foreign policy issue since 1943. And, as chairmen of Senate committees go, he is still a relatively young man.

Readers who do not agree with the thesis developed in these pages—and there will be many—will nevertheless appreciate the frankness, the candor, and the keen insight with which the author presents his views. Every thinking American who is really interested in our foreign policy, whether he be a hawk or a dove or, perhaps like many of us, finds himself somewhere in between, ought to read this important and challenging book.

Francis O. Wilcox, Dean
The Johns Hopkins School of Advanced
International Studies
Washington, November 7, 1966

Contents

Contents

THE
ARROGANCE
OF POWER

AMERICA is the most fortunate of nations—fortunate in her rich territory, fortunate in having had a century of relative peace in which to develop that territory, fortunate in her diverse and talented population, fortunate in the institutions devised by the founding fathers and in the wisdom of those who have adapted those institutions to a changing world.

For the most part America has made good use of her blessings, especially in her internal life but also in her foreign relations. Having done so much and succeeded so well, America is now at that historical point at which a great nation is in danger of losing its perspective on what exactly is within the realm of its power and what is beyond it. Other great nations, reaching this critical juncture, have aspired to too much, and by overextension of effort have declined and then fallen.

The causes of the malady are not entirely clear but its recurrence is one of the uniformities of history: power tends to confuse itself with virtue and a great nation is peculiarly susceptible to the idea that its power is a sign of God's favor, conferring upon it a special responsibility for other nations— to make them richer and happier and wiser, to remake them, that is, in its own shining image. Power confuses itself with virtue and tends also to take itself for omnipotence. Once imbued with the idea of a mission, a great nation easily assumes that it has the means as well as the duty to do God's work. The Lord, after all, surely would not choose you as His agent and then deny you the sword with which to work His will. German soldiers in the First World War wore belt buckles imprinted with the words *"Gott mit uns."* It was approximately under this kind of infatuation—an exaggerated sense of power and an imaginary sense of mission—that the Athenians attacked Syracuse and Napoleon and then Hitler invaded Russia. In plain words, they overextended their commitments and they came to grief.

I do not think for a moment that America, with her deeply rooted democratic traditions, is likely to embark upon a campaign to dominate the world in the manner of a Hitler or Napoleon. What I do fear is that she may be drifting into commitments which, though generous and benevolent in intent, are so far-reaching as to exceed even America's great capacities. At the same time, it is my hope—and I emphasize it because it underlies all of the criticisms and proposals to be made in these pages—that America will escape those fatal temptations of power which have ruined other great nations and will instead confine herself to doing only that good in the world which she *can* do, both by direct effort and by the force of her own example.

The stakes are high indeed: they include not only America's continued greatness but nothing less than the survival of the human race in an era when, for the first time in human history, a living generation has the power of veto over the survival of the next.

The Power Drive of Nations

When the abstractions and subtleties of political science have been exhausted, there remain the most basic unanswered questions about war and peace and why nations contest the issues they contest and why they even care about them. As Aldous Huxley has written:

> There may be arguments about the best way of raising wheat in a cold climate or of re-afforesting a denuded mountain. But such arguments never lead to organized slaughter. Organized slaughter is the result of arguments about such questions as the following: Which is the best nation? The best religion? The best political theory? The best form of government? Why are other people so stupid and wicked? Why can't they see how good and intelligent *we* are? Why do they resist our beneficent efforts to bring them under our control and make them like ourselves?[1]*

Many of the wars fought by man—I am tempted to say most—have been fought over such abstractions. The more I puzzle over the great wars of history, the more I am inclined to the view that the causes attributed to them—territory, markets, resources, the defense or perpetuation of great principles—were not the root causes at all but rather explanations or excuses for certain unfathomable drives of human nature. For lack of a clear and precise understanding of exactly what these motives are, I refer to them as the "arrogance of power" —as a psychological need that nations seem to have in order to prove that they are bigger, better, or stronger than other nations. Implicit in this drive is the assumption, even on the part of normally peaceful nations, that force is the ultimate proof of superiority—that when a nation shows that it has the stronger army, it is also proving that it has better people, better institutions, better principles, and, in general, a better civilization.

Evidence for my proposition is found in the remarkable discrepancy between the apparent and hidden causes of some modern wars and the discrepancy between their causes and ultimate consequences.

---

* Footnotes appear in the Notes section following the text (see pp. 259–264).

The precipitating cause of the Franco-Prussian War of 1870, for example, was a dispute over the succession to the Spanish throne, and the ostensible "underlying" cause was French resistance to the unification of Germany. The war was followed by the completion of German unification—which probably could have been achieved without war—but it was also followed by the loss of Alsace-Lorraine, the humiliation of France, and the emergence of Germany as the greatest power in Europe, which could not have been achieved without war. The peace treaty, incidentally, said nothing about the Spanish throne, which everyone apparently had forgotten. One wonders to what extent the Germans were motivated simply by the desire to cut those haughty Frenchmen down to size and have a good excuse to build another monument in Berlin.

The United States went to war in 1898 for the stated purpose of liberating Cuba from Spanish tyranny, but after winning the war—a war which Spain had been willing to pay a high price to avoid—the United States brought the liberated Cubans under an American protectorate and incidentally annexed the Philippines, because, according to President Mc-Kinley, the Lord told him it was America's duty "to educate the Filipinos, and uplift and civilize and Christianize them, and by God's grace do the very best we could by them, as our fellowmen for whom Christ also died."[2]

Isn't it interesting that the voice was the voice of the Lord but the words were those of Theodore Roosevelt, Henry Cabot Lodge, and Admiral Mahan, those "imperialists of 1898" who wanted America to have an empire just because a big, powerful country like the United States *ought* to have an empire? The spirit of the times was expressed by Albert Beveridge, soon thereafter to be elected to the United States Senate, who proclaimed Americans to be "a conquering race": "We must obey our blood and occupy new markets and if necessary new lands," he said, because "In the Almighty's infinite plan . . . debased civilizations and decaying races" must disappear "before the higher civilization of the nobler and more virile types of man."[3]

In 1914 all Europe went to war, ostensibly because the heir to the Austrian throne had been assassinated at Sarajevo, but really because that murder became the symbolic focus of the incredibly delicate sensibilities of the great nations of Europe. The events of the summer of 1914 were a melodrama of abnormal psychology: Austria had to humiliate Serbia in order not to be humiliated herself but Austria's effort at recovering self-esteem was profoundly humiliating to Russia; Russia was allied to France, who had been feeling generally humiliated since 1871, and Austria in turn was allied to Germany, whose pride required that she support Austria no matter how insanely Austria behaved and who may in any case have felt that it would be fun to give the German Army another swing down the Champs-Élysées. For these ennobling reasons the world was plunged into a war which took tens of millions of lives, precipitated the Russian Revolution, and set in motion the events that led to another world war, a war which took tens of millions more lives and precipitated the worldwide revolutions of our time, revolutions whose consequences are beyond the foresight of any of us now alive.

The causes and consequences of war may have more to do with pathology than with politics, more to do with irrational pressures of pride and pain than with rational calculations of advantage and profit. There is a Washington story, perhaps apocryphal, that the military intellectuals in the Pentagon conducted an experiment in which they fed data derived from the events of the summer of 1914 into a computer and that, after weighing and digesting the evidence, the machine assured its users that there was no danger of war. What this "proves," if anything, is that computers are more rational than men; it also suggests that if there is a root cause of human conflict and of the power drive of nations, it lies not in economic aspirations, historical forces, or the workings of the balance of power, but in the ordinary hopes and fears of the human mind.

It has been said that buried in every woman's secret soul is a drum majorette; it might also be said that in all of our souls there is a bit of the missionary. We all like telling people what to do, which is perfectly all right except that most people do not like being told what to do. I have given my wife some splendid suggestions on household management but she has been so consistently ungrateful for my advice that I have stopped offering it. The phenomenon is explained by the Canadian psychiatrist and former Director-General of the World Health Organization, Brock Chisholm, who writes:

> . . . Man's method of dealing with difficulties in the past has always been to tell everyone else how they should behave. We've all been doing that for centuries.
>
> It should be clear by now that this no longer does any good. Everybody has by now been told by everybody else how he should behave. . . . The criticism is not effective; it never has been, and it never is going to be. . . .[4]

Ineffective though it has been, the giving—and enforcement—of all this unsolicited advice has at least until recently been compatible with the survival of the human race. Man is now, however, for the first time, in a situation in which the survival of his species is in jeopardy. Other forms of life have been endangered and many destroyed by changes in their natural environment; man is menaced by a change of environment which he himself has wrought by the invention of nuclear weapons and ballistic missiles. Our power to kill has become universal, creating a radically new situation which, if we are to survive, requires us to adopt some radically new attitudes about the giving and enforcement of advice and in general about human and international relations.

The enormity of the danger of extinction of our species is dulled by the frequency with which it is stated, as if a familiar threat of catastrophe were no threat at all. We seem to feel somehow that because the hydrogen bomb has not killed us yet, it is never going to kill us. This is a dangerous assumption because it encourages the retention of traditional attitudes about world politics when our responsibility, in Dr. Chisholm's words, is nothing less than "to re-examine all of the attitudes of our ancestors and to select from those attitudes things which we, on our own authority in these present circumstances, with our knowledge, recognize as still valid in this new kind of world. . . ."⁵

The attitude above all others which I feel sure is no longer valid is the arrogance of power, the tendency of great nations to equate power with virtue and major responsibilities with a universal mission. The dilemmas involved are pre-eminently American dilemmas, not because America has weaknesses that others do not have but because America is powerful as no nation has ever been before, and the discrepancy between her power and the power of others appears to be increasing. One may hope that America, with her vast resources and democratic traditions, with her diverse and creative population, will find the wisdom to match her power; but one can hardly be confident because the wisdom required is greater wisdom than any great nation has ever shown before. It must be rooted, as Dr. Chisholm says, in the re-examination of "all of the attitudes of our ancestors."

It is a tall order. Perhaps one can begin to fill it by an attempt to assess the attitudes of Americans toward other peoples and some of the effects of America's power on small countries whom she has tried to help.

Innocents Abroad

There are signs of the arrogance of power in the way Americans act when they go to foreign countries. Foreigners frequently comment on the contrast between the behavior of Americans at home and abroad: in our own country, they say, we are hospitable and considerate, but as soon as we get outside our own borders something seems to get into us and wherever we are we become noisy and demanding and we strut around as if we owned the place. The British used to say during the war that the trouble with the Yanks was that they were "overpaid, oversexed, and over here." During a recent vacation in Mexico, I noticed in a small-town airport two groups of students on holiday, one group Japanese, the other American. The Japanese were neatly dressed and were talking and laughing in a manner that neither annoyed anybody nor particularly called attention to themselves. The Americans, on the other hand, were disporting themselves in a conspicuous and offensive manner, stamping around the waiting room in sloppy clothes, drinking beer, and shouting to each other as if no one else were there.

This kind of scene, unfortunately, has become familiar in many parts of the world. I do not wish to exaggerate its significance, but I have the feeling that just as there was once something special about being a Roman or a Spaniard or an Englishman, there is now something about the consciousness of being an American abroad, something about the consciousness of belonging to the biggest, richest country in the world, that encourages people who are perfectly well behaved at home to become boorish when they are in somebody else's country and to treat the local citizens as if they were not really there.

One reason Americans abroad may act as though they "own the place" is that in many places they very nearly do: American companies may dominate large segments of a country's economy; American products are advertised on billboards and displayed in shop windows; American hotels and snack bars are available to protect American tourists from foreign influence; American soldiers may be stationed in the country, and even if they are not, the population are probably well aware that their very survival depends on the wisdom with which America uses her immense military power.

The Arrogance of Power

I think that when any American goes abroad, he carries an unconscious knowledge of all this power with him and it affects his behavior, just as it once affected the behavior of Greeks and Romans, of Spaniards, Germans, and Englishmen, in the brief high noons of their respective ascendancies. It was the arrogance of their power that led nineteenth-century Englishmen to suppose that if they shouted at a foreigner loud enough in English he was bound to understand, or that now leads Americans to behave like Mark Twain's "innocents abroad," who reported on their travels in Europe that

> The people of those foreign countries are very, very ignorant. They looked curiously at the costumes we had brought from the wilds of America. They observed that we talked loudly at table sometimes. . . . In Paris they just simply opened their eyes and stared when we spoke to them in French! We never did succeed in making these idiots understand their own language.[6]

The Fatal Impact

Reflecting on his voyages to Polynesia in the late eighteenth century, Captain Cook later wrote that "It would have been better for these people never to have known us." In a book on European explorations of the South Pacific, Alan Moorehead relates how the Tahitians and the Australian aborigines were corrupted by the white man's diseases, alcohol, firearms, laws, and concepts of morality, by what Moorehead calls "the long down-slide into Western civilization." The first missionaries to Tahiti, says Moorehead, were "determined to recreate the island in the image of lower-middle-class Protestant England. . . . They kept hammering away at the Tahitian way of life until it crumbled before them, and within two decades they had achieved precisely what they set out to do."[7] It is said that the first missionaries to Hawaii went for the purpose of explaining to the Polynesians that it was sinful to work on

Sunday, only to discover that in those bountiful islands nobody worked on any day.

Even when acting with the best of intentions, Americans, like other Western peoples who have carried their civilizations abroad, have had something of the same "fatal impact" on smaller nations that European explorers had on the Tahitians and the native Australians. We have not harmed people because we wished to; on the contrary, more often than not we have wanted to help people and, in some very important respects, we have helped them. Americans have brought medicine and education, manufactures and modern techniques to many places in the world; but they have also brought themselves and the condescending attitudes of a people whose very success breeds disdain for other cultures. Bringing power without understanding, Americans as well as Europeans have had a devastating effect in less advanced areas of the world; without knowing they were doing it, they have shattered traditional societies, disrupted fragile economies and undermined peoples' self-confidence by the invidious example of their own power and efficiency. They have done this in many instances simply by being big and strong, by giving good advice, by intruding on people who have not wanted them but could not resist them.

The missionary instinct seems to run deep in human nature, and the bigger and stronger and richer we are, the more we feel suited to the missionary task, the more indeed we consider it our duty. Dr. Chisholm relates the story of an eminent cleric who had been proselyting the Eskimos and said: "You know, for years we couldn't do anything with those Eskimos at all; they didn't have any sin. We had to teach them sin for years before we could do anything with them."[8] I am reminded of the three Boy Scouts who reported to their scoutmaster that as their good deed for the day they had helped an old lady to cross the street.

"That's fine," said the scoutmaster, "but why did it take three of you?"

"Well," they explained, "she didn't want to go."

The good deed above all others that Americans feel qualified to perform is the teaching of democracy. Let us consider the results of some American good deeds in various parts of the world.

Over the years since President Monroe proclaimed his doctrine, Latin Americans have had the advantages of United States tutelage in fiscal responsibility, in collective security, and in the techniques of democracy. If they have fallen short in any of these fields, the thought presents itself that the fault may lie as much with the teacher as with the pupils.

When President Theodore Roosevelt announced his "corollary" to the Monroe Doctrine in 1905, he solemnly declared that he regarded the future interventions thus sanctified as a "burden" and a "responsibility" and an obligation to "international equity." Not once, so far as I know, has the United States regarded itself as intervening in a Latin American country for selfish or unworthy motives—a view not necessarily shared, however, by the beneficiaries. Whatever reassurance the purity of our motives may give must be shaken a little by the thought that probably no country in human history has ever intervened in another except for motives it regarded as excellent.

For all our noble intentions, the countries which have had most of the tutelage in democracy by United States Marines have not been particularly democratic. These include Haiti, which is under a brutal and superstitious dictatorship; the Dominican Republic, which languished under the brutal Trujillo dictatorship for thirty years and whose second elected government since the overthrow of Trujillo is threatened, like the first, by the power of a military oligarchy; and of course Cuba, which, as no one needs to be reminded, has replaced its traditional right-wing dictatorships with a communist dictatorship.

Maybe, in the light of this extraordinary record of accomplishment, it is time for us to reconsider our teaching methods. Maybe we are not really cut out for the job of spreading the gospel of democracy. Maybe it would profit us to concentrate on our own democracy instead of trying to inflict our particular version of it on all those ungrateful Latin Americans who stubbornly oppose their North American benefactors instead of the "real" enemies whom we have so graciously chosen for them. And maybe—just maybe—if we left our neighbors to make their own judgments and their own mistakes, and confined our assistance to matters of economics and technology instead of philosophy, maybe then they would begin to find the democracy and the dignity that have largely eluded them, and we in turn might begin to find the love and gratitude that we seem to crave.

Korea is another example. We went to war in 1950 to defend South Korea against the Russian-inspired aggression of North Korea. I think that American intervention was justified and necessary: we were defending a country that clearly wanted to be defended, whose army was willing to fight and fought well, and whose government, though dictatorial, was patriotic and commanded the support of the people. Throughout the war, however, the United States emphasized as one of its war aims the survival of the Republic of Korea as a "free society," something which it was not then and is not now. We lost 33,629 American lives in that war and have since spent $5.61 billion on direct military and economic aid and a great deal more on indirect aid to South Korea. The country, nonetheless, remained until recently in a condition of virtual economic stagnation and political instability. Only now is economic progress being made, but the truly surprising fact is that having fought a war for three years to defend the freedom of South Korea, most Americans quickly lost interest in the state of the ward for whom they had sacrificed so much. It is doubtful that more than a handful of Americans now know or care whether South Korea is a "free society."

We are now engaged in a war to "defend freedom" in South Vietnam. Unlike the Republic of Korea, South Vietnam has an army which fights without notable success and a weak, dictatorial government which does not command the loyalty of the South Vietnamese people. The official war aims of the United States government, as I understand them, are to defeat what is regarded as North Vietnamese aggression, to demonstrate the futility of what the communists call "wars of national liberation," and to create conditions under which the South Vietnamese people will be able freely to determine their own future.

I have not the slightest doubt of the sincerity of the President and the Vice-President and the Secretaries of State and Defense in propounding these aims. What I do doubt, and doubt very much, is the ability of the United States to achieve these aims by the means being used. I do not question the power of our weapons and the efficiency of our logistics; I cannot say these things delight me as they seem to delight some of our officials, but they are certainly impressive. What I do question is the ability of the United States or any other Western nation to go into a small, alien, undeveloped Asian nation and create stability where there is chaos, the will to fight where there is defeatism, democracy where there is no tradition of it, and honest government where corruption is almost a way of life.

In the spring of 1966 demonstrators in Saigon burned American jeeps, tried to assault American soldiers, and marched through the streets shouting "Down with American imperialists," while a Buddhist leader made a speech equating the United States with the communists as a threat to South Vietnamese independence. Most Americans are understandably shocked and angered to encounter expressions of hostility from people who would long since have been under the rule of the Viet Cong but for the sacrifice of American lives and money. Why, we may ask, are they so shockingly ungrateful? Surely they must know that their very right to parade and protest and demonstrate depends on the Americans who are defending them.

The answer, I think, is that "fatal impact" of the rich and strong on the poor and weak. Dependent on it though the Vietnamese are, American strength is a reproach to their weakness, American wealth a mockery of their poverty, American success a reminder of their failures. What they resent is the disruptive effect of our strong culture upon their fragile one, an effect which we can no more avoid having than a man can help being bigger than a child. What they fear, I think rightly, is that traditional Vietnamese society cannot survive the American economic and cultural impact.

The evidence of that "fatal impact" is seen in the daily life of Saigon. A *New York Times* correspondent reported—and his information matches that of other observers on the scene —that many Vietnamese find it necessary to put their wives or daughters to work as bar girls or to peddle them to American soldiers as mistresses; that it is not unusual to hear a report that a Vietnamese soldier has committed suicide out of shame because his wife has been working as a bar girl; that Vietnamese have trouble getting taxicabs because drivers will not stop for them, preferring to pick up American soldiers who will pay outrageous fares without complaint; that as a result of the American influx bar girls, prostitutes, pimps, bar owners, and taxi drivers have risen to the higher levels of the economic pyramid; that middle-class Vietnamese families have difficulty renting homes because Americans have driven the rents beyond their reach, and some Vietnamese families have actually been evicted from houses and apartments by landlords who prefer to rent to the affluent Americans; that Vietnamese civil servants, junior army officers, and enlisted men are unable to support their families because of the inflation generated by American spending and the purchasing power of the G.I.s. One Vietnamese explained to the *New York Times* reporter that "Any time legions of prosperous white men descend on a rudimentary Asian society, you are bound to have trouble." Another said: "We Vietnamese are somewhat xenophobe. We don't like foreigners, any kind of foreigners, so that you shouldn't be surprised that we don't like you."[9]

Sincere though it is, the American effort to build the foundations of freedom in South Vietnam is thus having an effect quite different from the one intended. "All this struggling and striving to make the world better is a great mistake," said George Bernard Shaw, "not because it isn't a good thing to improve the world if you know how to do it, but because striving and struggling is the worst way you could set about doing anything."[10]

One wonders how much the American commitment to Vietnamese freedom is also a commitment to American pride—the two seem to have become part of the same package. When we talk about the freedom of South Vietnam, we may be thinking about how disagreeable it would be to accept a solution short of victory; we may be thinking about how our pride would be injured if we settled for less than we set out to achieve; we may be thinking about our reputation as a great power, fearing that a compromise settlement would shame us before the world, marking us as a second-rate people with flagging courage and determination.

Such fears are as nonsensical as their opposite, the presumption of a universal mission. They are simply unworthy of the richest, most powerful, most productive, and best educated people in the world. One can understand an uncompromising attitude on the part of such countries as China or France: both have been struck low in this century and a certain amount of arrogance may be helpful to them in recovering their pride. It is much less comprehensible on the part of the United States—a nation whose modern history has been an almost uninterrupted chronicle of success, a nation which by now should be so sure of its own power as to be capable of magnanimity, a nation which by now should be able to act on the proposition that, as George Kennan said, "there is more respect to be won in the opinion of the world by a resolute and courageous liquidation of unsound positions than in the most stubborn pursuit of extravagant or unpromising objectives."[11]

The cause of our difficulties in Southeast Asia is not a deficiency of power but an excess of the wrong kind of power, which results in a feeling of impotence when it fails to achieve its desired ends. We are still acting like Boy Scouts dragging reluctant old ladies across streets they do not want to cross. We are trying to remake Vietnamese society, a task which certainly cannot be accomplished by force and which probably cannot be accomplished by any means available to outsiders. The objective may be desirable, but it is not feasible. As Shaw said: "Religion is a great force—the only real motive force in the world; but what you fellows don't understand is that you must get at a man through his own religion and not through yours."[12]

With the best intentions in the world the United States has involved itself deeply in the affairs of developing nations in Asia and Latin America, practicing what has been called a kind of "welfare imperialism." Our honest purpose is the advancement of development and democracy, to which end it has been thought necessary to destroy ancient and unproductive modes of life. In this latter function we have been successful, perhaps more successful than we know. Bringing skills and knowledge, money and resources in amounts hitherto unknown in traditional societies, the Americans have overcome indigenous groups and interests and become the dominant force in a number of countries. Far from being bumbling, wasteful, and incompetent, as critics have charged, American government officials, technicians, and economists have been strikingly successful in breaking down the barriers to change in ancient but fragile cultures.

Here, however, our success ends. Traditional rulers, institutions, and ways of life have crumbled under the fatal impact of American wealth and power but they have not been replaced by new institutions and new ways of life, nor has their breakdown ushered in an era of democracy and development. It has rather ushered in an era of disorder and demoralization because in the course of destroying old ways of doing things, we have also destroyed the self-confidence and self-reliance without which no society can build indigenous institutions. Inspiring as we have such great awe of our efficiency and wealth, we have reduced some of the intended beneficiaries of our generosity to a condition of dependency and self-denigration. We have done this for the most part inadvertently: with every good intention we have intruded on fragile societies, and our intrusion, though successful in uprooting traditional ways of life, has been strikingly unsuccessful in implanting the democracy and advancing the development which are the honest aims of our "welfare imperialism."

American Empire or American Example?

Despite its dangerous and unproductive consequences, the idea of being responsible for the whole world seems to be flattering to Americans and I am afraid it is turning our heads, just as the sense of universal responsibility turned the heads of ancient Romans and nineteenth-century British.

In 1965 Henry Fairlie, a British political writer for *The Spectator* and *The Daily Telegraph,* wrote what he called "A Cheer for American Imperialism."[13] An empire, he said, "has no justification except its own existence." It must never contract; it "wastes treasure and life"; its commitments "are without rhyme or reason." Nonetheless, according to Fairlie, the "American empire" is uniquely benevolent, devoted as it is to individual liberty and the rule of law, and having performed such services as getting the author released from a Yugoslav jail simply by his threatening to involve the American Consul, a service which he describes as "sublime."

What romantic nonsense this is. And what dangerous nonsense in the age of nuclear weapons. The idea of an "American empire" might be dismissed as the arrant imagining of a British Gunga Din except that it surely strikes a responsive chord in at least a corner of the usually sensible and humane American mind. It calls to mind the slogans of the past about the shot fired at Concord being heard 'round the world, about "manifest destiny" and "making the world safe for democracy," and the demand for "unconditional surrender" in World War II. It calls to mind President McKinley taking counsel with the Supreme Being about his duty to the benighted Filipinos.

The "Blessings-of-Civilization Trust," as Mark Twain called it, may have been a "Daisy" in its day, uplifting for the soul and good for business besides, but its day is past. It is past because the great majority of the human race is demanding dignity and independence, not the honor of a supine role in an American empire. It is past because whatever claim America may make for the universal domain of her ideas and values is balanced by the communist counter-claim, armed like our own with nuclear weapons. And, most of all, it is past because it never should have begun, because we are not God's chosen saviour of mankind but only one of mankind's more successful and fortunate branches, endowed by our Creator with about the same capacity for good and evil, no more or less, than the rest of humanity.

An excessive preoccupation with foreign relations over a long period of time is more than a manifestation of arrogance; it is a drain on the power that gave rise to it, because it diverts a nation from the sources of its strength, which are in its domestic life. A nation immersed in foreign affairs is expending its capital, human as well as material; sooner or later that capital must be renewed by some diversion of creative energies from foreign to domestic pursuits. I would doubt that any nation has achieved a durable greatness by conducting a "strong" foreign policy, but many have been ruined by expending their energies in foreign adventures while allowing their domestic bases to deteriorate. The United States emerged as a world power in the twentieth century, not because of what it had done in foreign relations but because it had spent the nineteenth century developing the North American continent; by contrast, the Austrian and Turkish empires collapsed in the twentieth century in large part because they had so long neglected their internal development and organization.

If America has a service to perform in the world—and I believe she has—it is in large part the service of her own example. In our excessive involvement in the affairs of other countries we are not only living off our assets and denying our own people the proper enjoyment of their resources, we are also denying the world the example of a free society enjoying its freedom to the fullest. This is regrettable indeed for a nation that aspires to teach democracy to other nations, because, as Edmund Burke said, "Example is the school of mankind, and they will learn at no other."[14]*

The missionary instinct in foreign affairs may, in a curious way, reflect a deficiency rather than an excess of national self-confidence. In America's case the evidence of a lack of self-confidence is our apparent need for constant proof and reassurance, our nagging desire for popularity, our bitterness and confusion when foreigners fail to appreciate our generosity and good intentions. Lacking an appreciation of the dimensions of our own power, we fail to understand our enormous and disruptive impact on the world; we fail to understand that no matter how good our intentions—and they are, in most cases, decent enough—other nations are alarmed by the very existence of such great power, which, whatever its benevolence, cannot help but remind them of their own helplessness before it.

Those who lack self-assurance are also likely to lack magna-

---

* The services America can perform in the world—other than that of her own example—are discussed in Chapter 11.

nimity, because the one is the condition of the other. Only a nation at peace with itself, with its transgressions as well as its achievements, is capable of a generous understanding of others. Only when we Americans can acknowledge our own past aggressive behavior—in such instances, for example, as the Indian wars and the wars against Mexico and Spain—will we acquire some perspective on the aggressive behavior of others; only when we can understand the human implications of the chasm between American affluence and the poverty of most of the rest of mankind will we be able to understand why the American "way of life" which is so dear to us has few lessons and limited appeal to the poverty-stricken majority of the human race.

It is a curiosity of human nature that lack of self-assurance seems to breed an exaggerated sense of power and mission. When a nation is very powerful but lacking in self-confidence, it is likely to behave in a manner dangerous to itself and to others. Feeling the need to prove what is obvious to everyone else, it begins to confuse great power with unlimited power and great responsibility with total responsibility: it can admit of no error; it must win every argument, no matter how trivial. For lack of an appreciation of how truly powerful it is, the nation begins to lose wisdom and perspective and, with them, the strength and understanding that it takes to be magnanimous to smaller and weaker nations.

Gradually but unmistakably America is showing signs of that arrogance of power which has afflicted, weakened, and in some cases destroyed great nations in the past. In so doing we are not living up to our capacity and promise as a civilized example for the world. The measure of our falling short is the measure of the patriot's duty of dissent.

: *Part I* :

THE
HIGHER
PATRIOTISM

What do we mean by patriotism in the context of our times? . . . A patriotism that puts country ahead of self; a patriotism which is not short, frenzied outbursts of emotion, but the tranquil and steady dedication of a lifetime. There are words that are easy to utter, but this is a mighty assignment. For it is often easier to fight for principles than to live up to them.

ADLAI STEVENSON
New York, August 27, 1952

1

The Citizen and the University

To CRITICIZE one's country is to do it a service and pay it a compliment. It is a service because it may spur the country to do better than it is doing; it is a compliment because it evidences a belief that the country can do better than it is doing. "This," said Albert Camus in one of his "Letters to a German Friend," is "what separated us from you; we made demands. You were satisfied to serve the power of your nation and we dreamed of giving ours her truth. . . ."[1]

In a democracy dissent is an act of faith. Like medicine, the test of its value is not its taste but its effect, not how it makes people feel at the moment but how it makes them feel and moves them to act in the long run. Criticism may embarrass the country's leaders in the short run but strengthen their hand in the long run; it may destroy a consensus on policy while expressing a consensus of values. Woodrow Wilson once said that there was "such a thing as being too proud to fight"; there is also, or ought to be, such a thing as being too confident to conform, too strong to be silent in the face of apparent error. Criticism, in short, is more than a right; it is an act of patriotism, a higher form of patriotism, I believe, than the familiar rituals of national adulation. If nonetheless the critic is charged with a lack of patriotism, he can reply with Camus, "No, I didn't love my country, if pointing out what is unjust in what we love amounts to not loving, if insisting that what we love should measure up to the finest image we have of her amounts to not loving."[2]

What is the finest image of America? To me it is the image of a composite, or better still a synthesis, of diverse peoples and cultures, come together in harmony but not identity, in an open, receptive, generous, and creative society. Almost two hundred years ago a Frenchman who had come to live in America posed the question "What Is an American?" His answer, in part, was the following:

> Here individuals of all nations are melted into a new race of men, whose labors and posterity will one day cause great change in the world. Americans are the western pilgrims, who are carrying along with them that great mass of arts, sciences, vigour, and industry, which began long since in the east; they will finish the great circle. The Americans were once scattered all over Europe; here they are incorporated into one of the finest systems of population which has ever appeared, and which will hereafter become distinct by the power of the different climates they inhabit. . . . The American is a new man, who acts upon new principles; he must therefore entertain new ideas and form new opinions. From involuntary idleness, servile dependence, penury, and useless labor, he has passed to toils of a very different nature, rewarded by ample subsistence.—This is an American. . . .[3]

With due allowance for the author's exuberance, I think that his optimism was not far off the mark. We are an extraordinary nation, endowed with a rich and productive land, a humane and decent political tradition and a talented and energetic population. Surely a nation so favored is capable of extraordinary achievement, not only in the area of producing and enjoying great wealth, in which area our achievements have indeed been extraordinary, but also in the area of human and international relations, in which area, it seems to me, our achievements have fallen short of our capacity and promise.

My question is whether America can close the gap between her capacity and performance. My hope and my belief are that she can, that she has the human resources to conduct her affairs with a maturity which few if any great nations have ever achieved: to be confident but also tolerant, to be rich but also generous, to be willing to teach but also willing to learn, to be powerful but also wise.

I believe that America is capable of all of these things; I also believe she is falling short of them. If one honestly thought that America was doing the best she is capable of doing at home and abroad, then there would be no reason for criticism. But if one feels certain that she has the capacity to be doing very much better, that she is falling short of her promise for reasons that can and should be overcome, then approbation is a disservice and dissent the higher patriotism.

The Fear of Dissent

The discharge of the *duty* of dissent is handicapped in America by an unworthy tendency to fear serious criticism of our government. In the abstract we celebrate freedom of opinion as part of our patriotic liturgy; it is only when some Americans exercise it that other Americans are shocked. No one of course ever criticizes the right of dissent; it is always this particular instance of it or its exercise under these particular circumstances or at this particular time that throws people into a blue funk. I am reminded of Samuel Butler's observation that "People in general are equally horrified at hearing the Christian religion doubted, and at seeing it practiced."[4]

Intolerance of dissent is a well-noted feature of the American national character. Louis Hartz attributes it to the heritage of a society which was "born free," a society which is unnerved by serious criticism because it has experienced so little of it.[5] Alexis de Tocqueville took note of this tendency over a hundred years ago: "I know of no country in which there is so little independence of mind and real freedom of discussion as in America." Profound changes have occurred since *Democracy in America* first appeared and yet it may be asked whether recognition of the right of dissent has gained substantially in practice as well as in theory. The malady in Tocqueville's view was one of democracy itself: ". . . The smallest reproach irritates its sensibility and the slightest joke that has any foundation in truth renders it indignant; from the forms of its language up to the solid virtues of its character, everything must be made the subject of encomium. No writer, whatever be his eminence, can escape paying this tribute of adulation to his fellow citizens."[6]

From small-town gatherings to high-policy councils Americans are distressed when a writer or a politician or even a private citizen interrupts all this self-congratulation and expresses himself with simple, unadorned candor. The problem is worsening, among other reasons, because more and more of our citizens earn their livings by working for corporations and other large organizations, few of which are known to encourage political and other forms of heterodoxy on the part of their employees. The result is that more and more Americans face the dilemma of how, if at all, an individual can safely exercise honest individual judgment, indeed retain his capacity for it, in an environment in which the surest route to advancement is conformity with a barren and oppressive orthodoxy.

The problem is acute in the federal bureaucracy, whose congenital inhospitality to unorthodox ideas, were its dimensions only known, would allay the anxieties of the most agitated superpatriot. In most if not all government agencies originality, especially at the lower levels, is regarded as a form of insolence or worse, and the most valued, therefore the most professionally rewarding, quality is "soundness," which has very nearly become a euphemism for pedantry and mediocrity. The State Department, for example, with which I have had some experience, has many intelligent, courageous, and independent-minded Foreign Service Officers, but I have had occasion to notice that there are also sycophants and conformists, individuals in whose minds the distinction between official policy and personal opinion has disappeared. That, I suppose, is the worst of it: the censorship of ideas after a while no longer needs to be imposed; it is internalized, and the individual who may have begun his career as an idealist, full of hopes and ideas, becomes his own censor, purging himself of "unsound" ideas before he thinks them, converting himself from dreamer to drone by the time he reaches that stage in his career at which he can expect to be entrusted with some responsibility.

This is unfortunate indeed because the most valuable public servant, like the true patriot, is one who gives a higher loyalty to his country's ideals than to its current policy and who therefore is willing to criticize as well as to comply.

Some time ago I met an American poet, Mr. Ned O'Gorman, who had just returned from a visit to Latin America sponsored by the State Department. He said, and previously had written, that he had been instructed by American Embassy officials in the countries he visited that if he were questioned, by students and intellectuals with whom he was scheduled to meet, on such "difficult" questions as the Dominican Republic and Vietnam, he was to reply that he was "unprepared." Poets, as we all know, are ungovernable people and Mr. O'Gorman proved no exception. At a meeting with some Brazilian students he finally rebelled, with the following result as he described it: ". . . the questions came, swirling, battering, bellowing from the classroom. Outside the traffic and the oily electric heat. But I loved it. I was hell bent for clarity. I knew they wanted straight answers and I gave them. I had been gorged to sickness with embassy prudence. The applause was long and loud. The embassy man was furious. 'You are taking money dishonestly,' he told me. 'If the government pays you to do this tour you must defend it and not damn it.' It did no good when I explained to him that if I didn't do what I was doing, *then* I'd be taking the money dishonestly...."[7]

A high degree of loyalty to the President's policy is a requirement of good order within the Department of State, but it escapes me totally why American diplomats should not be proud to have American poets and professors and politicians demonstrate their country's political and intellectual health by expressing themselves with freedom and candor. As O'Gorman put it, ". . . I spoke with equal force of the glory and the tragedy of America. And that is what terrified the Americans."[8]

Criticism and Consensus

We must learn to treat our freedom as a source of strength, as an asset to be shown to the world with confidence and pride. No one challenges the value and importance of national consensus, but consensus can be understood in two ways. If it is interpreted to mean unquestioning support of existing policies, its effects can only be pernicious and undemocratic, serving to suppress differences rather than to reconcile them. If, on the other hand, consensus is understood to mean a general agreement on goals and values but not necessarily on the best means of realizing them, then and only then does it become a lasting basis of national strength. It is consensus in this sense which has made America strong in the past. Indeed, much of our national success in combining change with continuity can be attributed to the vigorous competition of men and ideas within a context of shared values and generally accepted institutions. It is only through this kind of vigorous competition of ideas that a consensus of values can sometimes be translated into a true consensus of policy. Or as Mark Twain plainly put it: "It were not best that we should all think alike; it is difference of opinion that makes horse races."[9]

Freedom of thought and discussion gives a democracy two concrete advantages over a dictatorship in the making of foreign policy: it diminishes the danger of an irretrievable mistake and it introduces ideas and opportunities that otherwise would not come to light.

The correction of errors in a nation's foreign policy is greatly assisted by the timely raising of voices of criticism within the nation. When the British launched their disastrous attack on Egypt, the Labour Party raised a collective voice of indignation while the military operation was still under way; refusing to be deterred by calls for national unity in a crisis, Labour began the long, painful process of recovering Great Britain's good name at the very moment when the damage was still being done. Similarly, the French intellectuals who protested France's colonial wars in Indochina and Algeria not only upheld the values of French democracy but helped pave the way for the enlightened policies of the Fifth Republic which have made France the most respected Western nation in the underdeveloped world. It has been in the hope of performing a similar service for America on a very modest scale that I criticized American intervention in the Dominican Republic and that some of my colleagues and I have raised questions about the wisdom of American military involvement in Vietnam.

The second great advantage of free discussion to democratic policy-makers is its bringing to light of new ideas and the supplanting of old myths with new realities. We Americans are much in need of this benefit because we are severely, if not uniquely, afflicted with a habit of policy-making by analogy: North Vietnam's involvement in South Vietnam, for example, is equated with Hitler's invasion of Poland and a parley with the Viet Cong would represent "another Munich." The treatment of slight and superficial resemblances as if they were full-blooded analogies—as instances, as it were, of history "repeating itself"—is a substitute for thinking and a misuse of history. The value of history is not what it seems to prohibit or prescribe but its general indications as to the kinds of policies that are likely to succeed and the kinds that are likely to fail, or, as one historian has suggested, its hints as to what is likely not to happen. Mark Twain offered guidance on the uses of history: "We should be careful," he wrote, "to get out of an experience only the wisdom that is in it—and stop there; lest we be like the cat that sits down on a hot stove-lid. She will never sit down on a hot stove-lid again—and that is well; but also she will never sit down on a cold one anymore."[10]

There is a kind of voodoo about American foreign policy. Certain drums have to be beaten regularly to ward off evil spirits—for example, the maledictions regularly uttered against North Vietnamese aggression, the "wild men" in Peking, communism in general, and President de Gaulle. Certain pledges must be repeated every day lest the whole free world go to rack and ruin—for example, we will never go back on a commitment no matter how unwise; we regard this alliance or that as absolutely "vital" to the free world; and of course we will stand stalwart in Berlin from now until Judgment Day. Certain words must never be uttered except in derision—the word "appeasement," for example, comes as near as any word can to summarizing everything that is regarded by American policy-makers as stupid, wicked, and disastrous.

I do not suggest that we should heap praise on the Chinese Communists, dismantle NATO, abandon Berlin, and seize every opportunity that comes along to appease our enemies. I do suggest the desirability of an atmosphere in which unorthodox ideas would arouse interest rather than anger, reflection rather than emotion. As likely as not, new proposals carefully examined would be found wanting and old policies judged sound; what is wanted is not change itself but the capacity for change. Consider the idea of "appeasement": in a free and healthy political atmosphere it would elicit neither horror nor enthusiasm but only interest in what precisely its proponent had in mind. As Winston Churchill once said: "Appeasement in itself may be good or bad according to the circumstances. . . . Appeasement from strength is magnanimous and noble and might be the surest and perhaps the only path to world peace."[11]

In addition to its usefulness of redeeming error and introducing new ideas, free and open criticism has a third, more abstract but no less important function in a democracy: it is therapy and catharsis for those who are troubled by something their country is doing; it helps to reassert traditional values, to clear the air when it is full of tension and mistrust. There are times in public life as in private life when one must protest, not solely or even primarily because one's protest will be politic or materially productive, but because one's sense of decency is offended, because one is fed up with political craft and public images, or simply because something goes against the grain. The catharsis thus provided may indeed be the most valuable of freedom's uses.

The Vietnam Protest Movement

While not unprecedented, protests against a war in the middle of the war are a rare experience for Americans. I see it as a mark of strength and maturity that an articulate minority have raised their voices against the Vietnamese war and that the majority of Americans are enduring this dissent, not without anxiety, to be sure, but for the moment at least with better grace and understanding than would have been the case in any other war of the twentieth century.

It is by no means certain that the relatively healthy atmosphere in which the debate has been taking place will not give way to a new era of McCarthyism. Critics of the Vietnamese war are being accused of a lack of patriotism, and these accusations are coming not only from irresponsible columnists but, with increasing frequency, from the highest levels of government. This situation is likely to become worse. The longer the Vietnamese war goes on without prospect of victory or negotiated peace, the higher the war fever will rise; hopes will give way to fears, and tolerance and freedom of discussion will give way to a false and strident patriotism.

In Mark Twain's novel *The Mysterious Stranger* a benevolent and clairvoyant Satan said the following about war and its corrosive effects on a society:

There has never been a just one, never an honorable one—on the part of the instigator of the war. I can see a million years ahead, and this rule will never change in so many as half a dozen instances. The loud little handful —as usual—will shout for the war. The pulpit will— warily and cautiously—object—at first; the great, big, dull bulk of the nation will rub its sleepy eyes and try to make out why there should be a war, and will say, earnestly and indignantly, "It is unjust and dishonorable, and there is no necessity for it." Then the handful will shout louder. A few fair men on the other side will argue and reason against the war with speech and pen, and at first will have a hearing and be applauded; but it will not last long; those others will outshout them, and presently the anti-war audiences will thin out and lose popularity. Before long you will see this curious thing: the speakers stoned from the platform, and free speech strangled by hordes of furious men who in their secret hearts are still at one with those stoned speakers—as earlier—but do not dare to say so. And now the whole nation—pulpit and all—will take up the war-cry, and shout itself hoarse, and mob any honest man who ventures to open his mouth; and presently such mouths will cease to open. Next the statesmen will invent cheap lies, putting the blame upon the nation that is attacked, and every man will be glad of those conscience-soothing falsities, and will diligently study them, and refuse to examine any refutations of them; and thus he will by and by convince himself that the war is just, and will thank God for the better sleep he enjoys after this process of grotesque self-deception.[12]

Past experience provides little basis for confidence that reason can prevail in an atmosphere of mounting war fever. In a contest between a hawk and dove the hawk has a great advantage, not because it is a better bird but because it is a bigger bird with lethal talons and a highly developed will to use them. Without illusions as to the prospect of success we must try nonetheless to bring reason and restraint into the emotionally charged atmosphere in which the Vietnamese war is now being discussed. Instead of trading epithets about the legitimacy of debate and about who is and is not giving "aid and comfort" to the enemy, we would do well to focus calmly and deliberately on the issue itself, recognizing that all of us make mistakes and that mistakes can be corrected only if they are acknowledged and discussed, and recognizing further that war is not its own justification, that it can and must be discussed unless we are prepared to sacrifice our traditional democratic processes to a false image of national unanimity.

In fact, the protesters against the Vietnamese war are in good historical company. On January 12, 1848, Abraham Lincoln rose in the United States House of Representatives and made a speech about the Mexican War worthy of Senator Wayne Morse. Lincoln's speech was an explanation of a vote he had recently cast in support of a resolution declaring that the war had been unnecessarily and unconstitutionally begun by President Polk. "When the war began," said Lincoln, "it was my opinion that all those who, because of knowing too *little*, or because of knowing too *much*, could not conscientiously approve the conduct of the President, in the beginning of it, should, nevertheless, as good citizens and patriots, remain silent on that point, at least till the war should be ended." Only when he was provoked by the introduction of resolutions expressly endorsing the justice of the war and by what he called "the continual effort of the President to argue every silent vote given for supplies into an endorsement of the justice and wisdom of his conduct," Lincoln explained, did he cast his vote in favor of the resolution condemning the war. "I admit," he said, "that such a vote should not be given, in mere party wantonness, and that the one given, is justly censurable, if it have no other, or better foundation. I am one of those who joined in that vote; and I did so under my best impression of the *truth* of the case."[13]

That is exactly what the students and professors and politicians who oppose the Vietnamese war have been doing: they have been acting on their "best impression of the truth of the case." Some of our superpatriots assume that any war the United States fights is a just war, if not indeed a holy crusade, but history does not sustain their view. No reputable historian would deny that the United States has fought some wars which were unjust, unnecessary, or both—I would suggest the War of 1812, the Civil War, and the Spanish-American War as examples of wars that were at least unnecessary. In an historical frame of reference it seems to me logical and proper to question the wisdom of our present military involvement in Asia.

The wisdom and productivity of the protest movement of students, professors, clergy, and others may well be questioned, but their courage, decency, and patriotism cannot be doubted. At the very least the student protest movement of the sixties is a moral and intellectual improvement on the panty raids of the fifties. In fact it is a great deal more: it is an expression of the national conscience and a manifestation of traditional American idealism. As one university publication characterized it, the "new radical" movement "is not shallow and sophomoric, it is not based on the traditional formula of generational defiance, and it is not the result of an infusion of foreign ideologies. It is based instead on personal disenchantment and the feeling of these radicals that they must repudiate a corrupted vision of society and replace it with a purer one."[14]

No student generation in recent history has faced both brighter lifetime possibilities and greater short-term uncertainties than the present one. The bright possibilities are those afforded by a prosperous and dynamic America; the uncertainties are those of a cruel and costly war in Asia, a war which has already taken thousands of American lives, a war whose end is not in sight, a war which may indeed grow larger in scale and destructiveness. The central issue in the debate here at home—the issue on which all other questions turn—is whether the sacrifices imposed on the present generation of young Americans are justified by the stakes of the war, whether the diversion of hundreds of thousands of our young men from their homes and jobs and families will yield rewards of freedom and security commensurate with their sacrifices.

It is one of life's injustices that young men must fight the wars that older men begin. To a great extent, therefore, the lives and hopes of the present student generation turn on the wisdom and judgment of the men of an older generation to whom the people have entrusted political power. Surely, considering what they themselves have at stake, it is not improper for young people to question the wisdom and judgment of the makers of our foreign policy. Surely it is the right of citizens in a democracy, especially citizens of military age, to ascertain that the great decisions of war and peace are made with care and deliberation. The calling of public men to account unquestionably adds to their burdens, but the convenience of policy-makers is not sufficient reason for the shutting down of public discussion. The responsibilities of high office are burdensome indeed but they are borne, let it be remembered, by men who actively sought or freely accepted them, men who accepted not only the obligation to use power but the obligation to account for its use as well.

Protesters against the Vietnamese war have been held up to scorn on the ground that they wish to "select their wars," by which it is apparently meant that it is hypocritical to object to this particular war while not objecting to war in general. I fail to understand what is reprehensible about trying to make moral distinctions between one war and another, between, for example, resistance to Hitler and intervention in Vietnam. From the time of Grotius to the drafting of the United Nations Charter international lawyers have tried to distinguish between "just wars" and "unjust wars." It is a difficult distinction of law and an even more difficult one of morality, but it is certainly a valid problem and, far from warranting contempt, those who try to make that most pertinent distinction deserve our sympathy and respect.

There can be no solution to a problem until it is first acknowledged that there is a problem. When Mr. Bill Moyers reported with respect to the Vietnam protests the President's "surprise that any one citizen would feel toward his country in a way that is not consistent with the national interest,"[15] he was denying the existence of a question as to where, in fact, the national interest lies. The answer, one must concede, is elusive, but there is indeed a question and it is a sign of the good health of this nation that the question is being widely and clearly posed.

With due respect for the honesty and patriotism of the student demonstrations, I would offer a word of caution to the young people who have organized and participated in them. As most politicians discover sooner or later, the most dramatic expression of grievances is not necessarily the most effective. That would seem to be especially true in the United States, a country easily and excessively alarmed by expressions of dissent. We are, for better or worse, an essentially conservative society; in such a society soft words are likely to carry more weight than harsh words and the most effective dissent is dissent expressed in an orderly, which is to say a conservative manner.

For these reasons such direct action as the burning of draft cards probably does more to retard than to advance the views of those who take such action. The burning of a draft card is a symbolic act, really a form of *expression* rather than of *action,* and it is stupid and vindictive to punish it as a crime. But it is also an unwise act, unwise because it is shocking rather than persuasive to most Americans and because it exposes the individual to personal risk without political reward.

The student, like the politician, must consider not only how to say what he means but also how to say it persuasively. The answer, I think, is that to speak persuasively one must speak in the idiom of the society in which one lives. The form of protest that might be rewarding in Paris or Rome, to say nothing of Saigon or Santo Domingo, would be absolutely disastrous in Washington. Frustrating though it may be to some Americans, it is nonetheless a fact that in America the messages that get through are those that are sent through channels, through the slow, cumbersome institutional channels devised by the founding fathers in 1787.

The good order and democracy of our society therefore depend on the keeping open of these channels. As long as every tendency of opinion can get a full and respectful hearing from the elected representatives of the people, as long as the classroom from primary school to graduate school is a place where freedom of thought is welcomed and encouraged, the teach-ins and the draft-card burnings and the demonstrations are unlikely to become the principal forms of dissent in America. It is only when the Congress fails to challenge the Executive, when the opposition fails to oppose, when politicians join in a spurious consensus behind controversial policies, and when institutions of learning sacrifice traditional functions to the short-term advantages of association with the government in power, that the campuses and streets and public squares of America are likely to become the forums of a direct and disorderly democracy.

The University and the Government

Whatever the circumstances of the moment, whatever the demands of government and industry on the universities— and whatever the rewards for meeting these demands—the highest function of higher education is what might be called the teaching of things in perspective, toward the purposes of enriching the life of the individual, cultivating the free and inquiring mind, and advancing the effort to bring reason, justice, and humanity into the relations of men and nations. Insofar as the study of politics is pertinent to these ends, the university is properly a place in which scholars analyze existing public policies with a view to determining whether they advance or retard the realization of basic human objectives and whether and how they should be changed. Only insofar as the university is a place in which ideas are valued above their practical application, in which there is greater interest in contributing to the sum of human knowledge than in helping a government agency to resolve some practical problem, is the university meeting its academic responsibility to its students and its patriotic responsibility to the country.

Obviously there are great mutual benefits in relations between the universities and government, but when the relationship becomes too close, too extensive, and too highly valued by the universities, the higher functions of the university are in danger of being compromised. The danger goes far beyond contractual associations with the Central Intelligence Agency, which, unfortunate though they are, are so egregious that once they become known, there is a tendency to terminate them with all possible haste, although at a lasting cost to the integrity of the institutions involved. Nor is there great danger inherent in government-sponsored research of and by itself; on the contrary, government contracts bring needed money to the universities and needed intellectual resources to the government. The danger lies rather in the extent and the conditions, implicit as well as explicit, of these governmental associations: as long as they involve secondary functions for the university they are not harmful, but when they become primary areas of activity, when they become the major source of the university's revenue and the major source of the scholar's prestige, then the "teaching of things in perspective" is likely to be neglected and the universality of the university compromised. The harm, in short, lies less in what is done in relation to the government than in what is neglected as a result of it.

Not having been a professor for some years, I must make it clear that I am expressing strong suspicions rather than firm convictions about the effects of government on the universities. I suspect that when a university becomes very closely oriented to the current needs of government, it takes on some of the atmosphere of a place of business while losing that of a place of learning. The sciences are emphasized at the expense of the humanities, and within the humanities the behavioral school of social science at the expense of the more traditional—and to my mind more humane—approaches. Generally, I would expect an interest in salable information pertaining to current problems to be emphasized at the expense of general ideas pertaining to the human condition.

In such an atmosphere there can be little room for intellectual individualists whose interest is in making a contribution to the sum of human knowledge without regard to its immediate uses. The kind of professor needed in the government-oriented university is one, I suspect, who though technically brilliant is philosophically orthodox, because the true dissenter, the man who dissents about purpose and not just technique, is likely to lose a sale.

"Sound" scholars produce "sound" disciples. In a research-oriented university, especially a government-research-oriented university, I would expect, the student who is highly valued is the one who can contribute to production. Obviously the graduate student is a more valuable research assistant than the undergraduate and the scientifically-oriented student is more valuable than the one who is interested in history or philosophy. The latter, indeed, is likely to find himself relegated to the charge of the lower echelon of the faculty, those, that is, who are condemned to teach.

In lending itself too much to the purposes of government, a university fails of its higher purposes. It is not contributing to the re-examination of the ideas of our ancestors on which human survival depends; it is not dealing with the central problems of the first generation in human history which holds the power of life and death over its progeny; it is not, in Archibald MacLeish's phrase, trying to produce "an idea that mankind can hold to."[16] It is not, therefore, meeting its responsibilities to its students and to society.

How might some of these considerations guide the universities toward a constructive contribution in the current crisis of our foreign relations?

I most emphatically do not think that the universities should act like recruits called to the colors. I do not think that the humanities must now give way to military science, that civil engineering must give way to military engineering, or that history and philosophy must give way to computerized "war games."

Unless it conceives itself as nothing more than the servant of the party in power, the university has a higher function to perform. The university, it is true, cannot separate itself from the society of which it is a part, but neither can the community of scholars accept existing public policies as if they set limits on "responsible" inquiry, as if the scholar's proper function, and only proper function, were to devise the technical means of carrying these policies out. The proper function of the scholar is not to exclude certain questions in the name of practicality, or in the name of a spurious patriotism, but to ask all possible questions, to ask what has been done wisely and what has been done foolishly and what the answers to these questions imply for the future. It would be a fine thing indeed if, instead of spending so much of their time playing "war games," political scientists were asking how it came about that we have had for so long to devote so great a part of our resources to war and its prevention, and whether we are condemned by forces beyond our control to continue to do so. The scholar can ask what is wrong with the "other side," but he must not fail to ask as well what is wrong with our side, remembering always that the highest devotion we can give is not to our country as it is but to a concept of what we would like it to be.

2

The Senate and
the Senator

A REPRESENTATIVE ASSEMBLY, wrote John Stuart Mill, has the responsibility "to be at once the nation's Committee of Grievances and its Congress of Opinions; an arena in which not only the general opinion of the nation, but that of every section of it, and, as far as possible, of every eminent individual whom it contains, can produce itself in full light and challenge discussion; where every person in the country may count upon finding somebody who speaks his mind as well or better than he could speak it himself . . . ; where those whose opinion is overruled feel satisfied that it is heard, and set aside not by a mere act of will, but for what are thought superior reasons, . . ."[1]

The American Constitution entrusts these functions to the Congress and particularly, in matters of foreign relations, to the Senate, which has the responsibility to review the conduct of foreign policy by the President and his advisers, to render advice whether it is solicited or not, and to grant or withhold its consent to major acts of foreign policy. In addition the Congress has a traditional responsibility, in keeping with the spirit if not the precise words of the Constitution, to serve as a forum of diverse opinions and as a channel of communication between the American people and their government. The discharge of these functions is not merely a prerogative of the Congress; it is a constitutional obligation, for the neglect of which the Congress can and should be called to public account.

In recent years the Congress has not been fully discharging these responsibilities in the field of foreign relations. The reduced role of the Congress and the enhanced role of the President in the making of foreign policy are not the result merely of President Johnson's ideas of consensus; they are the culmination of a trend in the constitutional relationship between President and Congress that began in 1940, which is to say, at the beginning of this age of crisis.

The cause of the change is crisis. The President has the authority and resources to make decisions and take actions in an emergency; the Congress does not. Nor, in my opinion, should it; the proper responsibilities of the Congress are those spelled out by Mill—to reflect and review, to advise and criticize, to grant or withhold consent. In the last twenty-five years American foreign policy has encountered a shattering series of crises and inevitably, or almost inevitably, the effort to cope with these has been Executive effort, while the Congress, inspired by patriotism, importuned by Presidents, and deterred by lack of information, has tended to fall in line behind the Executive. The result has been an unhinging of traditional constitutional relationships; the Senate's constitutional powers of advice and consent have atrophied into what is widely regarded as, though never asserted to be, a duty to give prompt consent with a minimum of advice.

This situation is not fundamentally the fault of individuals. It is primarily the result of events, and the problem is not one of apportioning blame but of finding a way to restore the constitutional balance, of finding ways by which the Senate can discharge its *duty* of advice and consent in an era of permanent crisis.

Presidents must act in emergencies, especially when the country is at war, and of the last five Presidents only one has not had to wage a sizable war for at least a part of his period in office. Beset with the anxieties of a foreign crisis, no President can relish the idea of inviting opinionated and tendentious Senators into his high-policy councils. His reluctance is human but it is not in keeping with the intent of the Constitution. As representatives of the people Senators have the duty, not merely the right, to render advice, not on the day-to-day conduct of foreign policy, but on its direction and philosophy as these are shaped by major decisions. I conclude that when the President, for reasons with which we can all sympathize, does not invite us into his high-policy councils, it is our duty to infiltrate them as best we can.

A distinction, to be sure, must be made between the making and the conduct of foreign policy. In a number of speeches in recent years, I have deplored the tendency of Senators and Representatives to interfere excessively in the *conduct* of policy, by advising on and complaining about the routine activities of American diplomats, especially those below the top level, and by such practices as the use of the annual foreign-aid debate as an occasion to air extraneous grievances —extraneous, that is, to foreign aid—ranging from Ecuadoran incursions on the rights of California fishermen to proposals for the withdrawal of most-favored-nation trade treatment from Yugoslavia.

The philosophy and direction of foreign policy are a different matter altogether. It is ironic that the Congress, while steadily if erratically expanding its incursions on the day-to-day *conduct* of policy, where its influence is inappropriate and often mischievous, has just as steadily been resigning from its responsibilities in the *making* of policy. It is the latter trend which poses the more serious problems for the nation, and it is my hope, as I shall explain further, that through its extensive public hearings on Vietnam, China, and other issues, the Senate Foreign Relations Committee is contributing to a revival of the Senate's traditional authority in foreign affairs and thereby to the restoration of a proper constitutional balance between the Executive and the legislature. It is too soon, however, to judge whether the revival of debate in the Senate signals the beginning of a trend toward constitutional readjustment or is only a manifestation of widespread anxiety about the war in Vietnam.

Decline of the Senate

I have had some personal experiences which illustrate the extent to which the trend toward Executive predominance has gone and the extraordinary difficulty a Senator has in trying to discharge his responsibility to render useful advice and to grant or withhold his consent with adequate knowledge and sound judgment.

The Bay of Pigs. In the spring of 1961 I was invited to participate with President Kennedy's advisers in the deliberations preceding the Bay of Pigs expedition. The President's deference to the Chairman of the Senate Foreign Relations Committee was inspired not by constitutional considerations but by a coincidence. A few days previously, at the time of Congress's Easter recess, the President had let me hitch a ride to Florida on his plane. During the flight I heard his advisers discussing a plan for the invasion of Cuba. I was less than completely astonished because rumors of an invasion were widespread at the time and, in fact, I had already prepared a short memorandum advising against the project. I discussed the matter with President Kennedy on the plane, giving him a copy of my memorandum; upon my return to Washington he invited me to a meeting with himself and his senior advisers at which my reasons for opposing the invasion of Cuba were given a full and fair hearing.

It was a mark of President Kennedy's magnanimity that I was not subsequently banished from the Presidential plane, but neither did any subsequent trip have such interesting results. Nor, indeed, can this episode be regarded as a manifestation of the advice-and-consent function of the Senate; I was the only Senator involved in the fateful deliberations preceding the Bay of Pigs and my involvement was an accident.

The Cuban Missile Crisis. The Cuban missile crisis of 1962 more typically illustrated the respective roles of President and Congress in the making of a critical decision. Many of us at that time were in our home states campaigning for re-election. When the President called some of us back—the Congressional leadership, appropriate committee chairmen, and ranking minority members—we were not told the nature of the emergency about which we were to be consulted or informed, but of course we were able to guess the approximate situation. None of us aboard the Presidential plane which had been sent to pick us up on October 22, 1962, however, had any official knowledge of the crisis which in the following hours was to bring the world to the brink of nuclear war.

We convened at the White House at five P.M. and were briefed by the President and his advisers on the crisis and on the decisions *which had already been taken* on how to deal with it. When the President asked for comments, Senator Richard Russell of Georgia and I advocated the invasion of Cuba by American forces, I on the grounds that a blockade, involving as it might a direct, forcible confrontation with Russian ships, would be more likely to provoke a nuclear war than an invasion which would pit American soldiers against Cuban soldiers and allow the Russians to stand aside. Had I been able to formulate my views on the basis of facts since made public rather than on a guess as to the nature of the situation, I might have made a different recommendation. In any case, the recommendation which I made represented my best judgment at the time and I thought it my duty to offer it.

The decision to blockade Cuba had already been made. We had been summoned to the White House, as it turned out, not for a consultation but for a last-minute briefing. The meeting at the White House broke up after six P.M., and President Kennedy went on television at seven P.M. to announce his decision to the American people. In his book on President Kennedy, Theodore Sorensen refers to the temerity of those of us from the Congress who expressed opinions at the White House meeting as "the only sour note" in all of the decision-making related to the Cuban missile crisis.[2]

The Dominican Intervention. On the afternoon of April 28, 1965, the leaders of Congress were called once again to an emergency meeting at the White House. We were told that the revolution that had broken out four days before in the Dominican Republic was completely out of hand, that Americans and other foreigners on the scene were in great danger, and that United States Marines would be landed in Santo Domingo that night for the sole purpose of protecting the lives of Americans and other foreigners. (The Dominican intervention and its effects on the relations of the United States with Latin America are discussed in Chapter 4.) None of the Congressional leaders expressed disapproval of the action planned by the President.

Four months later, after an exhaustive review of the Dominican crisis by the Senate Foreign Relations Committee meeting in closed sessions, it was clear beyond reasonable doubt that although saving American lives may have been a factor in the decision to intervene on April 28, the major reason was a determination on the part of the United States government to defeat the rebel, or constitutionalist, forces whose victory at that time was imminent. Had I known in April what I knew in August, I most certainly would have objected to the American intervention in the Dominican Republic. I would have objected for a number of excellent reasons, not the least of which was the violation by the United States of the Charter of the Organization of American States, a treaty which had been solemnly ratified with the consent of the Senate.

The Gulf of Tonkin Resolution. Almost nine months before the Dominican intervention, on August 5, 1964, the Congress received an urgent request from President Johnson for the immediate adoption of a joint resolution regarding Southeast Asia. On August 2 the United States destroyer *Maddox* had reportedly been attacked without provocation by North Vietnamese torpedo boats in the Gulf of Tonkin, and on August 4 the *Maddox* and another destroyer, the *C. Turner Joy,* had reportedly been attacked again by North Vietnamese torpedo boats in international waters. In addition to endorsing the President's action in ordering the Seventh Fleet and its air units to take action against the North Vietnamese attacks, the resolution authorized the President "to take all necessary steps, including the use of armed force," against aggression in Southeast Asia.

Once again Congress was asked to show its support for the President in a crisis; once again, without questions or hesitation, it did so. The Senate Foreign Relations and Armed Services Committees endorsed the resolution after perfunctory hearings and with only one dissenting vote on the morning of August 6. After brief floor debate the resolution was adopted by the Senate on August 7 by a vote of 88 to 2 and by the House of Representatives on the same day by a vote of 416 to 0.

The joint resolution of August 7, 1964, was a blank check —so it has been interpreted—signed by the Congress in an atmosphere of urgency that seemed at the time to preclude debate. Since its adoption the Administration has converted the Vietnamese conflict from a civil war in which some American advisers were involved to a major international war in which the principal fighting unit is an American army of hundreds of thousands of men. Each time Senators have raised questions about successive escalations of the war, we have had the blank check of August 7, 1964, waved in our faces as supposed evidence of the overwhelming support of the Congress for a policy in Southeast Asia which in fact has been radically changed since the summer of 1964. We have also been told that we can exercise the option to withdraw the support expressed in the resolution at any time by concurrent resolution—an option so distasteful to most members of Congress, because it would surely be interpreted abroad as a repudiation of the President's leadership, as to be no option at all. Still, when the Senate on March 1, 1966, tabled Senator Morse's motion to rescind the resolution, the Administration chose to interpret this vote as an endorsement of its policy in Vietnam.

All this is very frustrating to some of us in the Senate but we have only ourselves to blame. Had we met our responsibility of careful examination of a Presidential request, had the Senate Foreign Relations Committee held hearings on the resolution before recommending its adoption, had the Senate debated the resolution and considered its implications before giving its overwhelming approval, and specifically had we investigated carefully and thoroughly the alleged unprovoked attacks on our ships, we might have put limits and qualifications on our endorsement of future uses of force in Southeast Asia, if not in the resolution itself then in the legislative history preceding its adoption. As it was, only Senators Morse of Oregon and Gruening of Alaska opposed the resolution.

As Chairman of the Foreign Relations Committee, I served as floor manager of the Southeast Asia resolution and did all I could to bring about its prompt and overwhelming adoption. I did so because I was confident that President Johnson would use our endorsement with wisdom and restraint. I was also influenced by partisanship: an election campaign was in progress and I had no wish to make any difficulties for the President in his race against a Republican candidate whose election I thought would be a disaster for the country. My role in the adoption of the resolution of August 7, 1964, is a source of neither pleasure nor pride to me today.

Many Senators who accepted the Gulf of Tonkin resolution without question might well not have done so had they foreseen that it would subsequently be interpreted as a sweeping Congressional endorsement for the conduct of a large-scale war in Asia. Literally, it can be so interpreted, but it must be remembered that the resolution was adopted during an election campaign in which the President was telling the American people that it would be a mistake for the United States to become involved in a major war in Asia while criticizing his opponent for proposing just that. This may explain the perfunctory debate of August 1964 but hardly excuses the Congress for granting such sweeping authority with so little deliberation. It was a mistake which I trust will not soon be repeated.

The Asian Doctrine. With such experiences in mind as those which I have described, I think it extremely important that the Senate consider the implications of the Johnson Administration's evolving "Asian Doctrine" before it becomes an irrevocable national commitment undertaken by the Executive without the consent or even the knowledge of the Senate.

Under the emerging "Asian Doctrine" the United States is taking on the role of policeman and provider for all of non-communist Asia. Defining Asia as "the crucial arena of man's striving for independence and order," the President, without reference to the United Nations or the obligation of other countries, declared in a speech in July 1966 "the determination of the United States to meet our obligations in Asia as a Pacific power," denounced those—whoever they may be—who hold to the view that "east is east and west is west and never the twain shall meet," and laid down certain "essentials" for peace in Asia, all requiring a predominantly American effort for the shaping of a "Pacific era."[3]

In a television interview on April 19, 1966, Vice-President Humphrey defined the Honolulu Declaration resulting from the President's meeting with Premier Nguyen Cao Ky of South Vietnam in February 1966 as a "Johnson Doctrine" for Asia, "a pledge to ourselves and to posterity to defeat aggression, to defeat social misery, to build viable, free political institutions, and to achieve peace. . . ." Acknowledging these to be "great commitments," the Vice-President went on to say: ". . . I think there is a tremendous new opening here for realizing the dream of the Great Society in the great area of Asia, not just here at home."

All this must come as a big surprise to Senators who have not even been informed of these sweeping commitments, much less asked for their advice and consent, but the President's close friend and biographer, Mr. William White, reported in one of his columns that the "Asian Doctrine" has been in the President's mind for five years, and Mr. White should know.[4] To the best of my knowledge, however, it has not been in the mind of the Senate, whose consent is required for treaties, or of the Congress as a whole, which is empowered by the Constitution not only to "declare war" and to "raise and support armies" but "to pay the debts and provide for the common defense and general welfare of the United States."

The Senate as a Forum of Debate

How then can the Senate discharge its constitutional responsibilities of advice and consent in an age when the direction and philosophy of foreign policy are largely shaped by urgent decisions made at moments of crisis? I have no definitive formula to offer but I do have some ideas as to how both the Senate as an institution and an individual Senator can meet their constitutional responsibilities.

The Senate as a whole, I think, should undertake to revive and strengthen the deliberative function which it has permitted to atrophy in the course of twenty-five years of crisis. Acting on the premise that dissent is not disloyalty, that a true consensus is shaped by airing differences rather than suppressing them, the Senate should again become, as it used to be, an institution in which the great issues of American politics are contested with thoroughness, energy, and candor. Nor should the Senate allow itself to be too easily swayed by Executive pleas for urgency and unanimity, or by allegations of "aid and comfort" to the enemies of the United States made by officials whose concern with such matters may have something to do with a distaste for criticism directed at themselves.

It is sometimes useful and occasionally necessary for Congress to express prompt and emphatic support for the President on some matter of foreign relations. It seems to me, however, that we have gone too far in this respect, to the point of confusing Presidential convenience with the national interest. It is perfectly natural for the President, pressed as he is to make decisions and take action in foreign relations, to overemphasize the desirability of promptness and unanimity. But the Senate has its own responsibilities, and however strongly feelings of patriotism may incline it to comply with the President's wishes, the higher patriotism deriving from its constitutional trust requires it to reply to the President in effect: "Mr. President, we will take your urgent request under immediate advisement; we will set aside our other legislative business and will proceed as rapidly as orderly procedure permits to hear testimony and to debate and act upon your request. We will not, however, except under conditions of national emergency, set aside the normal procedures of committee hearings and deliberation and debate on the Senate floor. We regret any inconvenience which this may cause you, but just as we are cognizant of your obligation to act, we know that you are cognizant of our obligation to inform ourselves and deliberate in order to be able to give you our best possible advice. We know you are aware that we render this advice not only in the hope that it will be a service to your Administration but also as an obligation to our constituents—an obligation, Mr. President, which we feel bound to meet even if, for one reason or another, our doing so subjects you to certain inconveniences."

It must be admitted that vigorous debate in the Senate can be misunderstood abroad. It seems reasonable to suppose that the debate on Vietnam has given the Viet Cong, the North Vietnamese, and the Chinese a distorted impression of internal divisions within the United States. I regret this effect very much, but I cannot accept the conclusion that it is necessary or proper to suspend the normal procedures of the Congress in order to give our adversaries an impression— an inaccurate impression—of American unanimity. I, as one Senator, am unwilling to acquiesce, actively or tacitly, to a policy that I judge to be unwise as the price of putting the best possible face on that policy. To do so would be to surrender the limited ability I have to bring influence to bear for what I would judge to be a wiser policy and would constitute a default on my constitutional responsibilities and on my responsibilities to the people of my state.

The major part of the burden of criticism in the Senate naturally falls to the opposition party. Under normal conditions, the duty is one which the opposition is only too glad to perform. Only occasionally does it happen that the party out of power is so feeble or so much in agreement with the President's policies or both that it fails to provide responsible and intelligent opposition. Under such unusual circumstances, when the proper opposition defaults, it seems to me that it is better to have the function performed by members of the President's party than not to have it performed at all.

The Committee on Foreign Relations

In the winter and spring of 1966 the Senate Committee on Foreign Relations engaged in an experiment in public education. The Committee made itself available as a forum for the meeting of politicians and professors and, more broadly, as a forum through which recognized experts and scholars could contribute to Congressional and public understanding of a number of aspects of the foreign relations of the United States, some short-term and specific, others long-term and general. During the second session of the 89th Congress the Committee, meeting in open session, heard testimony by specialists on Vietnam and the Vietnamese war, on China and her relations with the United States, on NATO and American relations with Western Europe; and finally, in an experiment that I believe to be unprecedented, the Committee heard testimony by distinguished psychiatrists and psychologists on some of the psychological aspects of international relations. It is my hope that these experiments have contributed to public education and also that they have made a beginning toward restoring the Senate to its proper role as adviser to the President on the great issues of foreign policy.

I believe that the public hearings on Vietnam, by bringing before the American people a variety of opinions and disagreements pertaining to the war and perhaps by helping to restore a degree of balance between the Executive and the Congress, strengthened the country rather than weakened it. The hearings were criticized on the ground that they conveyed an "image" of the United States as divided over the war. Since the country obviously *is* divided, what was conveyed was a fact rather than an image. I see no merit in the view that at the cost of suppressing the normal procedures of democracy, we should maintain an image of unity even though it is a false image.

The hearings on Vietnam were undertaken by the Senate Foreign Relations Committee in the hope of helping to shape a true consensus in the long run, even at the cost of dispelling the image of a false one in the short run. They were undertaken in the belief that the American people and their government would profit from an airing of views by forceful advocates from within and outside the government. They were undertaken in the belief that the best way to assure the prevalence of truth over falsehood is by exposing all tendencies of opinion to free competition in the market place of ideas. They were undertaken in something of the spirit of Thomas Jefferson's words:

> I know no safe depository of the ultimate powers of the society but the people themselves; and if we think them not enlightened enough to exercise their control with a wholesome discretion, the remedy is not to take it from them, but to inform their discretion.[5]

Many times in the past the Senate Foreign Relations Committee has served as the forum for a national debate and in some instances its proceedings have had the effect of translating a consensus of values into a consensus of policy as well. One notable instance was the debate on the nuclear test ban treaty in the summer of 1963. For three weeks the Foreign Relations Committee, with members of the Armed Services and Atomic Energy Committees also attending, met in open session to hear vigorous arguments for and against the treaty by witnesses from the government, from the universities, and from other areas of private life. Each day's discussion was transmitted to the American people through the press. The result was that the Foreign Relations Committee was able to serve simultaneously as both an organ of Senate deliberation and a forum of public education. In the course of those three weeks and the Senate floor debate that followed, support for the treaty steadily grew and the treaty was finally ratified by a vote of 81 to 19. Through the medium of open discussion and debate an existing consensus for peace as an objective was translated into a policy consensus for the test ban treaty as a means of advancing it.

The Foreign Relations Committee contemplates additional proceedings pertaining to major questions of American foreign policy. It is our expectation that these proceedings may generate controversy. If they do, it will not be because we value controversy for its own sake but rather because we accept it as a condition of intelligent decision-making, as, indeed, the crucible in which a national consensus as to objectives may be translated into a consensus of policy as well.

The Individual Senator

A Senator who wishes to influence foreign policy must consider the probable results of communicating privately with the Executive or, alternatively, of speaking out publicly. I do not see any great principle involved here: it is a matter of how one can better achieve what one hopes to achieve. For my own part, I have used both methods, with results varying according to circumstances. Other things being equal—which they seldom are—I find it more agreeable to communicate privately with Democratic Presidents and publicly with Republican Presidents.

Since 1961, when the Democrats came back to power, I have made recommendations to the President on a number of occasions through confidential memoranda. I have already referred to the memorandum I gave to President Kennedy regarding the Bay of Pigs.

In June 1961 I sent the President a memorandum protesting public statements on controversial political issues made by members of the armed forces under the sponsorship of right-wing organizations; it resulted in the issuance of an order by Secretary of Defense Robert McNamara restricting such activities and it also produced a lively Senate debate in which I was accused of wishing to "muzzle the military."

In April 1965 I sent President Johnson a memorandum containing certain recommendations on the war in Vietnam, recommendations which I reiterated thereafter in private conversations with high Administration officials. When it became very clear that the Administration did not find my ideas persuasive, I began to make my views known publicly in the hope, if not of bringing about a change in Administration policy, then at least of opening up a debate on that policy.

On the afternoon of September 15, 1965, I made a speech in the Senate criticizing the United States intervention in the Dominican Republic. That morning I had sent a copy of the speech to President Johnson, accompanied by a letter which read as follows:

Dear Mr. President:
Enclosed is a copy of a speech that I plan to make in the Senate regarding the crisis in the Dominican Republic. As you know, my Committee has held extensive hearings on the Dominican matter; this speech contains my personal comments and conclusions on the information which was brought forth in the hearings.

As you will note, I believe that important mistakes were made. I further believe that a public discussion of recent events in the Dominican Republic, even though it brings forth viewpoints which are critical of actions taken by your Administration, will be of long term benefit in correcting past errors, helping to prevent their repetition in the future, and thereby advancing the broader purposes of your policy in Latin America. It is in the hope of assisting you toward these ends, and for this reason only, that I have prepared my remarks.

On the basis of the testimony given in the Foreign Relations Committee, I have concluded that the primary cause of our mistakes in the Dominican Republic was faulty advice that was given to you in the critical last days of April 1965. I believe that it would have been extremely difficult for you to have made any decisions other than the ones that you made on the basis of the information that was given to you; this point is made in two different places in my speech. Nor is the purpose of this statement recrimination against those who seem to have committed errors of judgment; the officials involved are men of competence and integrity, who appear, however, in this instance, to have offered faulty recommendations. I am interested solely, as I know you are, in helping to lay the basis for more successful policies in the future.

Another purpose of my statement is to provide a measure of reassurance for those liberals and reformers in Latin America who were distressed by our Dominican actions, just as you did in your outstanding statement to the Latin American ambassadors on August 17. I believe that the people in Latin America whose efforts are essential to the success of the Alliance for Progress are in need of reassurance that the United States remains committed to the goals of social reform. I know that you are doing a great deal to provide such reassurance and one of my purposes in this speech will be to supplement your own efforts in this field.

Public—and, I trust, constructive—criticism is one of the services that a Senator is uniquely able to perform. There are many things that members of your Administration, for quite proper reasons of consistency and organization, cannot say, even though it is in the long term interests of the Administration that they be said. A Senator, as you well know, is under no such restriction. It is in the sincere hope of assisting your Administration in this way, and of advancing the objective of your policy in Latin America, that I offer the enclosed remarks.

My speech generated a controversy. A number of my colleagues in the Senate expressed support for my position; others disagreed. Much of the criticism, to my surprise and disappointment, was directed not at what I had said about the Dominican Republic and Latin America but at the propriety of my speaking out at all. Taken aback by the consternation caused by my breach of the prevailing consensus, I made the following remarks in the Senate on October 22, 1965:

There has been a good deal of discussion as to whether it is proper for the Chairman of the Senate Foreign Relations Committee to make a speech critical of an Administration of his own party which he generally supports. There is something to be said on both sides of this question and it is certainly one which I considered with care before deciding to make my speech on the Dominican Republic. I concluded, after hearing the testimony of Administration witnesses in the Committee on Foreign Relations, that I could do more to encourage carefully considered policies in the future by initiating a public discussion than by acquiescing silently in a policy I believed to be mistaken. It seemed to me, therefore, that, despite any controversy and annoyance to individuals, I was performing a service to the Administration by stating my views publicly.

I do not like taking a public position criticizing a Democratic Administration which in most respects I strongly support; I do not like it at all. Neither do I like being told, as I have been told, that my statement was "irresponsible" or that it has given "aid and comfort" to the enemies of the United States. I am quite prepared to examine evidence suggesting that my statement contained errors of fact or judgment; I am not prepared to accept the charge that a statement following upon many hours of listening to testimony in the Foreign Relations Committee and many more hours of examining and evaluating relevant documents was "irresponsible." Nor do I take kindly to the charge that I gave "aid and comfort" to the enemies of the United States. If that accusation is to be pressed—and I should hope it would not be—an interesting discussion could be developed as to whether it is my criticisms of United States policy in the Dominican Republic or the policy itself which has given "aid and comfort" to our enemies.

A Senator has a duty to support his President and his

party, but he also has a duty to express his views on major issues. In the case of the Dominican crisis I felt that, however reluctant I might be to criticize the Administration—and I was very reluctant—, it was nonetheless my responsibility to do so, for two principal reasons.

First, I believe that the Chairman of the Committee on Foreign Relations has a special obligation to offer the best advice he can on matters of foreign policy; it is an obligation, I believe, which is inherent in the chairmanship, which takes precedence over party loyalty, and which has nothing to do with whether the Chairman's views are solicited or desired by people in the executive branch.

Second, I thought it my responsibility to comment on United States policy in the Dominican Republic because the political opposition, whose function it is to criticize, was simply not doing so. It did not because it obviously approved of United States intervention in the Dominican Republic and presumably, had it been in office, would have done the same thing. The result of this peculiar situation was that a highly controversial policy was being carried out without controversy—without debate, without review, without that necessary calling to account which is a vital part of the democratic process. Again and again, in the weeks following the Committee hearing I noted the absence of any challenge to statements appearing in the press and elsewhere which clearly contradicted evidence available to the Committee on Foreign Relations.

Under these circumstances, I am not impressed with suggestions that I had no right to speak as I did on Santo Domingo. The real question, it seems to me, is whether I had the right not to speak.[6]

It is difficult to measure the effectiveness of a Senator's speech, because its effect may be something *not* done rather than some specific action or change of policy on the part of the Executive. Generally speaking, it seems to me that a Senator's criticism is less likely to affect the case in point than it is to affect some similar case in the future. I am inclined to believe, for example, that my criticism of the State Department in the summer of 1965 for its failure to give public support to the Firestone Tire and Rubber Company when that company was brought under right-wing attack for agreeing to engineer a synthetic-rubber plant in Rumania, while it did not revive that transaction, may have encouraged the State Department to give vigorous and timely support to a number of tobacco companies who were subsequently criticized by extremist groups for their purchases of tobacco from certain Eastern European communist countries. As to the effect of my Dominican speech, it may have been a factor in the Administration's subsequent support of democratic government in the Dominican Republic, repairing thereby some of the damage wrought by the intervention of April 1965 in support of the Dominican military. Its more significant results will be shown in the reaction of the United States government if it is again confronted with a violent revolution in Latin America.

As to my criticisms and those of my colleagues regarding the Vietnamese war, their effect remains to be seen. Thus far they have clearly failed to persuade the Johnson Administration to reconsider its policy of military escalation. It may be, for the time being, that those of us who deplore American involvement in the Vietnamese civil war will have to be content—in the manner of the British Labour Party at the time of Suez and of the French intellectuals who opposed the colonial wars of the Fourth Republic—with demonstrating to the world that America is not monolithic in its support of present policies, that there are other tendencies of opinion in the American democracy, tendencies which, though temporarily muted, are likely to reassert themselves and to influence American foreign policy in the future as they have in the past. This function alone gives meaning and purpose to the dissent on Vietnam.

Before considering how he will try to influence events, a politician must decide which events he proposes to influence and which he will leave largely to the determination of others.

The Senate consists of a hundred individuals with fifty separate constituencies and widely varying fields of individual knowledge and interest. There is little that a Senator can accomplish by his own efforts; if he is to have an effect on public policy, he must influence his colleagues. Sometimes, but not often, a colleague's support can be won by charm; it can certainly be lost by rudeness. Occasionally it can be won by persuasive rhetoric; more often it is gotten by trading your support on one issue for his on another, or simply by a general practice of limiting your own initiatives to matters of unusual interest or importance while otherwise accepting the recommendations of the committees. And in some instances a Senator may influence his colleagues by influencing their constituencies.

Some may regard this process of mutual accommodation as unethical. I do not regard it as unethical, because I do not place my own wishes and judgments on a plane above those of my colleagues. There are no areas of public policy in which I am absolutely sure of the correctness of my opinions, but there are some in which I am reasonably confident of my judgment; it is in these areas that I try to make a contribution. There are other areas in which my knowledge is limited, and in these I prefer to let others take the lead. There are still other areas in which I am proscribed from leadership or initiative by the strong preferences of my constituency.

A politician has no right to ask that he be absolved from public judgment; he may hope, however, that he will be judged principally on the basis of his performance in the areas of his principal effort. He may hope that he will be judged not as a saint or paragon but as a human being entrusted by his constituents with great responsibilities but endowed by the Lord with the same problems of judgment and temptation that afflict the rest of the human race.

Hampered though he is by human limitations, the American politician of the 1960s has responsibilities which no politician in any country in all history has had before. His is the world's most powerful nation at the moment in history when powerful nations have acquired the means of destroying the human race. All of the traditional attitudes of our ancestors, about war and peace, about the conflicts of nations and the brotherhood of man, have been called into question and are in need of re-examination. It is the responsibility of the politician to lead in that fateful re-examination; to do so surely is to act upon a higher patriotism. And, in so doing, in the words of Albert Camus, "if at times we seemed to prefer justice to our country, this is because we simply wanted to love our country in justice, as we wanted to love her in truth and in hope."[7]

Part II

REVOLUTION
ABROAD

What characterizes our time . . . is the way the masses and their wretched condition have burst upon contemporary sensibilities. We now know that they exist, whereas we once had a tendency to forget them. And if we are more aware, it is not because our aristocracy . . . has become better—no, have no fear—it is because the masses have become stronger and keep people from forgetting them.

ALBERT CAMUS
"Create Dangerously,"
December 1957

3

America
and Revolution

IN MANY PARTS of the world revolutions are being made and in many still-quiet places they are in the making, not by the silent and demoralized poor but by a new generation of powerful and charismatic leaders who are arousing the masses from their inertia, inspiring them with anger and hope, and giving them the discipline that turns numbers into strength. Some of these new revolutionaries are democrats but most of them are not. Their principal purpose in any case is to modernize rather than democratize and they are more interested in material results than in abstract ideas. Whatever ideology they begin with or profess, they soon enough discover that the success of their revolutions turns on social and economic achievement and that political ideals are of relevance only insofar as they advance or obstruct the struggle to modernize.

The question therefore remains whether the future course of revolution will be peaceful or violent, democratic or totalitarian. Present prospects, I think, are for more upheavals that are violent and undemocratic, because recent experiments in peaceful revolution have been disappointing and authoritarian methods seem to promise greater and faster results. (In making this observation, I would emphasize that I am anticipating violence, not welcoming it.) With few exceptions the nations that have tried to carry out social revolution by democratic means have faltered in their efforts, and there seems to be a growing conviction that the task of modernization is too large and too socially disruptive to be accomplished by democratic methods, a growing conviction that in a society in revolt, as in an army at war, there is no place for democracy except as a distant dream.

Events of the last two decades suggest that Americans have been overly sanguine about the possibilities of social revolution by peaceful means. The reconstruction of a traditional society requires great discipline and enormous human sacrifices: not only must the rich be persuaded to give up privileges which they regard as their birthright, but the poor, who have practically nothing, must be persuaded for a time to do with even less in order to provide investment capital. From what we know of history and human nature there is little reason indeed to expect people to make these sacrifices voluntarily; there is, on the contrary, a great deal of reason to expect the privileged classes of the emerging countries to use every available means to defend their privileges.

Revolution by peaceful means is an historical rarity. In the West, England, some of her colonial heirs, and a few of the smaller European countries made the transition from autocracy to democracy and from feudalism to modernism by more or less peaceful means, but these were countries, by and large, which enjoyed extraordinary advantages of wealth, location, or tradition. The other great European nations—notably France, Italy, Germany, and Russia—came to be what they are today only after violent internal upheavals; nor did any of these countries, it is interesting to note, escape some reversion to dictatorship after an initial experiment in democracy.

It requires the optimism of Dr. Pangloss to expect Asian and Latin American nations, beset as they are with problems of poverty and population unknown in Western

Europe and North America, to achieve by peaceful means what nations with vastly greater advantages were able to achieve only by violent revolution. History does not repeat itself and there is probably no such thing as an inevitability, but the past does suggest certain limits of probability and certain likelihoods. The likelihood that it suggests for the "third world" of Asia, Africa, and Latin America is not a smooth transition to democracy but an extended time of troubles, not a rapidly improving life for the ordinary man, but, for some societies, a period of intermittent progress under more or less democratic leadership, for others, continued stagnation or deterioration and, for still others, a period of painful sacrifices enforced by authoritarian leaders though mitigated in the better-run societies by some equity in the sharing of the sacrifices.

These prospects are probable rather than inevitable; they are anything but desirable. We must continue to do what we can—more indeed by far than we are doing now—to improve the chances of peaceful and democratic social revolution in the underdeveloped world. We would do well, however, to stop deluding ourselves about the likelihood of success. We would do well, for example, to stop proclaiming the triumph of the Alliance for Progress because five hundred thousand units of housing were built in Latin America in 1965—of which, in fact, only sixty thousand were attributable to the Alliance for Progress—when the more pertinent fact is that the number of families needing housing increased by one and a half million. We must stop fooling ourselves about economic progress in many of the countries that receive American aid and acknowledge that the magnitude of the problem is vastly disproportionate to what is being done or is now likely to be done to overcome it; we must face the fact that democratic methods are more often failing than succeeding in Asia, Africa, and Latin America, and that as rapidly growing populations continue to press on slowly growing economies, violent upheavals are not only possible but very likely indeed.

Unrevolutionary America

In confrontations with social revolution we Americans are emotionally and intellectually handicapped in three respects: first, by the fact that we ourselves are an unrevolutionary society; second, by the absence of a genuine feeling of empathy for revolutionary movements—which is the result not of hard-heartedness but of our own lack of experience with social revolution; and third, by a national mythology, cultivated in Fourth of July speeches and slick publications, which holds that we *are* a revolutionary society, that ours indeed was the "true" revolution which ought to be an inspiration for every revolutionary movement in the world.

We are never going to have much understanding of revolutions until we become clear on exactly what constitutes a revolution and what does not. Part of the problem is the imprecision of language. Just as the word "morality" can be used to describe attitudes of both tolerant humanitarianism and self-righteous puritanism, the word "revolutionary" can be applied to phenomena ranging from Robespierre's Terror to a newly marketed laundry soap. For purposes of clarity, therefore, I suggest the following distinction: true revolution is almost always violent and usually it is extremely violent; its essence is the destruction of the social fabric and institutions of a society and an attempt, not necessarily successful, to create a new society with a new social fabric and new institutions. The English reform acts of the nineteenth century, the American New Deal, and the Great Society were not revolutions; they were rather antidotes to revolution, timely measures of reform that met rising popular demands sufficiently to head off revolutionary pressures.

I do not know why some Americans take it so hard when it is suggested that their society is an unrevolutionary one. It seems to me that our essential conservatism is the result and the reward for one of the world's most strikingly successful experiments in popular government. We had one revolution, a limited but successful one, nearly two centuries ago, and then another revolution, a tragic and abortive one, a century later. Since then we have had no violent upheaval because we have not needed one, because our institutions have proven durable and flexible, capable of gradual and orderly change as America grew from an isolated society to the richest and most powerful nation in the world. Revolution after all is not in itself a blessing; it is the product of social and political failure and its sole merit is that it provides the means to dispose of atrophied institutions and to introduce the hope of social justice. Far from being distressed by the suggestion that ours is an unrevolutionary society, that fact should be taken as a mark of success and a reason for pride. Jefferson once asked, "What country before ever existed a century and a half without a rebellion?"[1] We have not yet reached that mark but we are approaching it; we are approaching it because the revolution of 1776 was a success; because the system it created has proven responsive to changing human needs.

Our lack of understanding, or empathy, for the great revolutions of our time is thus the result of success and good fortune. It is nonetheless an obstacle to perception and a problem of policy because our success has placed us outside of a large part of the common human experience. It is important, therefore, that we set aside false analogies and recognize the social revolutions of the "third world" as alien phenomena, as phenomena to which American experience has little relevance but which warrant nonetheless our sympathy and support.

The Anatomy of Revolution

As Crane Brinton pointed out in his classic study,[2] great revolutions are characterized by certain uniformities—not identities but similarities of phase and development. The study of these similarities can help Americans to understand phenomena that are outside their own experience. An examination of past revolutions—such as the English, French, or Mexican Revolutions—may also suggest that much of what we find shocking and barbarous in present-day China or Cuba, or Russia in the twenties and thirties, may have more to do with a particular stage of revolution than with communist ideology.

Great revolutions pass through more or less similar and identifiable stages. Eric Hoffer suggests that revolutions are prepared by "men of words"—intellectuals, that is, such as Rousseau, Mazzini, and Marx—carried to fulfillment by "fanatics"—such as Robespierre, Lenin, and Trotsky—and finally brought back to earth by "practical men of action"—men like Cromwell, Bonaparte, and Stalin.[3] In Crane Brinton's analysis, there is a tendency for great revolutions to be preceded by the demoralization of traditional ruling classes and thereafter to be characterized, first by the rule of moderates, whose very moderation makes them unable to cope with the violence which they themselves may have unleashed, then by the rule of extremists, whose extremism degenerates into terror and who then are displaced by more practical men who bring the society back to normalcy and routine, to the stage known in the French Revolution as "Thermidor."

The acute phase of any revolution is the rule of the extremists. They are brought to power by the dynamism of violent change, which, once begun, feeds upon itself, breeding fanaticism. As Brinton puts it, "The normal social roles of realism and idealism are reversed in the acute phases of a revolution."[4]

The extremists of great revolutions—English, French, Russian, Chinese, or Cuban—have demonstrated certain common characteristics, regardless of the ideology they have professed. First and foremost, whatever their beliefs, they have professed them with fanatical intolerance and a ruthless idealism that is used to justify acts of extreme cruelty against opponents. In addition, they all have practiced many of the same techniques of revolutionary action, including propagandizing, parading, street fighting, terrorism, non-violence, guerrilla warfare, and other techniques in varying combinations.

Once in power, the extremists tend to abandon or betray whatever previous interest they had in liberties and legalities and they proceed to carry out their programs, or try to, in an authoritarian manner. To some degree dictatorship is inherent in the revolutionary process—quite apart from the aims and ideology of the revolution—because revolution breaks down the laws and customs of a society and force becomes necessary to prevent anarchy. Robespierre described this particular phenomenon as the despotism of liberty against tyranny; Marx called it the dictatorship of the proletariat.

The extremists also tend to be ascetic and puritanical. When the Bolsheviks first came to power in Russia, people in the West predicted the reign of license and debauchery, but just like the Chinese today, the Bolsheviks turned out to be as prudish and aggressively virtuous as seventeenth-century Calvinists. Even today Russia is surely one of the world's most puritanical societies.

It is the effort to remake human nature, to force the soup steaming hot down the ordinary citizen's throat, that generates the terror in a revolution but ends with the moderation of Thermidor when it becomes clear that human nature will simply not allow itself to be instantaneously remade. The period of terror represents an overshooting of the revolutionary mark, a foredoomed effort to close the gap between human nature and human aspirations. The ordinary man is pushed to the limits of endurance; he longs for a return to routine; he becomes fed up with the steady diet of virtue and self-sacrifice and longs to be left alone with his ordinary pleasures and vices. Societies like individuals can endure only a limited dose of virtue and high ideals, only so much of the effort to bring heaven to earth. When they have had their fill, the revolution abates and the terror gives way to the Thermidorean reaction.

Thermidor does not mean the undoing of the revolution; it is rather a coming back to earth, an abatement of fanaticism, a reassertion of human nature and a return to everyday living. As Brinton wrote, "there is no eternal fanaticism or, at any rate, there has not yet been an eternal fanaticism. Christian and Moslem have not come to understand one another, but they have come to abstain from holy wars against one another. The odds are that even with Lenin and Stalin as its prophets, communism will prove a less intractable faith than Islam."[5]

Nationalism and Communism in the American View of Revolution

In Latin America and in Asia, where great revolutions have taken place and others may still occur, American policy has been weakened by a seeming inability to believe in the tractability of communism or the abatement of its fanaticism and by a permeating inability to understand why the peoples of these continents cannot remake their societies by the same orderly processes that have worked so well in the United States. The result is that despite our genuine sympathy for those who cry out against poverty and social injustice, and despite the material support which we give to many of the poor nations of the world, our sympathy dissolves into hostility when reform becomes revolution; and when communism is involved, as it often is, our hostility takes the form of unseemly panic.

On the basis of past and present American policies toward China and Vietnam, toward Cuba and the Dominican Republic, we seem to be narrowing our criteria of what constitute "legitimate" and "acceptable" social revolutions to include only those which meet the all but impossible tests of being peaceful, orderly, and voluntary—of being, that is, in what we regard as our own shining image. At the same time, owing no doubt to a view of communism as the fulcrum of a revolutionary process that will not be satiated until it dominates the world, our abhorrence for violence from the left has been matched by no such sensibilities when the violence comes from the right. Thus it has come about that our sympathy for social revolution in principle is increasingly belied by hostility in practice.

The American view of revolution is thus shaped by a simple but so far insuperable dilemma: we are simultaneously hostile to communism and sympathetic to nationalism, and when the two become closely associated, we become agitated, frustrated, angry, precipitate, and inconstant. Or, to make the point by simple metaphor: loving corn and hating lima beans, we simply cannot make up our minds about succotash.

The resulting ambivalence has weakened American foreign policy since the end of World War II. Insofar as communism and nationalism have confronted us as separate forces, United States policy has been largely successful. In such instances as the Soviet threat to Western Europe in the late forties and the Cuban missile crisis of 1962 the danger was clearly one of Soviet power and the United States had little difficulty in deciding on effective counter-action. In the case of the colonial revolution in most of Asia and Africa the United States took a strong lead in supporting national independence movements. Only in such instances as the Cuban Revolution and the war in Vietnam, in each of which communism and nationalism became closely associated with each other, or the Dominican Revolution, in which communism was feared but never proven to be a dominant influence, has the United States encountered cruel dilemmas in the shaping of policy and signal failures in its execution.

For complex reasons, deriving in large part from our early

postwar experience with Soviet communist imperialism, we have tended—and now more than ever are tending—to give our opposition to communism priority over our support for nationalism. The result has been that, with certain exceptions, we have strongly, and for the most part unsuccessfully, opposed those genuinely nationalist movements which have been controlled or influenced by communists. The most notable—and rewarding—exception has been Yugoslavia, whose national independence we have supported since 1948 with the result that it has posed a powerful barrier to Soviet aspirations in southeastern Europe—a more powerful barrier, it should be noted, than many non-communist governments have been able to erect.

Whatever wisdom or lack of it our emphasis on communism has had in the past, the realities of the present require a reversal of priorities as between opposing communism and supporting nationalism. The basis of the criticisms of American policy in Latin America and Southeast Asia to be set forth in succeeding chapters is my belief that American interests are better served by supporting nationalism than by opposing communism, and that when the two are encountered in close association it is in our interest to accept a communist government rather than to undertake the cruel and all but impossible task of suppressing a genuinely national movement.

Many Americans, probably including the highest officials in our government, are likely to be shocked by the contention that we can or should "accept" the establishment of a communist government anywhere in the world under any conceivable circumstances. One's attitude in this respect must depend on one's view of communism as a revolutionary ideology, on whether one views it as an implacable and unalterable design for world conquest or rather as something more subtle, flexible, and varying—varying according to a country's size, resources, and national character, the stage of its economic development and the stage of its revolution.

Communism as a Revolutionary Ideology

The evil in communism is not its doctrinal content, which at worst is utopian, but its fanatical certainty of itself, its messianic zeal, and its intolerance of dissent. Its evil is not in its anticipation of a world of happy and high-minded "toilers"—which is a benign if not a particularly enticing vision—but in its exorbitant demands upon human nature, in its intolerance of human weakness, in its unwillingness to accept man as he is and always has been. Out of this intolerance grows the egregious presumption of the true believer that he knows what is best for all men and, knowing what is best, has the right and the duty to force it upon them. The evil of men like Lenin and Mao Tse-tung is not their philosophy but their fervor, the fact, in the words applied by Crane Brinton to revolutionary extremists in general, that "they combine, in varying degrees, very high ideals and a complete contempt for the inhibitions and principles which serve most other men as ideals."[6]

If communism were both evil in doctrine and unalterable in practice, then there would be nothing for us to do except to engage the communist countries in relentless struggle until one ideology or the other was destroyed. There can be no compromise with unmitigated evil; compromise is a way of reconciling conflicting interests, based on the premise that interests, though opposed, are legitimate and entitled to a measure of satisfaction. If we assume that there is no legitimacy about the aims of communists, that there is no element of decency or humanity in communist societies, then any compromise must be regarded as a pact with the devil and our declared national policy of "building bridges" to the communist world must be regarded as a moral sellout. Indeed, if this view of communism were correct, honor and principle would require us to press the struggle by whatever means were necessary, including nuclear war, in order to destroy communism and establish the universal dominion of our own version of democracy.

I do not believe that this is an accurate view of communism, nor do I believe that it is accurate to equate communism with Nazism. Nazism was a psychotic aberration, a violent and degenerate romanticism; communism, for all its distortions in practice and for all the crimes committed in its name, is a doctrine of social justice and a product of Western civilization, philosophically rooted in humanitarian protest against the injustices of nineteenth-century capitalism. In the words of the religious journal *Christianity and Crisis*: "What is at stake in the case of communism is different from what was at stake in the case of national socialism. Stalinism had many of the worst features of Hitlerism, but it proved to be a passing phase of Soviet communism. It showed itself more open-ended than we had supposed, capable of varying degrees of humanization if not democratization. It is not monolithic, nor is it permanent slavery; and, in its later phases, cooperative as well as competitive coexistence becomes politically and morally possible. We doubt if such coexistence would have become possible with nazism."[7]

A very critical distinction must be made between communist philosophy and the fervor with which it is practiced. It is the latter which rightly offends us, and despite the fact that the doctrine itself has universal pretensions, messianism in practice is not so much a product of communism as it is a stage of revolution, a stage comparable to the period of terror in the French Revolution, a stage which the experience of past revolutions suggests is just about certain to be followed by a conservative reaction. The stage of revolutionary extremism actually has already passed in a number of communist countries, including the Soviet Union, whose commitment to world revolution is now more liturgical than political, so much so, in fact, that Russia can now properly be regarded as a conservative power in international relations, as a nation whose stake in the status quo is a far more important determinant of her international behavior than her philosophical commitment to world revolution.

Far from being unified in a design for world conquest, the communist countries are deeply divided among themselves, with widely varying foreign policies and widely varying concepts of their own national interests. Unless, therefore, we accept the view that communist ideology in itself constitutes a threat to the free nations, we are bound to regard communist countries as menacing or not, depending on whether their foreign policies are aggressive or benign. If we accept the premise that it is aggression rather than communism which endangers us, then it follows that the existence of a strong communist state which poses a barrier to expansion by an aggressive communist power may be more desirable from the viewpoint of American interests than a weak non-communist state whose very weakness forms a vacuum which invites conquest or subversion.

The point that I wish to make is not that communism is not a harsh and, to us, a repugnant system of organizing society, but that its doctrine has redeeming tenets of humanitarianism; that the worst thing about it is not its philosophy but its fanaticism; that history suggests the probability of an abatement of revolutionary fervor; that in practice fanaticism *has* abated in a number of countries including the Soviet Union; that some countries are probably better off under communist rule than they were under preceding regimes; that some people may even want to live under communism; that in general the United States has more to gain from the success of nationalism than from the destruction of communism; and finally—to anticipate the theme of the next several chapters—that it is neither the duty nor the right of the United States to sort out all these problems for the revolutionary and potentially revolutionary societies of Asia, Africa, and Latin America.

4

Revolution
in Latin America

Nowhere has the ambivalence in the American attitude toward revolution been more apparent and more troublesome than in the relations of the United States with Latin America. In Latin America as in Asia the United States, a profoundly unrevolutionary nation, is required to make choices between accepting revolution and trying to suppress it.

Caught between genuine sympathy for social reform on the one hand and an intense fear of revolution on the Cuban model on the other, we have thus far been unwilling, or unable, to follow a consistent course. On the one hand, we have made ourselves the friend of certain progressive democratic governments and have joined with Latin America in the Alliance for Progress, the purpose of which is social revolution by peaceful means. On the other hand, we have allowed our fear of communism to drive us into supporting a number of governments whose policies, to put it charitably, are inconsistent with the aims of the Alliance, and on three occasions—Guatemala in 1954, Cuba in 1961, and the Dominican Republic in 1965—we resorted to force, illegally, unwisely, and inasmuch as each of these interventions almost certainly strengthened the appeal of communism to the younger generation of educated Latin Americans, unsuccessfully as well.

The United States thus pursues two largely incompatible policies in Latin America—discriminating support for social reform and an undiscriminating anti-communism that often makes us the friend of military dictatorships and reactionary oligarchies. Anti-communism is increasingly being given precedence over support for reform. American policy-makers clearly prefer reformist democratic governments to economic oligarchies and military juntas as long as the former are aggressively anti-communist; but the slightest suspicion of communist support seems to be enough to discredit a reform movement in North American eyes and to drive United States policy-makers into the stifling embrace of the generals and the oligarchs.

Guided by a reflex bred into them by Fidel Castro, American policy-makers have developed a tendency to identify revolution with communism, assuming, because they have something to do with each other, as indeed they do, that they are one and the same thing, as indeed they are not. The pervading suspicion of social revolutionary movements on the part of United States policy-makers is unfortunate indeed because there is the strong possibility of more explosions in Latin America and, insofar as the United States makes itself the enemy of revolutionary movements, communism is enabled to make itself their friend. The anti-revolutionary bias in United States policy, which is rooted in the fear of communism on the Cuban model, can only have the effect of strengthening communism.

The Dominican Intervention

The Alliance for Progress encouraged the hope in Latin America that the United States would not only tolerate but actively support domestic social revolution. The Dominican intervention at least temporarily destroyed that hope.

The election on June 1, 1966, of Joachin Balaguer as President of the Dominican Republic, in an election regarded by most observers as having been fair and free, has been widely interpreted as a vindication of the American military intervention of April 1965, as proof that the intervention was necessary, justified, and wise. Those of us who criticized the American intervention must concede that a degree of order and stability in the Dominican Republic was restored more quickly than seemed likely in the spring and summer of 1965 and that credit for this properly belongs to United States diplomacy, to the Organization of American States, and to the Inter-American Force which remained in the Dominican Republic until the summer of 1966, as well as to the provisional government which held office from September 1965 to July 1966 and to the elected government which succeeded it.

That, however, is all that must or can be conceded. The facts remain that the United States engaged in a unilateral military intervention in violation of inter-American law, the "good neighbor" policy of thirty years' standing, and the spirit of the Charter of Punta del Este; that the Organization of American States was gravely weakened as the result of its use—with its own consent—as an instrument of the policy of the United States; that the power of the reactionary military oligarchy in the Dominican Republic remains substantially unimpaired; that the intervention alienated from the United States the confidence and good opinion of reformers and young people throughout Latin America, the very people, that is, whose efforts are essential to the success of peaceful revolution through the Alliance for Progress; and that confidence in the word and in the intentions of the United States Government has been severely shaken, not only in Latin America but in Europe and Asia and even in our own country.

Recovery from a disaster does not turn the disaster into a triumph. To regard the restoration of constitutional government in the Dominican Republic as a vindication of the intervention is like regarding the reconstruction of a burned-out house as a vindication of the fire. The effects of the Dominican intervention abroad have been described by a good friend of the United States, the former President of Colombia, Alberto Lleras Camargo, who was touring Europe at the time and who later wrote: ". . . The general feeling was that a new and openly imperialistic policy in the style of Theodore Roosevelt had been adopted by the White House and that, if there was intervention with Marines in the Hemisphere, against unequivocal standards of law, one could only expect—in Asia, in Africa, and in wherever— new acts of force and, perhaps, the escalation of the cold war to the hot in a very short time. . . ."[1]

The central fact about the intervention of the United States in the Dominican Republic was that we had closed our minds to the causes and to the essential legitimacy of revolution in a country in which democratic procedures had failed. The involvement of an undetermined number of communists in the Dominican Revolution was judged to discredit the entire reformist movement, like poison in a well, and rather than use our considerable resources to compete with the communists for influence with the democratic forces who actively solicited our support, we intervened militarily on the side of a corrupt and reactionary military oligarchy. We thus lent credence to the idea that the United States is the enemy of social revolution, and therefore the enemy of social justice, in Latin America.

The evidence is incontrovertible that American forces landed in Santo Domingo on April 28, 1965, not, as was and is officially contended, for the primary purpose of saving American lives but for the primary if not the sole purpose of defeating the revolution, which, on the basis of fragmentary evidence and exaggerated estimates of communist influence, was judged to be either communist-dominated or certain to become so. It is not my purpose here to review the complicated series of events surrounding the intervention but only to recall those salient facts which bear out the contention that the United States acted impetuously and unwisely in unseemly fear of an indigenous revolution in the Dominican Republic.

When the Dominican Revolution began on Saturday, April 24, 1965, the United States had three options available: first, it could have supported the Donald Reid Cabral government, a junta which had overthrown the freely elected government of Juan Bosch in September 1963 to the great consternation of the United States government at the time but with which the United States had since come comfortably to terms; second, it could have supported the revolutionary forces; and third, it could have done nothing.

The Administration chose the last course. When Cabral asked for United States intervention on Sunday morning, April 25, he was given no encouragement. He then resigned, and considerable disagreement ensued over the nature of the government to succeed him. The party of Juan Bosch, the PRD, or Dominican Revolutionary Party, asked for a "United States presence" at the transfer of government power but was given no encouragement. Thus, there began a chaotic situation which amounted to civil war in a country without an effective government.

What happened in essence was that the Dominican military refused to support Reid and were equally opposed to Bosch or other PRD leaders as his successor. The PRD, which had the support of some military officers, announced that Rafael Molina Urena, who had been president of the Senate during the Bosch regime, would govern as provisional president pending Bosch's return. At this point the military leaders delivered an ultimatum, which the rebels ignored, and at about 4:30 on the afternoon of April 25 the air force and navy began firing at the National Palace. Later in the day PRD leaders asked the United States Embassy to use its influence to persuade the air force to stop the attacks. The Embassy made it clear it would not intervene on behalf of the rebels, although on the following day, Monday, April

26, the Embassy did persuade the military to stop air attacks for a limited time.

This was the first crucial point in the crisis. If the United States thought that Reid was giving the Dominican Republic the best government it had had or was likely to get, why did the United States not react more vigorously to support him? On the other hand, if the Reid government was thought to be beyond salvation, why did the United States not offer positive encouragement to the moderate forces involved in the coup, if not by providing the "United States presence" requested by the PRD, then at least by letting it be known that the United States was not opposed to the prospective change of regimes or by encouraging the return of Juan Bosch to the Dominican Republic? In fact, according to available evidence, the United States government made no effort to contact Bosch in the initial days of the crisis.

The United States was thus at the outset unwilling to support Reid and unwilling to support if not positively opposed to Bosch. Events of the days following April 24 demonstrated that Reid had so little popular support that it can reasonably be argued that there was nothing the United States could have done, short of armed intervention, to save his regime. The more interesting question is why the United States was so reluctant to see Bosch returned to power. This is part of the larger question of why United States attitudes had changed so much since 1963 when Bosch, then in power, was warmly and repeatedly embraced and supported as few if any Latin American Presidents have ever been supported by the United States.

The next crucial point in the Dominican story came on Tuesday, April 27, when rebel leaders, including Molina Urena and the rebel military leader, Francisco Caamaño Deñó, called at the United States Embassy seeking mediation and negotiations. At that time the military situation looked very bad for the rebel, or constitutionalist, forces. The United States Ambassador, W. Tapley Bennett, who had been instructed four times to work for a cease-fire and for the formation of a military junta, felt he did not have the authority to mediate; mediation, in his view, would have been "intervention." Mediation at that point might have been accomplished quietly and peacefully. Twenty-four hours later the Ambassador was pleading for the Marines, and for over a year thereafter the United States was intervening as deeply as in the palmiest days of the Monroe Doctrine.

On the afternoon of April 27 General Wessin y Wessin's tanks seemed about to cross the Duarte bridge into the city of Santo Domingo and the rebel cause appeared hopeless. When the rebels felt themselves rebuffed at the American Embassy, some of their leaders, including Molina Urena, sought asylum in Latin American embassies in Santo Domingo. The United States government interpreted this development as evidence that the non-communist rebels had recognized growing Communist influence in their movement and were consequently abandoning the revolution. Molina Urena has said simply that he sought asylum because he thought the revolutionary cause hopeless.

A great opportunity was lost on April 27. Ambassador Bennett was in a position to bring possibly decisive mediating power to bear for a democratic solution, but he chose not to do so on the disingenuous ground that the exercise of his good offices at that point would have constituted "intervention." In the words of Mr. Murrey Marder of *The Washington Post*—one of the press people who, to the best of my knowledge, has not been assailed as "prejudiced" —"It can be argued with considerable weight that late Tuesday, April 27, the United States threw away a fateful opportunity to try to prevent the sequence that produced the American intervention. It allowed the relatively leaderless revolt to pass into hands which it was to allege were Communist."[2]

The overriding reason for this mistake was the conviction of United States officials, on the basis of evidence which was fragmentary at best, that the rebel movement was dominated by communists. A related and perhaps equally important reason for the United States Embassy's refusal to mediate on April 27 was the desire for and, at that point, the expectation of an anti-rebel victory. The United States officials on the scene therefore passed up an important opportunity to reduce or even eliminate communist influence by encouraging the moderate elements among the rebels and mediating for a democratic solution.

Owing to a degree of disorganization and timidity on the part of the anti-rebel forces anticipated by no one, including the United States Embassy and the rebels themselves, the rebels were still fighting on the morning of Wednesday, April 28. Ambassador Bennett thereupon urgently recommended that the anti-rebels under Air Force General de los Santos Cespedes be furnished fifty walkie-talkies from United States Defense Department stocks in Puerto Rico. Repeating this recommendation later in the day, Bennett said that the issue was one between Castroism and its opponents. The anti-rebels themselves asked for armed United States intervention on their side; this request was refused at that time.

During the day, however, the situation deteriorated rapidly, from the point of view of public order in general and of the anti-rebels in particular. In mid-afternoon of April 28 Colonel Pedro Bartolome Benoit, head of a junta which had been hastily assembled, asked again, this time in writing, for United States troops on the ground that intervention was the only way to prevent a communist takeover; no mention was made of the junta's inability to protect American lives. This request was denied in Washington and Benoit was thereupon told that the United States would not intervene *unless he said he could not protect American citizens present in the Dominican Republic.* Benoit was thus told in effect that if he said American lives were in danger, the United States would intervene. And that is precisely what happened.

It was at this point, on April 28, that the United States made its decision to act in violation of the Organization of American States Charter. That decision shaped subsequent events: the failure of the missions of John Bartlow Martin and McGeorge Bundy, the conversion of the United States force into an inter-American force, the enforced stalemate between the rebels under Caamaño Deñó and the junta of General Antonio Imbert Barreras, the OAS mediation, the tortuous and ultimately successful negotiations for a provisional government. In any case, the general direction of events was largely determined by the fateful decision of April 28. Once the Marines landed on that day, and especially after they were heavily reinforced in the days immediately following, the die was cast and the United States found itself deeply involved in the Dominican civil conflict, with its hemisphere relations complicated in a way that few could have foreseen and no one could have desired.

The United States intervened in the Dominican Republic for the purpose of preventing the victory of a revolutionary force which was judged to be communist-dominated. On the basis of Ambassador Bennett's messages to Washington, there is no doubt that the fear of communism rather than danger to American lives was his primary or sole reason for recommending military intervention. In fact, no American lives were lost in Santo Domingo until the Marines began exchanging fire with the rebels after April 28; reports of widespread shooting that endangered American lives turned out to be greatly exaggerated.

The question of the degree of communist influence is therefore crucial but it cannot be answered with certainty. The weight of the evidence is that communists did not participate in planning the revolution—indeed, there is some indication that it took them by surprise—but that they very rapidly began to try to take advantage of it and to seize control of it. The evidence does not establish that the communists at any time actually had control of the revolution.

There is little doubt that they had influence within the revolutionary movement, but the degree of that influence remains a matter of speculation.

The United States government, however, assumed almost from the beginning that the revolution was communist-dominated, or would certainly become so, and that nothing short of forcible opposition could prevent a communist takeover. In their panic lest the Dominican Republic become "another Cuba," some of our officials seem to have forgotten that virtually all reform movements attract some communist support, that there is an important difference between communist support and communist control of a political movement, that it is quite possible to *compete* with the communists for influence in a reform movement rather than abandon it to them, and, most important of all, that economic development and social justice are themselves the primary and most reliable security against communist subversion. The point I am making is not—most emphatically not—that there was no communist participation in the Dominican crisis, but simply that the Administration acted on the premise that the revolution was *controlled* by communists—a premise which it failed to establish at the time and has not established since.

Intervention on the basis of communist participation as distinguished from control of the Dominican Revolution was a mistake of panic and timidity which also reflects a grievous misreading of the temper of contemporary Latin American politics. Communists are present in all Latin American countries, and they are going to inject themselves into almost any Latin American revolution and try to seize control of it. If any group or any movement with which the communists associate themselves is going to be automatically condemned in the eyes of the United States, then we have indeed given up all hope of influencing even to a marginal degree the revolutionary movements and the demands for social change which are sweeping Latin America. Worse, if that is our view, then we have made ourselves the prisoners of the Latin American oligarchs who are engaged in a vain attempt to preserve the status quo—reactionaries who habitually use the term "communist" very loosely, in part out of emotional predilection and in part in a calculated effort to scare the United States into supporting their selfish and discredited aims.

The movement of the future in Latin America is social revolution. The question is whether it is to be communist or democratic revolution and the choice which the Latin Americans make will depend in part on how the United States uses its great influence. It should be very clear that the choice is not between social revolution and conservative oligarchy but whether, by supporting reform, we bolster the popular non-communist left, or, by supporting unpopular oligarchies, we drive the rising generation of educated and patriotic young Latin Americans to an embittered and hostile form of communism like that of Fidel Castro in Cuba.

We simply cannot have it both ways; we must choose between the objectives of the Alliance for Progress and a foredoomed effort to sustain the status quo in Latin America. The choice which we are to make is the principal unanswered question arising out of the unhappy events in the Dominican Republic and, indeed, the principal unanswered question for the future of our relations with Latin America.

Law and Revolution

Because the law is by its very nature a buttress of the status quo, it is rational for revolutionaries to try to overthrow it and for conservatives to try to uphold it. It is not rational for conservatives to play fast and loose with the law in a seizure of anti-revolutionary zeal. When they do, it is rather like the defenders of a besieged fort firing their artillery *through* the protecting walls instead of over them:

they may blow up some of the attackers on the other side but in the process they are making a nice opening through which the enemy can pour into the fort in their next attack. That is exactly what the United States did when it intervened unilaterally in the Dominican Republic.

Article 15 of the Charter of the Organization of American States says that "No State or group of States has the right to intervene, directly or indirectly, for any reason whatever, in the internal or external affairs of any other State." Article 17 states that "The territory of a State is inviolable; it may not be the object, even temporarily, of military occupation or of other measures of force taken by another State, directly or indirectly, on any grounds whatever."

These clauses are not ambiguous. They mean that, with one exception to be noted, all forms of forcible intervention are absolutely prohibited among the American states. It may be that the United States was unwise to accept this commitment at Bogotá in 1948; it is obvious from all the talk one hears these days about the "obsoleteness" of the principle of non-intervention that some United States officials regret our commitment to it. The fact remains that we are committed to it, not partially or temporarily or insofar as we find it compatible with our vital interests but almost absolutely. It represents our word and our bond and our willingness to honor the solemn commitments embodied in a treaty which was ratified by the Senate on August 28, 1950.

There are those who might concede the point of law but who would also argue that such considerations have to do with our ideals rather than our interests and are therefore of secondary importance. I do not believe that is true. We are currently fighting a war in Vietnam, largely, we are told, because it would be a disaster if the United States failed to honor its word and its commitment; the matter, we are told, is one of vital national interest. I do not see—I completely fail to see—why it is any less a matter of vital interest to honor a clear and explicit treaty obligation in the Americas than it is to honor the much more ambiguous and less formal promises we have made to the South Vietnamese.

The sole exception to the prohibitions of Articles 15 and 17 is spelled out in Article 19 of the OAS Charter, which states that "Measures adopted for the maintenance of peace and security in accordance with existing treaties do not constitute a violation of the principles set forth in Articles 15 and 17." Article 6 of the Rio Treaty states that "If the inviolability or the integrity of the territory or the sovereignty or political independence of any American State should be affected by an aggression which is not an armed attack or by an extra-continental or intra-continental conflict, or by any other fact or situation that might endanger the peace of America, the Organ of Consultation shall meet immediately in order to agree on the measures which must be taken in case of aggression to assist the victim of the aggression or, in any case, the measures which should be taken for the common defense and for the maintenance of the peace and security of the Continent."

The United States thus had legal recourse when the Dominican crisis broke on April 24, 1965. We could have called an urgent session of the Council of the OAS for the purpose of invoking Article 6 of the Rio Treaty. But we did not do so. The Administration has argued that there was no time to consult the OAS, although there was time to "consult"—or inform—the Congressional leadership. The United States thus intervened in the Dominican Republic unilaterally—and illegally.

Advising the Latin American countries of our action after the fact did not constitute compliance with the OAS Charter or the Rio Treaty; nor, indeed, would *advising* them before the fact have constituted compliance. One does not comply with the law by notifying interested parties in advance of one's intent to violate it. Inter-American law requires consultation for the purpose of shaping a *collective decision*. Only on the basis of advance consultation and agreement could we have undertaken a legal intervention in the Dominican Republic.

Whatever lingering doubts Latin Americans may have held about the willingness of the United States to violate the OAS Charter after the Dominican intervention were soon resolved by the United States House of Representatives. On September 20, 1965, with the tacit consent of the Executive branch, the House of Representatives adopted a resolution calling for the unilateral use of force against any threat of communism in the hemisphere, which is to say, in clear and open violation of the OAS Charter. The United States was promptly rewarded for the House of Representatives' action by unanimous expressions of outrage in Latin America, including resolutions of condemnation adopted by the Congresses of Colombia and Peru and by the Latin American Parliament representing fourteen countries. The Colombian Congress by unanimous vote adopted a resolution calling the action of the United States House of Representatives "openly regressive and contrary to the juridical and political system of Latin America."

It is possible, had we consulted with our Latin American partners about the Dominican Revolution in the manner prescribed by the Rio Treaty, that they would have delayed a decision; it is possible that they would have refused to authorize collective intervention. My own feeling is that the situation in any case did not justify military intervention except for the limited purpose of evacuating United States citizens and other foreigners, but even if it seemed to us that it did, we should not have undertaken it without the advance consent of our Latin American allies. We should not have done so because the word and the honor of the United States were at stake just as much—at least as much—in the Dominican crisis as they are in Vietnam and Korea and Berlin and all the places around the globe which we have committed ourselves to defend.

There is a more general reason, already referred to, for compliance with the law. The United States is a conservative power in the world in the sense that most of its vital interests are served by stability and order. Law is the essential foundation of stability and order both within societies and in international relations. As a conservative power the United States has a vital interest in upholding and expanding the reign of law in international relations. Insofar as international law is observed, it provides us with stability and order and with a means of predicting the behavior of those with whom we have reciprocal legal obligations. When we violate the law ourselves, whatever short-term advantage may be gained, we are obviously encouraging others to violate the law; we thus encourage disorder and instability and thereby do incalculable damage to our own long-term interests.

There are those who defend United States unilateral intervention in the Dominican Republic on the ground that the principle of non-intervention as spelled out in the OAS Charter is obsolete. The argument is unfortunate on two grounds. First, the contention of obsoleteness justifies an effort to bring about changes in the OAS Charter by due process of law, but it does not justify violation of the Charter. Second, the view that the principle of non-intervention is obsolete is one held by certain United States officials; most Latin Americans would argue that, far from being obsolete, the principle of non-intervention was and remains the heart and core of the inter-American system. Insofar as it is honored, it provides them with something that many in the United States find it hard to believe they could suppose they need: protection from the United States.

Many North Americans seem to believe that, while the United States does indeed "participate" in Latin American affairs from time to time, sometimes by force, it is done with the best of intentions, usually indeed to protect the Latin Americans from intervention by somebody else, and therefore cannot really be considered "intervention." The trouble with this point of view is that it is not shared by our neighbors to the south. Most of them do think they need protection from the United States and the history of the Monroe Doctrine and the "Roosevelt Corollary" suggest that their fears are not entirely without foundation. "Good intentions" are not a very sound basis for judging the fulfillment of contractual obligations. Just about everybody, including the communists, believes in his own "good intentions." It is a highly subjective criterion of national behavior and has no more than a chance relationship to good results. With whatever justice or lack of it, many Latin Americans are afraid of the United States; however much it may hurt our feelings, they prefer to have their security based on some more objective standard than the good intentions of the United States.

The standard on which they rely most heavily is the principle of non-intervention; however obsolete it may seem to certain United States officials, it remains vital and pertinent in Latin America. When we violate it, we are not overriding the mere "letter of the law"; we are violating what to Latin Americans is its vital heart and core.

Two Revolutions: Cuba and Mexico

The dominant force in Latin America is the aspiration of increasing numbers of people to personal and national dignity. In the minds of the rising generation there are two principle threats to that aspiration: reaction at home and domination from abroad. As a result of its actions in the Dominican Republic, its ready accommodation to the rule of conservative oligarchies and military dictators and its active support for such regimes through military assistance,* the United States has allowed itself to become associated with both. We have thereby offended the dignity and self-respect of young and idealistic Latin Americans, many of

---

* Military assistance is discussed in Chapter 11.

whom may wonder whether the United States will not one day intervene against social revolutions in their own countries, whether they will not one day find themselves facing United States Marines across barricades in their own home towns.

There are two available models—two prototypes—for the struggle against reaction and foreign domination in Latin America: the Cuban and the Mexican. Which of the two will commend itself to the new generation of active, articulate, reformist Latin Americans will depend to an important degree on the attitude of the United States toward future revolutionary movements. I think, therefore, that there is something to be learned from a re-examination of the Cuban and Mexican Revolutions.

Both Cuba and Mexico had thoroughgoing social revolutions in this century. Both were violent; both inflicted suffering and injustice on great numbers of innocent people; both, in their initial stages, provoked unsuccessful military intervention by the United States. The Cuban Revolution, in Crane Brinton's frame of reference, is still under the rule of extremists, although their extremism may be abating. Mexico, long past its Thermidor and now a one-party democracy, maintains friendly and dignified relations with the United States despite the fact—I rather think *because* of the fact—that it is freer of United States influence than most Latin American countries.

However impure the Marxism of the Cuban Revolution, it is unquestionably Cuban. Chairman Khrushchev is said to have told President Kennedy at Vienna that he did not consider Fidel Castro to be a "real" communist; no one has persuasively suggested that he is not a "real" Cuban nationalist, albeit a violent, undemocratic, and anti-American Cuban nationalist.

Castro, according to American and European visitors, is highly popular with the Cuban people. Mr. C. K. McClatchy of the *Sacramento Bee* visited Cuba in the summer of 1965 and reported that Fidel, as he is generally called, is a national hero. He is admired because he can cut sugar cane faster than any other Cuban, because he can hit a baseball like Mickey Mantle, because he can talk longer and more eloquently than any man alive. He is admired, said McClatchy, because he "personifies the revolution."[3]

How can it be that a government which suppresses individual liberties, a government which immediately upon winning power executed its enemies after kangaroo trials held in a stadium, a government which held the courageous men of the Bay of Pigs for ransom by the United States, can be anything but feared and detested by its own people? The answer, I think, lies in such facts as the following, as reported by McClatchy:

Before the revolution there was only one small strip of public beach among the twenty-two miles of beaches surrounding Havana; now all beaches are open to the public and they are enjoyed by thousands of Cubans who did not have access to them before.

Education has been drastically revamped. Illiteracy has been greatly reduced and there are twice as many schools now as before the revolution. A Havana University student told Mr. McClatchy: "Before only the children of the rich could come. Now everyone who is qualified is admitted."

Formerly landless peasants now work on cooperatives or have been given small plots of expropriated land. State workers receive housing, medical care, and a wage.

Almost everybody above school age has a job; before the revolution the level of unemployment was about 20 percent, one of the highest in the world.

Most important of all is the sense of dignity and national pride associated with the revolution. After six decades of being an economic colony of the United States, Cubans, despite economic failures and severe shortages of certain consumer goods, are immensely proud of Castro's successful defiance of the North American giant. The continuing hostility of the United States undoubtedly strengthens Castro's aura of courageous independence.

Perhaps there never was a chance for peaceful democratic revolution in Cuba. Explaining in an interview with Herbert Matthews on October 29, 1963, how and why he became a Marxist-Leninist, Castro said that he had entered college imbued with the ideas of his birth and upbringing as the son of a landowner educated by Jesuits. He read Marxist literature while a student and then in 1953, at his trial for participating in the student attack on the Moncada Barracks in Santiago, he outlined what he called "a very radical revolution," but, as he told Matthews, "I thought that it could be done under the Constitution of 1940 and within a democratic system." His conversion, Castro said, was "a gradual process, a dynamic process in which the pressure of events forced me to accept Marxism as the answer to what I was seeking." Castro said that the American reaction to his "agrarian reform" of May 1959 "made me realize that there was no chance to reach an accommodation with the United States." "So," said Castro, "as events developed, I gradually moved into a Marxist-Leninist position. I cannot tell you just when, the process was so gradual and natural."[4]

The Cuban Revolution shows some signs that it may be emerging from extremism into its period of Thermidor. The process, as pointed out in Chapter 3, is one that other great revolutions have gone through: the French Revolution was finally institutionalized by the Third Republic, the Russian Revolution by Stalin and perhaps more even by Khrushchev. In each case the transition was characterized not by the abandonment of revolutionary ideology but by its gradual transformation from practical policy to patriotic liturgy.

A more relevant example for Latin America is the Mexican Revolution, which broke out in 1910 but began to be institutionalized only after a decade of extreme violence marked by lootings, burnings, and anti-religious atrocities. The Mexican Revolution was a class war in which landlords were murdered and foreign properties expropriated. In the first years of the revolution the United States invaded Mexico twice, once by sea at Veracruz to avenge an insult to the flag, once by land in fruitless pursuit of the bandit Pancho Villa.

The United States was diverted from Mexico by its involvement in the First World War, but after the war there was mounting agitation to occupy Mexico and suppress the revolution. President Coolidge, a man endowed with the virtue of humility, avoided intervention and sent to Mexico City an emissary, Dwight Morrow, who successfully negotiated the issue of expropriated American oil and mineral rights. Then, in a flourish of good will, Morrow persuaded Charles A. Lindbergh to fly his plane to Mexico City.

Mexico is now politically stable and its economy is developing at an impressive rate. Mexico disagreed with the United States over the Dominican intervention and, prior to that, over the expulsion of Cuba from the Organization of American States; in addition, the Mexicans maintain diplomatic relations with Cuba and operate an airline between Mexico City and Havana. Mexico is also on better terms with the United States than most of the countries of Latin America, not, I think, in spite of its independence but *because* of its independence. It was this independence, I feel sure, that made it possible and natural for the Mexican people to receive President Johnson with friendliness and enthusiasm; and it was the fact that he cannot be suspected of being an American puppet that made it possible and natural for President Diaz Ordaz to join his people in that warm welcome. The relations of the two countries are characterized by mutual respect and self-respect, and it all began when the United States came to terms with the Mexican Revolution forty years ago.

I am not so incautious as to predict that relations between the United States and the Cuban Revolution will come to the same happy outcome, but neither would I rule it out. The point that I wish to make, however, is that the United States has already come to terms with one great social revolution in Latin America, with highly rewarding results for both parties, and that this experience has important and obvious implications for our future relations with a continent where further revolution, peaceful or violent, is a certainty.

Charting a New Course in Inter-American Relations

It is not too late for the United States to play an important and effective role in helping Latin Americans to achieve their aspirations to democracy and social justice. These aims after all are the same as those which we seek for ourselves in our own society. Although we are an unrevolutionary society, we have traditionally been sympathetic to the aspirations of people all over the world to democracy and social justice. Despite a strand of harsh puritanism in our national character, I continue to believe that there is a stronger strand of democratic humanism, an elemental decency which has motivated us, despite grievous lapses, to seek social justice in our own society and to encourage it in others, not only because this was the prudent and politic thing to do but also, and perhaps primarily, because it was the decent thing to do.

It is thus in keeping with that which is best in our own character, and it is unquestionably in our interests that we make ourselves the friend of social revolution in Latin America. It will require a renewed commitment and increased contributions to the Alliance for Progress. It will also require a drawing-away from military and economic oligarchies, whatever the short-term advantages of supporting them. It may require the acceptance of gradual expropriation of American-owned enterprises. It will certainly require the acceptance of great and rapid change, not all of it necessarily by peaceful means.

It will also require acceptance of the fact that Latin America is coming into its own in the world and can no longer be regarded as the special ward of the United States. We must be prepared to see the Latin American countries, whose channels to the outside world have traditionally run through Washington, enter into new relationships with Europe and with Asia and Africa, some of which may not be much to our liking. We must recognize that paternalism is no longer a workable basis for our relations with Latin America, that, as President Edouardo Frei Montalva of Chile said during a visit to France in the summer of 1965, the people of Latin America "desire true political and economic independence; they want a system without hegemony."

The United States is a world power with world responsibilities and to it the inter-American system represents a sensible way of maintaining law and order in the region closest to the United States. To the extent that it functions as we want it to function, one of the inter-American system's important advantages is that it stabilizes relations within the Western Hemisphere and thus frees the United States to act on its global responsibilities. To Latin Americans, on the other hand, the inter-American system is politically and psychologically confining. It has the effect, so to speak, of cooping them up in the Western Hemisphere, giving them the feeling that there is no way to break out of the usually well-intentioned but often stifling embrace of the United States. In their hearts, I have no doubt, most Latin Americans would like to be free of us, just as a son or daughter coming of age wishes to be free of an overprotective parent. A great many of those Latin Americans for whom Castro still has some appeal are attracted not, I feel sure, because they are infatuated with communism, but because Cuba, albeit at the price of dependency on the Soviet Union, has broken out of the orbit of the United States.

It is in the nature of things that small nations do not live comfortably in the shadow of large and powerful nations, regardless of whether the latter are benevolent or overbearing. Belgium has always been uncomfortable about Germany and France; Ireland has never been able to work up much affection for Great Britain. And in recent years some of the Eastern European governments have demonstrated that despite the communist ideology which they share with the Soviet Union, they still wish to free themselves as much as they can and as much as they dare from the overbearing power of Russia. It is natural and inevitable that Latin American countries should have some of the same feelings toward the United States.

Perhaps, then, the foremost immediate requirement for a new and more friendly relationship between Latin America and the United States in the long run is not closer ties and new institutional bonds but a loosening of existing ties and institutional bonds. It is an established psychological principle—or, for that matter, just common sense—that the strongest and most viable personal bonds are those which are voluntary, a voluntary bond being, by definition, an arrangement which one is free to enter or not to enter. I do not see why the same principle should not operate in relations between nations. If it does, it would follow that the first step toward stronger ties between Latin America and the United States would be the creation of a situation in which Latin American countries would be free, and would feel free, to maintain or sever existing ties as they see fit and, perhaps more important, to establish new arrangements, both among themselves and with nations outside the hemisphere, in which the United States would not participate.

I think further that it would be a fine thing if Latin American countries were to undertake a program of their own for "building bridges" to the world beyond the Western Hemisphere—to Europe and Asia and Africa, and to the communist countries if they wish. Such relationships, to be sure, would involve a loosening of ties to the United States in the immediate future, but in the long run, I feel sure, they would make for both happier and stronger bonds with the United States—happier because they would be free, stronger because they would be dignified and self-respecting as they never had been before.

Underlying these recommendations—for a coming to terms with social revolution and for a loosening of the tight bonds between the United States and Latin America—is the hope that by wise and timely action the United States can influence revolutionary forces in a constructive direction. Many Latin Americans, including an impressive number of the younger Catholic clergy, are striving to make a reality of the "revolution in freedom" proclaimed by President Frei of Chile. There is a chance that with our sympathy and help they will succeed, although neither the historical odds nor the scale of the effort being made under the Alliance for Progress provide much basis for optimism.

The hard fact of the matter is that conditions are deteriorating in Latin America at a pace and on a scale that outweigh all current efforts to reverse the tide. As the pressures of uncontrolled population growth mount, more and more Latin Americans are likely to adopt the attitude of a despairing young father in the Lima slums—he could as well have been living in Rio or Recife, in a Haitian village or the mountains of Bolivia—who told an American writer: "I would rather grab a gun and impose my kind of justice than see my children starve."[5]

Somewhere in the mountains of Colombia there lies in an unmarked grave the body of a young priest who had been shot down at the head of a communist guerrilla band. His name was Camilo Torres and he was a member of one of Colombia's most aristocratic families. Having asked to be relieved of his clerical duties, he went into the hills in November 1965, because, he said, "Every sincere revolutionary must recognize the way of arms as the only way that remains." One may hope that Father Torres was wrong but he may have been right. The day after he died placards appeared on the walls of the university in Bogotá. They said:

CAMILO! WE SHALL NOT WEEP FOR YOU
WE SHALL AVENGE YOU

5

The
Vietnamese Revolution

WHILE THE Alliance for Progress falters, American soldiers are fighting and dying in another revolution—or, more exactly, in an Asian civil war which has been expanded into a conflict between the United States and Asian communism.

The war in Vietnam has divided and troubled the American people as has no other war of the twentieth century. Many of our people, perhaps a majority, regard the war as necessary and just but many others are doubtful and troubled: some are unconvinced that the Saigon government is worth saving; some fear that the United States has inadvertently taken over the role of the old European colonial powers; some simply cannot understand what vital interests are served by sending American soldiers to fight and die in a civil war almost ten thousand miles away from their own country.

Why are Americans fighting in Vietnam? For much the same reason, I think, that we intervened militarily in Guatemala in 1954, in Cuba in 1961, and in the Dominican Republic in 1965. In Asia as in Latin America we have given our opposition to communism priority over our sympathy for nationalism because we have regarded communism as a kind of absolute evil, as a totally pernicious doctrine which deprives the people subjected to it of freedom, dignity, happiness, and the hope of ever acquiring them. I think that this view of communism is implicit in much of American foreign policy; I think it is the principal reason for our involvement in Vietnam and for the emergence of an "Asian Doctrine" under which the United States is moving toward the role of policeman for all of Southeast Asia.

It is said that we are fighting against North Vietnam's aggression rather than its ideology and that the "other side" has only to "stop doing what it is doing" in order to restore peace. But what are the North Vietnamese doing, except participating in a civil war, not in a foreign country but on the other side of a demarcation line between two sectors of the same country, a civil war in which Americans from ten thousand miles across the ocean are also participating? What are they doing that is different from what the American North did to the American South a hundred years ago, with results that few of my fellow Southerners now regret?

What exactly is their crime? They are harsh in their treatment of their own people and cruel in their conduct of the war, but these attributes hardly distinguish them from the South Vietnamese for whom we are fighting. The crime of the North Vietnamese that makes them America's enemy is that they are communists, practitioners of a philosophy we regard as evil. When all the official rhetoric about aggression and the defense of freedom and the sanctity of our word has been cited and recited, we are still left with two essential reasons for our involvement in Vietnam: the view of communism as an evil philosophy and the view of ourselves as God's avenging angels, whose sacred duty it is to combat evil philosophies.

The view of communism as an evil philosophy is a distorting prism through which we see projections of our own minds rather than what is actually there. Looking through the prism, we see the Viet Cong who cut the throats of village chiefs as savage murderers but American flyers who incinerate unseen women and children with napalm as valiant fighters for freedom; we see Viet Cong defections as the rejection of communism but the much greater number of defections from the Saigon Army as expressions of a simple desire to return to the farm; we see the puritan discipline of life in Hanoi as enslavement but the chaos and corruption of life in Saigon as liberty; we see Ho Chi Minh as a hated tyrant but Nguyen Cao Ky as the defender of freedom; we see the Viet Cong as Hanoi's puppet and Hanoi as China's puppet but we see the Saigon government as America's stalwart ally; and finally, we see China, with no troops in South Vietnam, as the real aggressor while we, with hundreds of thousands of men, are resisting foreign intervention.

These perceptions are not patently wrong but they are distorted and exaggerated. It is true that whatever the fault may be on our side, the greater fault is with the communists, who have indeed betrayed agreements, subverted unoffending governments, and generally done a great deal to provoke our hostility. It is *our* shortcoming, however, that we have the power to overcome and, in so doing, to set a constructive example for our adversaries. As the more powerful belligerent by far, we are better able to take the initiative in showing some magnanimity, but we are not doing so. Instead we are treading a strident and dangerous course, a course that is all but unprecedented in American history.

The Asian Doctrine

Except for the Monroe Doctrine, the United States has traditionally rejected policies of unilateral responsibility for entire regions and continents. In the nineteenth century the United States played almost no part in European politics and only a marginal role in Asia, preferring to regard itself as an example of progress and democracy which others might imitate or not as they saw fit. In the twentieth century events beyond our control brought us into two world wars and imposed upon us responsibilities far beyond our borders. Until quite recently, however, our policies for meeting those commitments have been guided by two extremely important qualifying principles: first, that these responsibilities were limited to certain countries and certain purposes; second, that they would be discharged collectively either under the United Nations or in cooperation with our allies.

The emerging "Asian Doctrine" represents a radical departure in American foreign policy in that it is unilateral and virtually unlimited in its objectives. Without reference to the United Nations and with only perfunctory reference to the non-functioning Southeast Asia Treaty Organization, the United States on its own has undertaken to win a victory for its protégés in the Vietnamese civil war and thereupon to build a "Great Society" in Asia, whatever that might turn out to mean.*

American policy in Europe after World War II consisted of collective measures for the containment of Soviet power. Though financed by the United States, the Marshall Plan was shaped and largely executed as a cooperative program for European economic recovery. Although American military power was pre-eminent the North Atlantic Treaty Organization was created as and has remained a system for the collective defense of Europe and the North Atlantic. We did not talk in those days of a "New Deal" or a "Fair Deal" for Europe; we were satisfied to support economic reconstruction and to restrain Soviet power.

The Korean War was fought under the auspices of the United Nations for an ultimately limited purpose. The United States provided most of the forces from the outside, but a great many other members of the United Nations sent

---

* Statements of the President and the Vice-President defining an "Asian Doctrine" are cited in Chapter 2, pp. 52–53.

troops and the United Nations itself took part in the direction of the war. After the abandonment of the disastrous attempt to occupy North Korea, which brought hundreds of thousands of Chinese soldiers into the conflict, the war was fought for the limited purpose of repelling a clear act of aggression which had been incited by Stalinist Russia.

In Vietnam the United States is fighting virtually alone and for vague purposes in a war which is not an international conflict but an insurrection in one part of a divided country supported by the other part. Aside from the token forces provided by Australia and New Zealand for their own political purposes, the only other outside force in Vietnam besides the large American army is a Korean force of forty thousand men heavily subsidized by the United States. Except for peace proposals offered by the Secretary-General, the United Nations plays no part in the war and is generally ignored by the belligerents; indeed, many members of the United Nations are extremely critical of the American involvement in Vietnam, and it is most unlikely that if a vote were taken, the United States could muster a majority in the General Assembly in support of its policy. As for the SEATO Treaty, three of its seven members provide no active support for the American military effort, and at least one, France, is extremely critical of American policy.

American war aims have escalated with the fighting. A few years ago a handful of American advisers were committed to support a South Vietnamese counter-insurgency effort with the clearly stated stipulation that it was up to the South Vietnamese themselves to win or lose their battle with the Viet Cong. When they had virtually lost, the United States changed its policy and sent its own army to take over the war. Since early 1965 the American military effort has expanded from counter-insurgency to a large-scale ground and air war, and the American political commitment has grown into an "Asian Doctrine" which implies an American commitment not only to win the Vietnamese war but also to establish a popular, stable, and democratic government in Saigon and then to protect it indefinitely; to maintain massive American military power in Southeast Asia in order to provide permanent protection against attack or subversion for all of the non-communist countries of the region; and finally, to provide enormous amounts of economic aid in order to bring the dream of the "Great Society" to hundreds of millions of Asians.

It is ironic that at the same time that the vestiges of the Monroe Doctrine are being fitfully liquidated the United States should be formulating a similar doctrine of pre-eminent American responsibility for Asia. One wonders whether the "Asian Doctrine" will reap for the United States as rich a harvest of affection and democracy as has the Monroe Doctrine. One wonders whether China will accept American hegemony as gracefully as Cuba and the Dominican Republic have accepted it. And one wonders whether anyone ever thought of asking the Asians if they really want to join the Great Society.

The occasion for this potentially massive American involvement in Asia is of course the war in Vietnam, but its genesis is the priority of anti-communism over sympathy for nationalism in American policy and the terrible difficulties we encounter when confronted with a communist party which is also an indigenous nationalist party. It seems pertinent, therefore, to review the national origins of Vietnamese communism and to consider what these may imply for the United States.

National Communism in Vietnam

At the heart of the Vietnam tragedy is the fact that the most powerful nationalist movement in that country is one which is also communist. Ho Chi Minh is not a mere agent of Communist China, much less of the "international communist conspiracy" that we used to hear so much about. He is a bona-fide nationalist revolutionary, the leader of his country's rebellion against French colonialism. He is also a communist, and that is the essential reason why since at least 1950 he has been regarded as an enemy by the United States.

It was during the chaotic final months of World War II that Ho Chi Minh emerged as the leader of the Vietnamese nationalist movement. Ho had traveled far and done many things since leaving Vietnam as a kitchen boy on a French ship in 1912. He had been to France and England, to Africa and America. He had tried without success to promote the cause of Vietnamese nationalism at the Paris Peace Conference of 1919, and in 1920 he had been a founding member of the French Communist Party. Since then he has been a dedicated communist but always a Vietnamese communist. "This means," as Bernard Fall wrote, "that Ho is probably equipped with an instinctive Vietnamese fear of Chinese domination (no matter what its color) just as most observers agree that to Khrushchev *any* Germany might be slightly suspect."[1]

Ho Chi Minh spent the twenties and the thirties attending Communist Party schools in the Soviet Union, working with the communist army in China, and agitating against French rule in Indochina. In 1941 Ho organized the Viet Minh as a communist-dominated Vietnamese nationalist movement. Although it engaged in no major warfare against the Japanese, the Viet Minh engaged in espionage and guerrilla activities under a program of fighting both Japan and Vichy and working for the independence of Vietnam. The Chiang Kai-shek government arrested Ho and imprisoned him for a year but released him in 1943 because he was found to be the only Vietnamese leader with effective contacts throughout Vietnam for espionage work. The Viet Minh thereafter was subsidized and supported by the Chinese Nationalist government. By 1945 the Viet Minh had built an army of about ten thousand under the leadership of Vo Nguyen Giap, now the Defense Minister of North Vietnam.

Negotiations between the Viet Minh and France begun in September 1945 culminated in an agreement on March 6, 1946, under which France recognized the "Democratic Republic of Vietnam" as a "free state with its own government, parliament, army and finances, forming part of the Indochinese federation and the French Union." The French pledged themselves to a referendum to determine whether the three sections of the country, Tonkin, Annam, and Cochinchina, should be united, and the Vietnamese in turn agreed to the stationing of fifteen thousand French troops north of the 16th Parallel, with the stipulation that they would be progressively replaced by Vietnamese troops within five years.

Ho Chi Minh went to France in the late spring of 1946 to negotiate a final agreement implementing the accord of March 6. France, it must be remembered, was at that time in the throes of the crisis surrounding the birth of the Fourth Republic; its diplomacy reflected the confusion, stubbornness and penetrating sense of injury characteristic of a great nation which had been cruelly humiliated—behavior, one might note parenthetically, which is understandable for France in 1946 or for China in 1966 but absolutely grotesque for a nation at the peak of its wealth and power like the United States. The negotiations, in any case, soon reached an impasse, with the French insisting on a French-led Indochinese federation whose diplomacy and armed forces would remain under the substantial control of Paris.

Diplomacy then came to an end. Incidents of violence mounted in late 1946. On November 20 French forces attacked the Viet Minh at Haiphong, killing six thousand Vietnamese and opening the first Indochinese war, which was to last until 1954.

This outline, highly abbreviated though it is, illustrates a most important fact—the merger of nationalism and communism in Vietnam under the leadership of Ho Chi Minh. It is not meaningful to speak of the Viet Minh as more nationalist than communist or as more communist than nationalist; it is both. The merger is a misfortune from the viewpoint of American interests and preferences, but it is also a fact, a fact with which we can and should come to terms. Even today, after all that America has done to sustain the South Vietnamese government, there is only one politician whose name is known to peasants all over Vietnam: Ho Chi Minh.

It is important to be very clear about what is meant by "nationalism." It has been best described by Hans Kohn as a "state of mind" which regards the nation as "the ideal form of political organization and the nationality as the source of all creative cultural energy and of economic well being."[2] Understood in this way, nationalism is not necessarily humane or democratic, socially constructive or responsive to individual needs. It is merely powerful—powerful in a sense of being able to mobilize the loyalty and active support of vast numbers of ordinary people. When one describes Ho Chi Minh or the Viet Minh or the Viet Cong as "nationalist," it is not to be inferred that they are regarded as saints. Far from it: they have demonstrated again and again that they are fanatical and cruel, but they have also shown that they are patriots, that they have identified themselves with the nation and its mystique, with that "state of mind" which more than any other in our time inspires ordinary people to acts of loyalty, bravery, and self-sacrifice.

For our purposes, the significance of Ho Chi Minh's nationalism is that it is associated with what Bernard Fall has called "the 2,000-year-old distrust in Vietnam of everything Chinese."[3] Vietnamese communism is therefore a potential bulwark—perhaps the only potential bulwark—against Chinese domination of Vietnam. It is for this reason that I believe that we should try, if it is not yet too late, to come to terms with North Vietnam and the Viet Cong. I shall suggest in Chapter 9 how it seems to me this might be done.

America in Vietnam

How did it happen that America, the foremost advocate of colonial liberation after World War II, who set an example by liberating its own Philippine colony in 1946, allowed itself to be drawn into a colonial war and then a civil war in Indochina?

President Roosevelt's attitude toward Indochina during the war years was one of traditional American anti-colonialism. In a memorandum sent to Cordell Hull in January 1944, Roosevelt wrote: "France has had the country—thirty million inhabitants—for nearly one hundred years, and the people are worse off than they were at the beginning. . . . France has milked it for one hundred years. The people of Indo-China are entitled to something better than that."[4]

In the postwar years American enthusiasm for Vietnamese nationalism declined as rapidly as American concern with communism grew, which is to say very rapidly indeed. To an indeterminate but undoubtedly significant degree, the initial American involvement in Vietnam was influenced by two extraneous factors: Korea and McCarthy. After North Korea invaded South Korea in a direct and unambiguous act of aggression, the United States, understandably but inaccurately, came to regard the French war in Indochina as analogous to the war in Korea, overlooking extremely important considerations of nationalism and anti-colonialism. This view of the Indochinese war was reinforced by the McCarthy hysteria at home, which fostered undiscriminating attitudes of fear and hostility toward communism in all its forms. Not only were Americans disinclined in the late forties and early fifties to make distinctions among communist movements (with the notable exception of Yugoslavia), but at that time the communist world looked very much more like a monolith than it did a few years later. It was under these circumstances that the United States began indirect military assistance to the French in Indochina at the end of 1950. In September 1951 the United States signed an agreement for direct economic assistance to Vietnam and in October 1952 the two hundredth American ship carrying military aid arrived in Saigon.

The Eisenhower Administration went to the brink in 1954 but then decided against United States military intervention. The decision against intervention was taken largely on the advice of General Matthew Ridgway, then Army Chief of Staff. In his memoirs published in 1956 General Ridgway relates how he concluded, on the basis of a report by a team of Army experts, that it would be disastrous for the United States to intervene with ground forces in Indochina. General Ridgway wrote: "We could have fought in Indochina. We could have won, if we had been willing to pay the tremendous cost in men and money that such intervention would have required—a cost that in my opinion would have eventually been as great as, or greater than, that we paid in Korea. In Korea, we had learned that air and naval power alone cannot win a war and that inadequate ground forces cannot win one either. It was incredible to me that we had forgotten that bitter lesson so soon—that we were on the verge of making that same tragic error. That error, thank God, was not repeated."[5]

The Geneva Agreements were signed in July 1954. They explicitly prohibited the introduction into Vietnam of additional military forces and explicitly provided that general elections would be held in Vietnam by July 1956. They also explicitly stated that the demarcation line between North and South Vietnam at the 17th Parallel was "provisional and should not in any way be interpreted as constituting a political or territorial boundary," a fact which is overlooked by those who maintain that North Vietnam is engaged in aggression against a *foreign* country rather than supporting a domestic insurrection. In its unilateral statement of July 21, 1954, the United States indicated, with respect to the Accords, that it would "refrain from the threat or use of force to disturb them," and further stated that the United States would "continue to seek to achieve unity through free elections, supervised by the U.N. to insure that they are conducted fairly."

It is not useful to try to assign degrees of guilt to each side for violations of the Geneva Accords. It suffices to note that there have been violations by all concerned, including the United States, which, in violation of its commitment of 1954, supported President Ngo Dinh Diem in his refusal to hold the elections provided for in the Geneva Accords, presumably because he feared that the communists would win. Whatever short-term advantages the many violations of the Geneva Agreements by both sides have brought their perpetrators, their cumulative effect has been the destruction of each side's trust in the word of the other, greatly complicating present prospects for a new agreement. Hanoi's stubborn and puzzling refusal to negotiate may therefore reflect neither a preference for war nor confidence in victory but simply an unwillingness to believe that a negotiated settlement would be honored.

Through a series of small steps, none extremely important or irrevocable in itself, the United States gradually took over the French commitment in South Vietnam after the French withdrawal. The United States Military Assistance Advisory Group took over the training of the South Vietnamese Army in 1955 and thereafter the United States became increasingly committed to the Diem regime by means of economic and military support and public statements. In 1960 President Eisenhower increased the number of American military advisers from 327 to 685. Further increases followed and by February 1962 the number of United States military personnel in South Vietnam had reached four thousand. Step by step, as it became increasingly clear that the South Vietnamese Army was being defeated, the American commitment increased. The result has been that through a series of limited escalations, each one of which has been more or less compatible with the view that the war was not our war and would have to be won or lost by the South Vietnamese themselves, the war has indeed become our war. Gradually, almost imperceptibly, the commitment to support the South Vietnamese in a war which it was said *they* must either win or lose was supplanted by a commitment, as Secretary McNamara has put it, "to take all necessary measures within our capability to prevent a Communist victory."[6]

The United States is now involved in a sizable and "openended" war against communism in the only country in the world which won freedom from colonial rule under communist leadership. In South Vietnam as in North Vietnam, the communists remain today the only solidly organized political force. That fact is both the measure of our failure and the key to its possible redemption.

So-called "wars of national liberation" are political wars, whose outcomes depend on a combination of political and military factors. The communist guerrillas in Malaya could not have been beaten without hard fighting, but neither, in all probability, could they have been beaten had Malaya not been given its independence. The Hukbalahaps were defeated in the Philippines primarily because of the political isolation imposed on them by the reforms of President Ramon Magsaysay. The major reason for the success of the Viet Cong in South Vietnam has not been aid from the North but the absence of a cohesive alternative nationalist movement in the South. Both the success of the communists in South Vietnam and their failure in India, Burma, Malaya, Indonesia, and the Philippines strongly suggest that "wars of national liberation" depend for their success more on the weakness of the regime under attack than on the strength of support from outside.

The Vietnamese Revolution

Our search for a solution to the Vietnamese war must begin with the general fact that nationalism is the strongest single political force in the world today and the specific fact, arising from the history to which I have referred, that in Vietnam the most effective nationalist movement is communist-controlled. We are compelled, therefore, once again to choose between opposition to communism and support of nationalism. I strongly recommend that for once we give priority to the latter. The dilemma is a cruel one, and one which we must hope to avoid in the future by timely and unstinting support of non-communist nationalist movements, but it is too late for that in Vietnam. I strongly recommend, therefore, that we seek to come to terms with both Hanoi and the Viet Cong, not, to be sure, by "turning tail and running," as the saying goes, but by conceding the Viet Cong a part in the government of South Vietnam along the lines to be spelled out in Chapter 9.

Present realities require a revision of priorities in American policy. The basis of my criticisms of American policy in Southeast Asia and Latin America is a belief that American interests are better served by supporting nationalism than by opposing communism, and that when the two are encountered in the same political movement it is in our interest to accept a communist role in the government of the country concerned rather than to undertake the cruel and all but impossible task of suppressing a genuinely nationalist revolution. In Vietnam we have allowed our fear of communism to make us once again the enemy of a nationalist revolution, and in that role we have wrought havoc.

6

The
Vietnam Fallout

THE HAVOC wrought by American involvement is by no means confined to Vietnam. Its effects are being felt all over the world and I venture to guess that in the long run the Vietnamese war will have as significant an impact on our relations with Europe as it will on our future position in Southeast Asia; and perhaps the most important effects of the war will be felt here at home—in our national attitudes and the priorities of public policy. In this chapter I shall discuss the fallout effects of the Vietnamese war in three areas: our relations with the Soviet Union and Eastern Europe, relations with our allies in Western Europe and elsewhere, and the impact within the United States.

The Fallout in the East

An Eastern European diplomat told me that he regarded the Vietnamese war as remote to the concerns of his own country except when he read statements in the American press celebrating the number of *"communists"* killed in a particular week or battle. Then, he said, he was reminded that America considered itself to be at war not merely with some Vietnamese rebels but with communism in general, and that America, therefore, must be considered hostile to all communists, including himself, and all communist countries, including his own.

Soviet diplomats not only admit but are at pains to volunteer the view that relations between the United States and the Soviet Union are "frozen." One Soviet diplomat, asked what was being done to prevent a deterioration of Soviet-American relations while the war continued, scornfully replied, "What relations? in ballet?"[1]

I think these comments fairly well express the fallout effect of the Vietnamese war on American relations with Eastern Europe and the Soviet Union. As has happened all too many times in the past, ideology is intruding upon interest, acting as a conduit of hostility from one part of the world to another. It is a mark of relative maturity on both sides that the impulses of conflict thus conveyed have been fairly weak so far, that neither we nor the Russians have been willing to expand the Vietnamese war into a general revival of the cold war, but we are certainly moving in that direction. The ideological aspect of the Vietnamese war is slowly undermining good relations between the United States and Eastern Europe; the détente, whose progress was generating such optimism before the expansion of the Vietnamese war, has been arrested and a slow, steady erosion has set in. How far it will go, and with what unfortunate results, will be determined by the future course and scale of the war in Vietnam.

One of the principal reasons why things are not a lot worse than they are is the restraint shown by the Russians with respect to the war. They are providing the North Vietnamese with a steady flow of supplies, including the ground-to-air missiles used against American aircraft, but they show no inclination, thus far, to participate directly in the war, and even their anti-American propaganda is comparatively mild. If positions were reversed, if the Russians were conducting daily bombing raids against an American ally, it is just about inconceivable that we would confine ourselves to providing equipment to the country under attack. If we did, one can well imagine the field day the superpatriots would have charging our government with cowardice and treason. My feeling about the matter is that the Russians are frightened of us, not only because of our enormous power but also because of our erratic behavior in such places as Vietnam and the Dominican Republic, which may make our policies seem, from their viewpoint, dangerously unpredictable.

What is wrong with that? it may be asked. Isn't it a fine thing to keep the Russians guessing? What is wrong with it is that it puts Soviet-American relations on an exceedingly unstable basis. Though not as powerful as the United States, Russia is a very great power and she is unlikely to be restrained indefinitely by fear of the United States. As long as the Vietnamese war is fought on its present scale, the Russians may remain essentially outside of the conflict, although that is by no means certain. But if the war is significantly expanded, the Russians will be increasingly goaded by the Chinese for standing aside while the Americans devastate a Soviet ally. With their prestige thus impaired, fear could give way to anger and the Russians might then take the enormous risk of direct intervention in the war.

For the present the main fallout effect of the war on East-West relations is the loss of the opportunities associated with the American policy of building bridges to the East. The significance of that loss is great indeed; it amounts to the suspension of significant progress toward normal relations between the two great nations which hold the power of life and death over all of humanity. One may hope that a positive evolution of Soviet-American relations will be resumed, but it certainly cannot be counted upon.

Soviet-American cooperation in bringing about the cease-fire in the India-Pakistan war in September 1965 is one example of the kind of beneficial collaboration that the Vietnamese war makes increasingly difficult. That cooperation—or "parallelism," as it was called—was possible because the Kashmir war was one of the very few international conflicts of the postwar era, and perhaps the most important, in relation to which Russia and America had similar interests. As a result of their shared interest in a cease-fire that would humiliate neither India nor Pakistan while also having the effect of restraining China, the Soviet Union and the United States brought decisive influence to bear for the acceptance by both sides of the United Nations Security Council's cease-fire resolution. In so doing they breathed a bit of life back into the United Nations in the wake of the fiasco over Article 19. Just as the Article 19 controversy—in which the Americans demanded and the Russians refused to make compulsory payments for the costs of the United Nations peace forces in the Middle East and the Congo—illustrated the inability of the organization to function when the United States and the Soviet Union are set against each other, the Kashmir crisis showed that the United Nations could function in the manner intended by its architects when the two great powers were in substantial agreement.

There are other areas of the world and other kinds of issues on which the Russians and Americans could collaborate through the United Nations, but for the fallout from Vietnam. Even at the time of the Kashmir war, however, American officials were at pains to describe their cooperation with the Russians as a policy of "parallelism," using that word, apparently, to dispel the notion that any similarity in Soviet and American interests could be more than an accident and to reassure people in general that the cold war was still on. Since the end of the Kashmir war and the restoration of Vietnam to its position of unchallenged primacy on the international agenda the United Nations, excluded from a meaningful peace-seeking role, has again become impotent and demoralized.

One notable casualty of the Vietnamese war was a consular

convention between the Soviet Union and the United States signed in June 1964 and still unratified by the Senate in mid-1966 although it had been reported favorably by the Foreign Relations Committee on August 3, 1965. The convention is essentially an arrangement for the facilitation of travel and the orderly conduct of business between the Soviet Union and the United States. In addition to the normal provisions of consular conventions, it contains special provisions guaranteeing notification about and access to American citizens detained in the Soviet Union, thus giving Americans some protection against arbitrary Soviet police methods. The treaty also grants consular officials the same immunity from prosecution for felonies accorded to diplomats; they can, however, be expelled promptly if they engage in improper activities. Opposition to this sensible treaty developed after its approval by the Foreign Relations Committee. Mr. J. Edgar Hoover was widely quoted as having said that the establishment of Soviet consulates would make the work of the Federal Bureau of Investigation "more difficult," and the "Liberty Lobby," a right-wing extremist organization, deluged Senators with mail denouncing the treaty. The treaty thereafter was held back by the Senate leadership for fear of an embarrassing defeat. A number of my colleagues have told me privately that they know the treaty is a good one but they just don't want to vote on it now—"not," as one Senator said, "while this war is going on."

Another straw in an ill wind was the rupture in 1965 of negotiations between the Rumanian government and the Firestone Tire and Rubber Company for the design and engineering of two synthetic-rubber plants as the result of pressures applied in an anti-communist crusade conducted by a junior extremist organization and a Firestone competitor. It was contended, among other things, that the tires which the Rumanian plants would produce eventually would be used by the Viet Cong. In a Senate speech on July 26, 1965, I suggested that "the probable result of this affair will be that instead of a healthy profit for Firestone, a solid gain for our balance of payments, and a positive step forward in the building of bridges to the East, the United States will have earned a harvest of ill will and a reputation for being quite incapable of executing policies decided upon by the President and the Department of State." Several months after the Firestone fiasco, a group of American tobacco companies were brought under similar right-wing attacks for their purchases of tobacco from Eastern European communist countries. On that occasion the State Department gave prompt, public support, as it had not done for Firestone, and the tobacco companies were able to fend off their right-wing attackers.[2]

Other proposals for improved relations between the United States and communist countries have been put on ice. A legislative proposal by President Johnson for liberalized and expanded trade with the communist countries lies pigeonholed in a Congressional committee which refuses even to hold hearings on it. Outer Mongolia, a Soviet-oriented country with which the United States has had virtually no contact, felt constrained to reject an American gift of $25,000 for flood relief, which may have been an American gesture toward the establishment of the diplomatic relations hitherto desired by Outer Mongolia. On the other hand, an agreement for the opening of direct air service between New York and Moscow has been reached, and there is some hope for a ban on underground nuclear tests and even more for a treaty which would limit the spread of nuclear weapons.

On balance, however, the Vietnamese war thus far has had three major "fallout" effects on East-West relations: first, it has generated a degree of mistrust and antagonism toward the United States on the part of Eastern European nations which otherwise are most anxious to expand economic, cultural and even political relations with the West; second, it has weakened the drive of the Eastern European countries toward greater independence of the Soviet Union; third, it has put a severe strain on the Soviet-American détente—if indeed one can still speak of a détente—reducing whatever hope there may have been for substantive agreements in many fields. Relations, if not overtly hostile, have indeed, as the Russians say, become "frozen"—frozen in the direction of active hostility.

East-West relations now hinge on the war in Vietnam. If it goes on indefinitely, or if it is greatly escalated, it will destroy prospects for accommodation on issues ranging from trade to the future of Germany, and eventually it may bring the Russians, to say nothing of the Chinese, into direct conflict with the United States. If these things happen, then the fallout from Vietnam will indeed be far more destructive than the war itself.

The fact that Soviet-American relations are not worse than they are, and that some limited accommodations seem possible, is almost certainly attributable to China, whose hostility seems to have caused the Russians to despair of reconciliation and to turn, therefore, slightly toward the West. As long as the Vietnam war continues, that process cannot go very far, but if there were no war, it might go very far indeed—farther perhaps than anyone can now anticipate.

The Fallout in the West

Vietnam has become the key factor in America's relations with both allies and neutrals. American officials are in many instances more concerned with what a country's leaders say or think about American policy in Vietnam than with more relevant matters such as the particular country's internal development or contribution to the security of its own region. "Realists" that we are, proud and often boastful of the universality of our commitments—to the extent indeed that in testimony before the Senate Preparedness Subcommittee on August 25, 1966, the Secretary of State has declared that the United States would use force against any aggressor even in the absence of a defense treaty, an American military presence, or any form of Congressional approval—we have become nonetheless a one-issue participant in world affairs, hungering after a kind word or some token of support, for either of which we are more than willing to pay a handsome reward.

Nevertheless, our major allies are not supporting us in Vietnam. A few countries do have strong words of encouragement for us; they see America doing its "duty" as leader of the free world and, while their own young men go to school, get jobs, and raise families, they are quite reconciled to having American boys fight and die in the jungles of Southeast Asia, because if Americans were not fighting and dying in Vietnam, they tell us, America's friends in other parts of the world—they themselves, for example—might lose "confidence" in her. We are very grateful for this support. Other countries, dependent on the United States for their defense or for monetary support, for economic aid or for export markets, have found silence to be the better part of discretion; occasionally they have some mild praise for us, which makes us feel happy, and occasionally they have a mild reproach, which makes us feel angry and injured. Still others, who by reason of economic self-sufficiency, strong leadership, or a highly developed sense of national dignity do not feel the need to please the United States, are openly critical of American policy in Vietnam; the leaders of these countries, who do not understand that they are supposed to feel "secure" because Americans are fighting in Vietnam, are regarded as "senile" or "eccentric" by American officials, who profess "sadness" and "puzzlement" but never—heaven forbid—anger in the face of such ingratitude and apostasy.

There are three possible explanations for the refusal of almost all of America's friends to participate in the war, each of which, if valid, suggests that there is something wrong with American policy. First, they may believe that it simply does not matter, from the viewpoint of their own security, who wins the Vietnamese war. Or, second, they may believe that their security is affected but there is no point in becoming involved because the United States, under what has been called the "Rusk Doctrine," is unilaterally committed to resist any and all threats to the free world and will take all the risks and accept all the costs regardless of what anyone else does. Finally, our allies and other friends may have judged that it is neither necessary nor possible for a Western army to fight a successful land war on the Asian mainland and that their security, and ours, can be defended from the islands and waters off the coast of Asia where American sea and air power are dominant.

It is contended by American policy-makers that if the United States makes major concessions in Vietnam, the credibility of our other guarantees and commitments will be undermined and countries which depend on American support, from Thailand to Germany, will lose faith in the United States. There may be something in this but not much. In fact, many of America's allies are more inclined to worry about an undue American preoccupation with Vietnam than to fear the consequences of an American withdrawal, provided that withdrawal were orderly and based on a negotiated agreement.

Although because of their country's exposed position and the vulnerability of Berlin some Germans may feel reassured by the demonstration of America's willingness to fight for an ally, one also hears German commentators expressing the fear that in its preoccupation with Asia the United States may be losing interest in Germany and Berlin. A leading professor of the Free University of Berlin wrote of the American involvement in Vietnam: "They have made a major, long-term commitment on the Asian mainland, which is bound to reduce their concern for Europe and may lead to reduction of their forces there, without consulting their European allies. As a result, they have undermined the confidence of these allies at a critical moment. . . ."[3] That of course is exactly the opposite of the intended effect of America's war policy. Since this statement was made, the United States has in fact withdrawn some troops from Germany, without consulting the Germans.

I suspect that the American involvement in Vietnam has something to do with the current crisis in NATO. President de Gaulle has said as much, for example, in his press conference of February 21, 1966, in which he cited as one reason for his decision to withdraw French forces from NATO what he perceives to be a danger that the United States may drag its European partners into non-European wars. One detects in Europe a growing uneasiness about American policy, a feeling that the United States is becoming unreliable and that it may be better—safer, that is—to keep the Americans at a distance. One detects in the French withdrawal from NATO a great deal more than General de Gaulle's idiosyncrasies; the French action may be representative of a widespread loss of European confidence in American policy and judgment.

It is difficult for an American to look at his country as a foreigner may see it. I would guess that many a European or Asian or African or Latin American looking at America today feels overawed rather than reassured by our tremendous power—by the power of our nuclear weapons and rockets and the power of the world's greatest and possibly fastest growing economy. In an irrational but human way they may be more appalled than impressed by the existence of such great power, even though they are dependent on it for their own security. And, far from being reassured by the uses of American military power in Vietnam, by the spectacle of American bombs falling on Vietnamese jungles and villages in a volume equal to that of the bombing of Germany's great industrial cities at the height of World War II, our friends abroad may be puzzled both by the destructiveness of American power and its apparent ineffectiveness. It is possible that the violence and inconclusiveness of the war have raised doubts in many minds abroad as to whether it is not worse to be saved than to be abandoned by the United States. They may even be thinking in terms of the pungent Chinese proverb: "In shallow waters dragons become the sport of shrimps."

I am inclined to wonder too if the current reluctance of our allies to accept responsibilities outside of their own regions is not indirectly related to the American military involvement in Southeast Asia. Insofar as that involvement implies a willingness on the part of the United States to act as a global policeman, even though it must do so with no more than token support from a few allies, others may be encouraged to believe that, even if their interests are involved in crises like the war in Vietnam, there is really no need to get involved because the Americans will take care of it anyway. Why not, therefore, concentrate on more agreeable matters at home and let the Americans sacrifice the lives and pay the costs since apparently they are willing to do it?

This suspicion may be unkind, but I do not think it is unfounded. It is perfectly natural for a nation, like an individual, to let someone else do a hard job or bear some disagreeable burden. What is not perfectly natural—what is in fact a very puzzling question indeed—is why the other party is *willing* to do it.

The reason, I think, is an excess of pride born of power. Power has a way of undermining judgment, of planting delusions of grandeur in the minds of otherwise sensible people and otherwise sensible nations. As I have said earlier, the idea of being responsible for the whole world seems to have dazzled us, giving rise to what I call the arrogance of power, or what the French, perhaps more aptly, call "le vertige de puissance," by which they mean a kind of dizziness or giddiness inspired by the possession of great power. If then, as I suspect, there is a relationship between the self-absorption of some of our allies and the American military involvement in Vietnam, it may have more to do with American vanity than with our friends' complacency. Thus, by taking on foreign responsibilities for which it is ill-equipped, America not only strains her resources but encourages other nations to neglect their responsibilities, which neglect of course can only lead to added burdens for the United States. With this thought in mind, I turn now to what may be the most fateful of all of the fallout effects of the Vietnamese war: its effects on the American people and nation.

The Fallout at Home

The war in Southeast Asia has affected the internal life of the United States in two important ways: it has diverted our energies from the Great Society program which began so promisingly, and it has generated the beginnings of a war fever in the minds of the American people and their leaders.

Despite brave talk about having both "guns and butter," the Vietnamese war has already had a destructive effect on the Great Society. The 89th Congress, which enacted so much important domestic legislation in 1965, enacted much less in 1966, partly, it is true, because of the unusual productivity of its first session but more because the Congress as a whole lost interest in the Great Society and became, politically and psychologically, a "war Congress."

There is a kind of Gresham's Law of public policy: fear drives out hope, security precedes welfare, and it is only to the extent that a country is successful in the prevention of bad things that it is set free to concentrate on those pursuits which renew the nation's strength and bring happiness into the lives of its people. For twenty years beginning in 1940 America was greatly preoccupied with external dangers and accordingly neglectful of those aspects of domestic life which require organized public programs and sizable public expenditures. The reason for this, of course, was the exacting demands of two world wars and an intractable cold war, which required the massive diversion of resources from community life to national security. We felt ourselves compelled to turn

away from our hopes in order to concentrate on our fears and
the public happiness became a luxury to be postponed to
some distant day when the dangers besetting us would have
disappeared.

In the early 1960s a trend and an event coincided which
seemed to create the opportunity for a revision of priorities
on our national agenda. The trend—after if not before the
Cuban missile crisis of 1962—was one toward relative stability
in international relations, based on a fragile, tacit agreement
between the great powers to live together in peaceful, or
competitive, coexistence. The event was the coming to office
in the United States of a creative new Administration, eager
to arrange a détente with the Russians and eager as well to
use a respite from international crisis to devise imaginative
new programs for the betterment of American life. During
the three years of his Administration, President Kennedy put
forward imaginative and well-conceived plans for the improvement of health and education, for the conquest of poverty, pollution, and blight, and for the spiritual enrichment
of American life.

President Johnson embraced and expanded upon these
innovations. Elected in 1964 by a great popular majority and
supported by a great Congressional majority, President Johnson used his extraordinary talent for leadership to make the
first session of the 89th Congress the most productive in a
generation. With a degree of partisan harmony that would
have seemed inconceivable a few years before, the Congress
in 1965 adopted sweeping legislation to expand education, to
provide health care to the aged, to combat urban and rural
poverty, to renew our cities and purify our streams, and to
meet many other long-neglected problems. It seemed that
the United States might be about to undergo something of a
social revolution.

Then came Vietnam. The war had been going on for many
years but before 1965 it had been a small and distant war and,
as our leaders repeatedly assured us, a war which would be

won or lost by the Vietnamese themselves. Then, in the first months of 1965 if not earlier, it became clear that the Saigon government was about to lose the war and we intervened with a large army, changing our role from adviser to principal belligerent. As a result of this radical change in American policy in Southeast Asia, we have had, after so brief an interlude, to turn back once again from our hopes to our fears, from the renewal of national resources to the avoidance of international disaster.

Vigorously executed and adequately funded, the legislation adopted by the 89th Congress can open the way to an era of abundance and opportunity for all Americans, but for the present at least the inspiration and commitment of the Great Society have disappeared. They have disappeared in the face of our deepening involvement in Vietnam, and although it may be contended that the United States has the material resources to rebuild its society at home while waging war abroad, it is already being demonstrated that we do not have the mental and spiritual resources for such a double effort. Politicians, like other people, have only one brain apiece, and it stands to reason that if they spend all their time thinking about one thing they are not going to be thinking about something else. The President simply cannot think about implementing the Great Society at home while he is supervising bombing missions over North Vietnam; nor is the Congress particularly inclined to debate, much less finance, expanded domestic programs when it is involved in debating, and paying for, an expanding war; nor can the American people be expected to think very hard or do very much about improving their schools and communities when they are worried about casualty lists and the danger of a wider war.

My own view is that there is a kind of madness in the facile assumption that we can raise the many billions of dollars necessary to rebuild our schools and cities and public transport and eliminate the pollution of air and water while also spending tens of billions to finance an "open-ended" war in

Asia. But even if the material resources can somehow be drawn from an expanding economy, I do not think that the spiritual resources will long be forthcoming from an angry and disappointed people.

As I have already suggested,* the effectiveness of foreign policy depends on the strength of the nation and the strength of the nation depends less on its actions abroad than on the development, use, and renewal of its own resources, both material and human. The education of our children, the rehabilitation of our cities and the making available of jobs for all who want to work have everything to do with the strength of our country and everything to do, therefore, with the success of our foreign policy. To argue, as was done in the forties and fifties and is now being done again, that the postponement of these things is the necessary price of national security is exactly the same as saying that the price of security is the slow erosion of the foundations of security—clearly an untenable position. Foreign and domestic policy are in fact inseparable; in the long run an effective policy abroad depends upon a healthy society at home.

There is something unseemly about a nation conducting a foreign policy that involves it in the affairs of most of the nations in the world while its own domestic needs are neglected or postponed, just as there is something unseemly about an individual carrying all the burdens of the Community Chest and the PTA while his own children run wild and his household is in disarray. There is something fishy about this kind of behavior, something hidden and unhealthy. I do not think that a man can be genuinely responsible in one area of his life and neglectful in another. I am more inclined to believe that the man who makes the best contribution to his community is the one who begins by meeting his responsibilities to himself and to his own family. By analogy, it seems to me unnatural and unhealthy for a nation to be engaged

---

See Introduction, pp. 20–21.

in global crusades for some principle or ideal while neglecting the needs of its own people; indeed, it seems far more likely that the nation that does most to benefit humanity in the long run is the nation that begins by meeting the needs of that portion of humanity which resides within its own frontiers.

It should be very clear that what is called for is not a wholesale renunciation by the United States of its global responsibilities. That would be impossible even if it were desirable. What is needed is a redress in the heavy imbalance on the side of foreign commitment that has prevailed for the last twenty years—a redress of the kind so hopefully begun by Presidents Kennedy and Johnson but now suspended as America once again turns her energies to making war.

The turning away from constructive pursuits after so brief an interlude is the first and at present more conspicuous fallout effect of the war on American life. The second, no less damaging, is the stirring up of a war fever in the minds of our people and leaders. It is only just now getting under way, but as the war goes on, as the casualty lists grow longer and affect more and more American homes, the fever will rise and the patience of the American people will give way to mounting demands for an expanded war, for a lightning blow that will get it over with at a stroke. The American people have already registered their approval, if the polls are to be believed, of the bombing of oil installations in Hanoi and Haiphong, not, I think, out of bellicosity but in the vain hope that these air strikes would shorten the war. If the war continues for a long time, the demand for expanded hostilities will rise, first perhaps for a blockade of the North Vietnamese ports; then, if that does not work, for an all-out attack on the North Vietnamese air bases; then, if the North Vietnamese withdraw their planes to Chinese bases, for a strike against China; and then we will have a general Asian war if not a global nuclear war.

There has already been a marked change in the kinds of things we think about and talk about in America and there can be no doubt that the major cause of the change is the war. Almost every day millions of Americans see stories and pictures of battle on the front pages of their newspapers and on their television screens. All this war news must have its effects: the diversion of attention from domestic pursuits, the gradual dehumanizing of the enemy, rising levels of tension, anger, war-weariness, and bellicosity.

In the first week of March 1966 United States Marines and South Vietnamese troops engaged North Vietnamese forces in a bloody fight designated "Operation Utah." Mr. Joseph Galloway of United Press International filed the following report on an incident in Operation Utah:

We stood on the hill and cheered and whistled and shouted advice:

"Kill the son of a bitch. . . . Get him. . . . what's the matter with you jarheads."

The lone communist was about 50 yards away from us, just below the next ridge, running and dodging, trying to make his way to the top. About 30 Marines were chasing him up the scrub-covered hill.

It was like watching a ball game from the upper deck of Yankee Stadium. We were above the communist and his pursuers and could see every move clearly.

The Marines on the ridge across the way were below their target and could not see him well. They fired time and time again at him.

Suddenly one of the bullets struck. The communist dropped to the ground. He lost his rifle as he fell.

"They breezed him, they breezed him," one of the cheering section beside me shouted. "Naw, there he goes," another Marine said. "He's up and running again . . . get him . . . get him."

Another bullet knocked the communist off his feet, and a second time he got up. He was moving slower when the third and fourth bullets slammed into his body and knocked him down again. But still he moved, crawling up and over the crest of the hill.

Nobody could tell whether he lived or died. The Marines chasing him went no further than the ridge top.[4]

The dehumanizing of the enemy is a characteristic of all wars. What Mr. Galloway described in his dispatch was the killing not of a man but of something abstract or something subhuman, a "communist," and it was "like watching a ball game from the upper deck of Yankee Stadium." The possibility that *he* may have regarded himself as a patriot fighting to free his country from foreign invaders would never of course have occurred to anyone in the "cheering section."

On April 20, 1966, Secretary of Defense McNamara appeared before the Senate Foreign Relations Committee to testify on the foreign-aid bill. With respect to Vietnam he said he thought "we should be proud of what we are doing." The Secretary is proud of the large number of aircraft and helicopters we have deployed, of our ability to transport and supply an army of hundreds of thousands of men ten thousand miles from home. It is an impressive achievement, I admit, but what is forgotten in all this pride, in this treating of a war machine as an end in itself, is the *purpose* of our army and its equipment, which is to kill people and destroy whole villages as well as the bridges and roads of North Vietnam.

Under normal circumstances most people would immediately and instinctively say "no" if asked whether they were proud of their country's ability to kill and destroy. But in a war all that changes, and in the course of dehumanizing an enemy—and this is the ultimate fallout from any war—a man dehumanizes himself. It is not just the naturally bellicose, the thwarted or the twisted personalities, that become dehumanized in a war. It is everyman: the good and decent citizen who looks after his children, who is considerate of his neighbors and kind to animals. It is he who ultimately prays the obscene "War Prayer" of Mark Twain:

. . . O Lord our God, help us to tear their soldiers to

bloody shreds with our shells; help us to cover their smiling fields with the pale forms of their patriot dead; help us to drown the thunder of the guns with the shrieks of their wounded, writhing in pain; help us to lay waste their humble homes with a hurricane of fire; help us to wring the hearts of their unoffending widows with unavailing grief; help us to turn them out roofless with their little children to wander unfriended the wastes of their desolated land in rags and hunger and thirst, sports of the sun flames of summer and the icy winds of winter, broken in spirit, worn with travail, imploring Thee for the refuge of the grave and denied it—for our sakes who adore Thee, Lord, blast their hopes, blight their lives, protract their bitter pilgrimage, make heavy their steps, water their way with their tears, stain the white snow with the blood of their wounded feet! We ask it, in the spirit of love, of Him Who is the Source of Love, and Who is the ever-faithful refuge and friend of all that are sore beset and seek His aid with humble and contrite hearts. Amen.[5]

Behind the "War Prayer" is the arrogance of power, the presumption of the very strong who confuse power with wisdom and set out upon self-appointed missions to police the world, to defeat all tyrannies, to make their fellow men rich and happy and free. Great nations in the past have set out upon such missions and they have wrought havoc, bringing misery to their intended beneficiaries and destruction upon themselves.

America is showing some signs of that fatal presumption, that overextension of power and mission, which has brought ruin to great nations in the past. The process has hardly begun, but the war which we are now fighting can only accelerate it. If the war goes on and expands, if that fatal process continues to accelerate until America becomes what she is not now and never has been, a seeker after unlimited power and empire, the leader of a global counter-revolution, then Vietnam will have had a mighty and tragic fallout indeed.

7

The
Chinese Revolution

THERE IS AN unacknowledged presence in all that we think
and say and do in connection with Vietnam: the presence
of China. We wage war against the Viet Cong and North
Vietnam but we regard them as instruments of China, and
it is China and Chinese communism that we regard as the
real threat to the security of Southeast Asia. If it were not
for our concern with China and what she might do, with
Chinese communism and its possible spread, it might be
a relatively easy matter to come to terms with our enemies
in Vietnam. Thus our prospects in Vietnam cannot be
separated from our attitude toward China and China's
attitude toward us. Separate and indigenous though it is,
the Vietnamese Revolution is related to the Chinese Revolution and, for reasons that I shall suggest, a durable settlement in Vietnam is unlikely except in the context of at least
a limited accommodation between the United States and
China.

The Chinese Revolution, an epochal event in the history
of Asia and the world, is still at flood tide, still confident of
its ability to remake human nature, still messianic in its
aims if not in its actions, still filled with passionate hostility
to its foreign enemies, real and imaginary, still, in Crane

Brinton's frame of reference, in its period of extremism, still unready for that coming down to earth which we call Thermidor.

The Chinese Revolution is more than a rebellion of the new against the old within China, comparable to the rising of the French republicans against the *ancien régime* or of the Russian communists against the tsarist regime. It is also the rebellion of a proud and ancient civilization against foreign powers—"barbarians" to the Chinese—who set upon China in the nineteenth century with a fatal impact on China's economy, institutions, and national pride.

China and the West: The Fatal Impact

When at last China began to adopt Western techniques and Western technology, it was not out of a desire to become Westernized in the way in which Japan had become Westernized; still less did it demonstrate affection for the West. It was rather the precursor to one of the great revolutions of history, an effort to use Western techniques to throw off the power of the West, to "use foreign ways to protect Chinese ideas." Over half a century ago, in 1903, a group of young scholars passed through the provincial town of Neichiang on their way to Europe to study. These young men, the local newspaper commented, would bring back science, which would save China and make her strong and able to lift her head again. "We have been insulted enough," the newspaper said. "We have been treated with contempt enough. Now we shall stand on our own, equal to other nations, and those that have come to despoil us will return where they properly belong, to their own lands, and leave us in peace."[1]

The measure of China's humiliation and anger is her great and ancient pride. China's pride is the product of a civilization which owed very little to contacts with foreigners, one which, until a century ago, had no important links with any civilization as powerful and developed as hers. The absence of any rival centers of culture and power instilled in the Chinese their sense of belonging to a civilization rather than to a state and also was responsible for their view of all foreigners as tributaries and barbarians.

China's historic pride is built on a great deal more than simple chauvinism. Before the time of Christ the Chinese had developed the principles and methods which were to hold together their empire until the twentieth century. In science and technology, as well as government, China was well ahead of Europe by the time Marco Polo visited her in the thirteenth century. China became the center of civilization in Eastern Asia and the model for smaller states, such as Korea and Vietnam, whose rulers accepted the obligation of tribute to the Chinese Emperor as their suzerain. When European merchants and missionaries and buccaneers first came to China, they did not come to a land of primitives and pagans. They came upon a rich and ancient civilization, but one which had fallen behind in its technology, especially its military technology, in part because, having been so powerful and secure for so long, the Chinese simply could not believe they might be attacked. The result was that they were thrown open to exploitation by foreigners whose ignorance of China was just about total and whose power, in any case, vastly exceeded their wisdom.

The behavior of Europeans who went to China confirmed the Chinese view of them as "barbarians," while until the nineteenth century the Chinese, in their ethnocentric pride, remained aloof, uninterested in the West and unable to believe that the "barbarians" could possibly have anything of value to offer. When King George III of England offered to send a permanent ambassador to Peking in 1793, Ch'ien-lung, the Emperor, grandly replied:

> As to the request made in your memorial, O King, to send one of your nationals to stay at the Celestial Court to take care of your country's trade with China, this is

not in harmony with the state system of our dynasty and will definitely not be permitted. . . . The Celestial Court has pacified and possessed the territory within the four seas. Its sole aim is to do its utmost to achieve good government and to manage political affairs, attaching no value to strange jewels and precious objects. . . . As a matter of fact, the virtue and prestige of the Celestial Dynasty having spread far and wide, the kings of the myriad nations come by land and sea with all sorts of precious things. Consequently, there is nothing we lack, as your principal envoy and others have themselves observed. We have never set much store on strange or ingenious objects, nor do we need any more of your country's manufactures. . . .[2]

The West was not so easily to be put off. In the course of the nineteenth century Western soldiers and traders and missionaries were to reduce China to a semi-colonial status, and the shock of this experience was to spawn the Chinese revolution, now still at flood tide. "So complete was the disaster," says Professor John Fairbank of Harvard University, "that a new order had to be built from the ground up. Western doctrines of all kinds were tried out. The thing that proved effective was the Leninist type of party dictatorship, an elite recruited under discipline according to a new orthodoxy, organized something like an old Chinese secret society, united in the effort to seize power and recreate a strong state. This nationalistic aim overrode every other consideration. The kind of Western individualism propagated by our missionaries had no chance."[3]

Under the Western impact an empire that had been superior to all others in its world was not only humbled but threatened with extinction. Words like "extraterritoriality" and "unequal treaties" are far too antiseptic, far too bland, to describe China's humiliation by Western imperialism. In human terms, the coming of Western civilization to China in the nineteenth century meant the plundering of China's wealth by foreigners and the reduction of most of the Chinese to a humiliating and inferior status in their own country. Missionaries were immune from Chinese law and treated the Chinese as heathen, except of course for the converts who also claimed immunity from Chinese law and used the power conferred by their foreign association to intimidate their fellow citizens. Foreign goods were exempted by treaty from internal toll taxes imposed by the Manchu Dynasty to pay for the Taiping Rebellion of the mid-nineteenth century, with the result that Western companies destroyed their Chinese competitors in the sale of such products as timber, oil, tobacco, and of course opium. Each of China's disastrous nineteenth-century wars with the West was followed by the levy of a huge indemnity or some further incursion on the economic life of the country.

It would be hard to imagine a more immoral purpose for a war than that of the Opium War of 1839–1842, the first of China's conflicts with the West, which was precipitated by the effort of the Chinese government to stop British traders from selling opium to the Chinese people. The destructive narcotic was destroying the health and the lives of alarming numbers of Chinese addicts but it was also a source of great profit to foreign and Chinese opium merchants. British businessmen were the major foreign dealers in opium but Americans, French, and others also participated; opium became an important factor in the trade balance between some Western countries and China. When the Chinese government tried to ban the import of opium in 1839, the British refused to pledge their compliance, whereupon a number of incidents occurred culminating in war between China and England.

There is both pathos and pride in the vain appeal of the Commissioner Lin Tse-hsü to Queen Victoria:

> . . . Even though the barbarians may not necessarily intend to do us harm, yet in coveting profit to an extreme, they have no regard for injuring others. Let us ask, where is your conscience? I have heard that the smoking of opium is very strictly forbidden by your country; that is because the harm caused by opium is clearly understood. Since it

is not permitted to do harm to your own country, then even less should you let it be passed on to the harm of other countries—how much less to China! Of all that China exports to foreign countries, there is not a single thing which is not beneficial to people: they are of benefit when eaten or of benefit when used, or of benefit when resold: all are beneficial. Is there a single article from China which has done any harm to foreign countries?[4]

The great Queen was unmoved and under the Nanking Treaty of 1842, which ended the Opium War, China was forced to cede Hong Kong, open five treaty ports for British trade, accept tariffs that could not be changed without Britain's consent and, in addition, pay an indemnity to compensate the British for lost opium and for expenses incurred in the war.

Following the British example, other powers exacted concessions from China through persuasion and the threat of force. The United States, for example, signed a treaty with China in 1844 under which the United States acquired trading privileges and extraterritoriality for both civil and criminal cases.

The Opium War and the Treaty of Nanking exposed China's vulnerability and opened the way to extensive exploitation by foreign powers. In the 1850s the British Prime Minister Lord Palmerston judged that "The time is fast approaching when we shall be obliged to strike another blow in China." In Palmerston's words, "these half-civilized governments such as those of China, Portugal, Spanish America . . . require a dressing down every eight or ten years to keep them in order."

The Chinese got many a "dressing down" in the years that followed. The British and French fought another war with China in 1856. Under the treaties of Tientsin new concessions were granted and old ones enlarged. The European powers acquired new trading ports and additional authority over Chinese tariffs as well as other privileges. The Chinese were required to pay indemnities, and there was also an article in one of the treaties guaranteeing the protection of missionaries, since, in the words of the treaty, "the Christian religion, as professed by Protestants and Roman Catholics, inculcates the practice of virtue, and teaches man to do as he would be done by."

The Chinese refused to ratify these treaties. Hostilities were renewed and the British burned the Emperor's summer palace in Peking. Under the Peking Convention of 1860 more ports were opened, more indemnities were paid, and the Chinese were compelled to cede Kowloon to England.

The treaties of 1842 and 1844 and of 1858 and 1860, known for fairly obvious reasons as the "unequal treaties," formed the basis of China's relations with the West until the Second World War.

The Chinese also had their difficulties with the Russians. In 1858, while the Chinese were beset with British and French attacks from the sea and the Taiping Rebellion in the interior, the Russians presented the Chinese with certain territorial demands. The Chinese were forced thereupon to cede to Russia all of the hitherto Chinese territories north of the Amur River. In 1860 the Russians demanded and received additional territory on the Pacific coast, including the area at which the port of Vladivostok was subsequently established. Under these two treaties Russia deprived China of a territory larger than Texas.

In the last decade of the nineteenth century Japan joined the Western powers in their depredations against China. Japan attacked China in 1894 and under the Treaty of Shimonoseki, which ended that war, Japan exacted large cessions of territory as well as extensive commercial privileges. Pressure by the European powers forced the Japanese to withdraw some of their demands, notably for Port Arthur on the Liaotung Peninsula, but Japan acquired the island of Taiwan and extensive trade privileges, and of course China was compelled to pay an indemnity.

Having joined with the powers in forcing Japan to return the Liaotung Peninsula to China, Germany now demanded a "reward." The Chinese failed to see the equity of this claim but were brought around when the Germans landed troops. China was thereupon forced to lease the port and bay of Kiaochow to Germany for ninety-nine years and was also forced to yield commercial privileges on the Shantung Peninsula.

The other powers also sought "rewards." Russia demanded and received the lease of Port Arthur and Dairen and the right to build a railroad across Manchuria. France, which had forced China to recognize French authority in Indochina in the 1880s, demanded and received in 1898 an extensive sphere of influence in South China, including the lease of Kwangchow Bay for ninety-nine years. The British, not to be outdone, now demanded and acquired control of the Chinese maritime customs, lease of a naval station at Weihaiwei, and the extension of the lease of Kowloon to ninety-nine years.

China had become a virtual colony with many masters. "Yet," said Sun Yat-sen, then a rising revolutionary, in a truly memorable historical understatement, "none of the masters feels responsible for its welfare."

The Society of the Righteous and Harmonious Fists, better known as the Boxers, was a secret organization composed largely of poverty-stricken peasants. Their grievances might well have been directed against the Manchu rulers of China, but government officials had no great difficulty in persuading the Boxers that the foreigners were the cause of the misery of the people. With great savagery, the Boxers fell upon foreigners and their Chinese cohorts in 1900; they were especially merciless toward missionaries and their Chinese converts. The Boxers went on a rampage against the foreigners in Peking, besieging the foreign legations.

An international rescue force made up of Japanese, Russians, British, Germans, French, and Americans was sent to relieve the legations. The commander of the allied force, Field Marshal Count Von Waldersee, was under instructions from the Kaiser "to give no quarter and to take no prisoners," so that "no Chinese will ever again dare to look askance at a German."

The allies proved the equal of the Boxers in their ferocity. The defeated Chinese were compelled to sign a new treaty under which the foreign powers received the right to station troops in their legation sites, a new Chinese tariff system was imposed, an indemnity of $333 million was to be paid, and the Chinese were obliged to punish "war criminals."

The United States returned a large part of the $25 million which was its share of the Boxer indemnity with the provision that the fund be used to educate Chinese students in the United States. Many Americans have regarded this as an act of extraordinary philanthropy. The United States thereafter announced its Open Door policy toward China. The Open Door policy purported to preserve the territorial integrity of China and to safeguard for all nations equal commercial access to China. Limited and ineffective as it was, the Open Door policy induced the Chinese to think of the United States as the only major foreign power which might be thought of as their friend and possible protector. The Open Door remained the basis of American policy toward China until the communists came to power in 1949 and closed China's door.

Political history hardly begins to convey the human effects of Western imperialism on the Chinese people. Something of the meaning of life in China under the impact of Western imperialism is conveyed by a Chinese engineer's account of his return to China in 1913 with his Belgian wife and son. He wrote as follows:

> In Shanghai it was agony, for there it was only too plain that in my own country I was nothing but an inferior, despised being. There were parks and restaurants and hotels I could not enter, although she could. I had no rights on the soil of a Chinese city which did not belong to the Chinese; she had rights by reason of something called skin.
>
> We boarded the English steamer from Shanghai to

Hankow; the first class was for Europeans only, and there was no other steamer. Marguerite leaned her arms on the railings and stared at the river. She was in first class, with our son. I went second class. I had insisted it should be so. "It is too hot for you here below."[5]

Some years earlier as a student in Shanghai the young man had written to his brother about his inability to understand the Europeans:

They always bewilder me. At once most ruthless in the pursuit of their interests, caring nothing for the wholesale misery they bring, at the same time their papers are full of verbiage of their nobility, rightness and the good they do. They become indignant at our public executions, and our cruelty to dogs. Yet the record of their lootings and killings in our country shows no such correct compassion. . . . They are illogical and incomprehensible, my brother. . . . They never know what they want, except that they always want more. Unbelievably rapacious, they yet weep tears when they give money to beggars. . . .[6]

China in Revolution

The Chinese revolutions of the twentieth century were in great part spawned by the ravages of the West. Finding themselves militarily inferior to the West but unshaken in their faith in the superiority of their own civilization, the Chinese undertook, first through the unsuccessful democratic revolution of Sun Yat-sen, then through the successful communist revolution of Mao Tse-tung, to acquire those Western techniques of science and technology, of political organization and military power, which would make it possible to expel the West from China. It is ironic and significant that the Western political doctrine which China finally adopted was one which the West itself had rejected.

China is still in the full tide of the longest and possibly the most complete revolution of the twentieth century. From 1911 until 1949 the country was in constant war and chaos. Before order was restored by the communists virtually all of China's ancient institutions and values had been shattered: the Imperial Dynasty, the classical system of education, Confucian ideas about the family and society.

The republic failed but the Russian Revolution had a profound impact on a demoralized China as an apparent model for converting a feudal society into a powerful modern nation almost overnight. The Kuomintang made some progress toward unifying the country in the twenties and thirties and, but for the Japanese war, the Nationalists might have established their authority as a viable government of China. The communists, on the other hand, as Professor Benjamin Schwartz of Harvard has pointed out, built up a strong base in the countryside and won patriotic support, especially from young intellectuals, by actively fighting the Japanese while the Kuomintang remained passive, waiting for the Americans to overwhelm Japan.[7] Greatly assisted by the incompetence and demoralization of the Kuomintang, the Chinese Communists emerged from the Second World War as the proponents of a genuine Chinese nationalism.

It is generally agreed by experts on China that the communist regime has rooted itself in solid foundations of nationalism. Professor C. P. Fitzgerald explains that Mao Tse-tung in effect has made Marxist ideas Chinese. These ideas are radically transforming Chinese society but have had much less significance for China's relations with the outside world than was once expected. Fitzgerald writes:

> The Chinese view of the world has not fundamentally changed: it has been adjusted to take account of the modern world, but only so far as to permit China to occupy, still, the central place in the picture. To do

this it was necessary to accept from the West a new doctrine to replace the inadequate Confucian teaching, which was too limited. After a long struggle China found that the doctrine which suited her was the one which the West had repudiated: and it may well be that this in itself was a reason for making communism, the outcast of Western origin, welcome in China. . . .[8]

China has thus had two simultaneous revolutions in this century: one a domestic revolution which is almost totally reconstructing Chinese life and society, albeit within a familiar context of authoritarianism, the other a revolution against foreigners which is not so much revising China's relations with the outside world as trying to *restore* them to something resembling their character in the days of imperial greatness. While revolutionizing her society at home, China seems to be retaining, or more accurately to be reviving, her traditional view of her role in the world.

As between China's foreign and domestic revolutions, the emphasis, according to experts, has been and remains on the latter. Communist China's leaders, according to Professor John Lindbeck of Harvard University, are specialists in domestic affairs but amateurs in international relations. Although they regard developments in China as "part of a larger transnational historic movement," the fundamental task which they have set for themselves, the one which absorbs by far the greater part of their resources and their attention, is the industrialization and social transformation of China.[9] In testimony before the Senate Foreign Relations Committee Professor Morton Halperin made the same point. The Chinese leaders, he believes, "are anxious to turn in and focus their efforts even more than they have in the past on the domestic concerns of the Chinese revolution. . . . I believe that if the Chinese can become convinced that they do not face imminent threat of an American nuclear attack, they are likely to withdraw even more from the world while continuing to issue revolutionary proclamations and concentrate on their internal difficulties and opportunities.[10]

The Theory and Practice
of Chinese Foreign Policy

These expert opinions are not easily reconciled with the official American view that China is embarked upon a campaign of unlimited conquest on the model of German aggression in the thirties. The basis currently cited in support of this view of China's intentions is the doctrine enunciated in September 1965 by the Chinese Minister of Defense, Lin Piao. The Lin Piao doctrine divides the world into two parts: the "cities," so-called, consisting of the United States, Western Europe, and the Soviet Union, and the "rural areas" of Asia, Africa, and Latin America, which, according to Lin, will gradually surround and conquer the cities in the same way that the Chinese Communists started from the countryside and gradually took over all of continental China.

All this, in Churchill's eloquent phrase, is "jaw jaw." It is a terrifying doctrine no doubt, but it is only a doctrine, not an existing fact. The Chinese have a ferocious vocabulary but surely some distinction must be made between what they say and what they do, and between what they might like to do and what they are able or likely to be able to do. In Vietnam itself, one must remember, the United States had some three hundred thousand troops as of mid-1966 while the Chinese had only work teams supporting the North Vietnamese. Some experts, far from regarding the Lin doctrine as a plan of Chinese aggression, have interpreted it as a formula for *indigenous* revolution, implying that the Chinese expect other countries to make their own revolutions with no more than marginal Chinese support.

The ferocity of Peking's language has obscured the fact that in practice China has tolerated a high degree of independence on the part of her neighbors, including those—perhaps especially those—which are not under the military protection of the United States. Burma, for example, though weak and non-aligned, remains independent and, so far as one can tell, untroubled by her Chinese neighbor. North Vietnam, despite its dependency on China for economic and logistical support for the prosecution of the war, remains substantially in command of its own affairs; and it seems logical to suppose that if there were no war, if there were normal relations with the United States, North Vietnam would be even more independent of China. The experience of North Korea is particularly interesting: during and after the Korean War the North was occupied by hundreds of thousands of Chinese troops; then in 1958, despite the fact that there was no outside pressure to compel them to do so, the Chinese withdrew from North Korea, whereupon the North Koreans purged many pro-Chinese officials from their government and acquired substantial freedom of action in their relations with both China and the Soviet Union. In August 1966 the North Korean government publicly proclaimed its intention to build communism neither in the Russian nor the Chinese way but in its own "Korean" way, and since then the North Koreans have given strong indications of aligning themselves with Russia in the Sino-Soviet dispute. One does not know, of course, but the thought that the Chinese, despite their colorful language, may actually not wish physically to subjugate their neighbors may be less "unthinkable" on examination than at first glance it appears to be.

Once again, there appears to be a discrepancy between myth and reality, between the American perception and a situation as it actually exists. Once again, it seems to me, the source of the distortion is the ideological prism through which America looks at the world. China is considered to be aggressive not on the basis of what her leaders do but rather on the basis of what they say or on the basis of their presumed intentions. China is not judged to be aggressive because of her actions; she is *presumed* to be aggressive because she is communist.

America and China

Between America, perhaps the most unrevolutionary country in the world, and China, the most revolutionary, there lies a chasm of ignorance and misunderstanding. On February 10, 1966, there was a discussion of China in the British House of Lords. In a most interesting speech Lord Kennet said: "Those two countries understand each other so little. America speaks all of peace, but bombs China's neighbor. China watches her actions, and ignores her words. China speaks all of war, but there is not a single Chinese soldier outside China. America listens to her words, and ignores her actions. It is historically determined."[11]

I hope that the failures of communication between China and the United States are not "historically determined," or at least not historically unalterable. In a modest way the Senate Foreign Relations Committee has been trying, through a series of public hearings, to establish some basis for communication between China and the United States.* Some pertinent questions have been raised and partially answered by experts who have testified before the Committee, such questions, for example, as the following: What kind of people are the Chinese? To what extent are they motivated by national feeling? To what extent by ideology? Why are the Chinese Communist leaders so hostile to the United States and why do they advocate violent revolution against most of the world's governments? To what extent is their view of the world distorted by isolation and the memory of ancient grievances? To what extent, and with what effect on their government, do the Chinese people share with Americans and with all other peoples what Aldous Huxley has called the "simple human preference for life and peace?"

We must seek answers to these questions if we are to

---

* See Chapter 2, pp. 56–57.

reverse what increasingly appears to be a drift toward war between China and the United States. We must gain some understanding of the great Chinese Revolution—of its origins, the stage of extremism in which it seems to be suspended, and its prospects for abating into Thermidor. Other violent revolutions have run their course and come to a kind of normalcy and the experts agree that at some time in the future, perhaps when a new generation of leaders succeeds Mao and his colleagues, perhaps only after two or three generations, China will become a more or less normal society with more or less normal relations with the outside world.

If we assume that the Chinese Revolution is permanently frozen in its extremist stage, that Chinese communism, unlike Russian communism, is implacably hostile to us, then I suppose it would be logical for us to take the first good excuse that comes along to strike a devastating military blow against China while she is still relatively weak, especially against her incipient nuclear capacity. There are a number of compelling reasons—even setting aside the strong possibility of a global nuclear war—why such action, the waging of a "preventive" war against China, would be one of the greatest disasters, perhaps the greatest disaster, in American history. First, it would disable China temporarily but not permanently while converting her present enmity into an enduring fury. Second, it would outrage the conscience of peoples all over the world, including, I would expect, the American people. Third, a pre-emptive war in "defense" of freedom would surely destroy freedom, because one simply cannot engage in barbarous action without becoming a barbarian, because one cannot defend human values by calculated and unprovoked violence without doing mortal damage to the values one is trying to defend. And finally, to assume that Chinese communism is unalterably committed to our destruction is to assume that a whole branch of humanity is immune from one of the basic facts of human nature, the fact of change and changeability: it is completely reasonable to anticipate change in China—and in every other society for that matter—because change is the law of life, if indeed there is a law of life.

The more pertinent questions for America are whether, by being so hostile, we are not helping to perpetuate the extremist phase of the Chinese Revolution and whether, by trying to draw China out of isolation, we could not encourage her progress toward moderation. My own view is that American hostility is probably prolonging the extremist phase of the Chinese Revolution, and my hope is that one day soon we will moderate our hostility and offer to China the hand of friendship, knowing full well that it is almost certain to be rejected but knowing as well that honest and repeated offers of friendship may weaken the Chinese image of a hostile America and hasten the day of China's Thermidor.

China's ancient pride may be an obstacle to communication, but it also provides the opportunity to breach the barrier of mistrust and hostility by treating China with the respect that is her due as a great and ancient civilization. Today China stands isolated, mistrustful and hostile toward the outside world; her whole history has contributed to the view of herself as a superior civilization set upon by hostile barbarians. In the wake of so tragic and unique a national experience, one can hardly be sanguine about immediate prospects for drawing China into the community of nations as a trustworthy and responsible partner. With a great deal of patience and perception on our part, however, China may be brought to alter her view of herself as the celestial empire in a world of barbarians; she may come, very gradually, to see herself as one of a number of great civilizations, with much to offer but also much to gain in relations with the outside world.

I am well aware that what I propose is something more, perhaps a great deal more, than reciprocity. I do so in the belief that in her own national interest and in the interest of peace, America as the stronger nation—stronger in wealth, stronger in arms, and stronger in political tradition

—has an obligation of magnanimity toward a nation just emerging from a century of crisis and humiliation. It is small-minded and unworthy when American officials reply to proposals for initiatives toward China by citing the number of futile encounters in Warsaw or by demanding to know "what they have offered us." "Magnanimity in politics," said Edmund Burke, "is not seldom the truest wisdom; and a great empire and little minds go ill together."[12]

If we can bring ourselves to act toward China with understanding and generosity, we will be on the way to a solution of the great problems that beset us in Eastern Asia. The prospects for an honorable and lasting peace in Vietnam have everything to do with China and her relations with the outside world, because China is the paramount power of Asia. Nothing that we say or do can make her otherwise.

Part III

RECONCILING HOSTILE WORLDS

. . . not a balance of power, but a community of power; not organized rivalries, but an organized common peace.

WOODROW WILSON
Address to the Senate,
January 22, 1917

8

Human Nature and International Relations

THERE ARE THREE WAYS of considering the effects of human nature on the behavior of nations. There is the approach of the moralist or theologian who weighs behavior against moral standards, notes the discrepancy, and then prescribes certain changes in behavior. There is the approach of the behavioral scientist, who accepts the game of politics as it is played, studies the behavior of the players with a view to prediction and hopes to use the data thus derived to give "our side" the advantage in the game. Finally, there is the approach of the humanist, who weighs human behavior against human *needs,* notes the discrepancy, notes as well the irrational elements in human nature and the limitations these impose, and then tries to find ways, within those limitations, of narrowing the gap between behavior and needs.

Civilizing the Competitive Instinct

The approach of the humanist is the one commended in this chapter, as applied to the discrepancy between man's unrestrained competitive instinct and his hope of survival at this first moment in human history when the means of violence at man's disposal have become sufficient to destroy his species. Unlike other forms of life which have faced the danger of extinction, we have had some choice in the matter, having ourselves invented the instruments that threaten us with distinction. This fact, to be sure, tells at least as much about man's folly as it does about his creative genius, but it also suggests that having created the conditions for our own collective death, we at least retain some choice about whether it is actually going to happen. Clearly, a radical change in traditional behavior is required. The question of our age is whether a change radical enough to close the gap between traditional political behavior and the requirements of survival is possible *within the limits* imposed by human nature.

It is hard to believe in the destruction of the human race. Because we have managed to avoid a holocaust since the invention of nuclear weapons only a little more than twenty years ago, the danger of its occurrence now seems remote, like Judgment Day, and references to it have become so frequent and familiar as to lose their meaning; the prospect of our disappearance from the earth has become a cliché, even something of a bore. It is a fine thing of course that the hydrogen bomb has not reduced us all to nervous wrecks, but it is not a fine thing that finding the threat incredible, we act as though it did not exist and go on conducting international relations in the traditional manner, which is to say, in a manner that does little if anything to reduce the possibility of a catastrophe.

Neither the government nor the universities are making the best possible use of their intellectual resources to deal with the problems of war and peace in the nuclear age. Both seem by and large to have accepted the idea that the avoidance of nuclear war is a matter of skillful "crisis management," as though the techniques of diplomacy and deterrence which have gotten us through the last twenty years have only to be improved upon to get us through the next twenty or a hundred or a thousand years.

The law of averages has already been more than kind to us and we have had some very close calls, notably in October 1962. We escaped a nuclear war at the time of the Cuban missile affair because of President Kennedy's skillful "crisis management" and Premier Khrushchev's prudent response to it; surely we cannot count on the indefinite survival of the human race if it must depend on an indefinite number of repetitions of that sort of encounter. Sooner or later the law of averages will turn against us; an extremist or incompetent will come to power in one major country or another, or a misjudgment will be made by some perfectly competent official, or things will just get out of hand without anyone being precisely responsible as happened in 1914. None of us, however,—professors, bureaucrats, or politicians —has yet undertaken a serious and concerted effort to put the survival of our species on some more solid foundation than an unending series of narrow escapes.

We have got somehow to try to grasp the idea of universal destruction—by some means other than actually experiencing it. We have got somehow to grasp the idea that man's competitive instinct, unalterable an element of human nature though it may be, must nonetheless be restrained, regulated or redirected in such a way that it no longer threatens to explode into universal, final violence.

The first step toward control of the competitive instinct is to acknowledge it. It is no use to declare it immoral or obsolete and to decree its abolition because, like sex, hunger, death, and taxes, it just won't go away. Nor does it make sense to accept unrestrained competitiveness as an unalterable fact of life, to resign ourselves to the game of nuclear politics as insane but inevitable and to focus our efforts on computerized war games aimed at making sure that we "get there first with the most," because even if our adversary "gets there" second and with much less, it is likely to be enough to wipe us out.

We can neither abolish nor totally accept national rivalries; we have got, somehow, to put them under some restraints, just as we have brought the rivalries of business and other groups within our own society under restraints in order to protect the community and, indeed, in order to perpetuate *competition,* which under conditions of unregulated rivalry would soon enough be ended with the elimination of the small and weak groups by the big and strong ones. In foreign politics as in domestic economics, competitive instincts are natural and, within limits, creative; but so prone are they to break out of those limits and to wreak havoc when they do that we must seek some means to confine them to their proper sphere, as the servant and not the master of civilization.

It may be that some idea as to where that sphere begins and where it ends, as to where the possibilities of human nature begin to conflict with the needs of human survival and as to whether and how the two can be reconciled, can be gotten from the study of psychology. If it be granted that the ultimate source of war and peace is human nature, then it follows that the study of politics is the study of man and that if politics is ever to acquire a new character, the change will not be wrought either in computers or in revival meetings but through a better understanding of the needs and fears of the human individual. It is a curious thing that in an era when interdisciplinary studies are favored in the universities, little has been done to apply the insights of individual and social psychology to the study of international relations.

Psychology, Ideology, and Political Behavior

Man's beliefs about how societies should be organized and related to each other are called ideologies. An understanding of the psychological roots of ideology would provide us with insight and perspective on our own political beliefs as well as those of others. To what extent, one might ask, are ideological beliefs the result of a valid and disinterested intellectual process and to what extent are they instilled in us by conditioning and inheritance? Or, to put the question another way, why exactly is it that, like Gilbert and Sullivan's Englishmen, every one of whom was miraculously born a "little Liberal" or a "little Conservative," most young Russians grow up believing in communism and most young Americans grow up believing in democracy, or, for that matter, what accounts for the coincidence that most Arabs believe in Islam and most Spaniards in Catholicism?

We must acquire some perspective about our beliefs about things. If, as psychologists suggest, the sources of ideological belief are largely accidental and irrational, the political implications are enormous. Ideologies are supposed to explain reality to people and to inspire them with political ideals for which they should be, and usually are, willing to fight and die. Yet it seems obvious that almost all of us acquire our ideological beliefs not principally as the result of an independent intellectual process but largely as the result of an accident of birth. If you happen to be born in the United States, the chances are overwhelming that you will grow up believing in democracy; if you happen to be born in Russia or China, the chances are just as great that you will grow up believing in communism. It would seem to follow that if the United States should fight a war with Russia or China, the basic issue would not be between two competing political philosophies but between two great societies made up of hundreds of millions of people, most of whom had little more choice in their ideological beliefs than in the color of their eyes and hair. It seems, to say the least, an arbitrary reason for killing hundreds of millions of people in a nuclear war.

Psychologists say that the appeal of an ideology is that it shields the individual from the painful fact that his life is a minor event in the ongoing universe. It helps us to connect our lives to some larger purpose and also helps to "organize the world for us," giving us a picture, though not necessarily an accurate picture, of reality. A person's world-view, or ideology, is said to filter the signals that come to him, giving meaning and pattern to otherwise odd bits of information. Thus, for example, when a Chinese and an American put radically different interpretations on the Vietnamese war, it is not necessarily because one or the other has chosen to propound a wicked lie but rather because each has filtered information from the real world through his ideological world-view, selecting the parts that fit, rejecting the parts that do not, and coming out with two radically different interpretations of the same events.

Ideology influences perception, perception shapes expectation, and expectation shapes behavior, making for what is called the self-fulfilling prophecy. Thus, for example, China, fearing the United States but lacking power, threatens and blusters, confirming the United States in its fears of China and causing it to arm against her, which in turn heightens Chinese fears of the United States. Professor Gordon Allport of Harvard made the point some years ago that ". . . while most people deplore war, they nonetheless *expect* it to continue. And what *people expect determines their behavior. . . .* The indispensable condition of war," wrote Professor Allport, "is that people must *expect* war and must prepare for war, before, under war-minded leadership, they make war. It is in this sense that 'wars begin in the minds of men.'"[1]

Another striking psychological phenomenon is the tendency of antagonists to dehumanize each other. To most Americans China is a strange, distant, and dangerous nation, not a society made up of more than seven hundred million individual human beings but a kind of menacing abstraction. When Chinese soldiers are described, for example, as "hordes of Chinese coolies," it is clear that they are being thought of not as people but as something terrifying and abstract, or as something inanimate, like the flow of lava from a volcano. Both China and America seem to think of each other as abstractions: to the Chinese we are not a society of individual people but the embodiment of an evil idea, the idea of "imperialist capitalism"; and to most of us China represents not people but an evil and frightening idea, the idea of "aggressive communism."

Obviously, this dehumanizing tendency helps to explain the savagery of war. Man's capacity for decent behavior seems to vary directly with his perception of others as individual humans with human motives and feelings, whereas his capacity for barbarous behavior seems to increase with his perception of an adversary in abstract terms. This is the only explanation I can think of for the fact that the very same good and decent citizens who would never fail to feed a hungry child or comfort a sick friend or drop a coin in the church collection basket can celebrate the number of Viet Cong killed in a particular week or battle, talk of "making a desert" of North Vietnam or of "bombing it back into the Stone Age" despite the fact that most, almost all, of the victims would be innocent peasants and workers, and can contemplate with equanimity, or even advocate, the use of nuclear weapons against the "hordes of Chinese coolies." I feel sure that this apparent insensitivity to the incineration of thousands of millions of our fellow human beings is not the result of feelings of savage inhumanity toward foreigners; it is the result of not thinking of them as humans at all but rather as the embodiment of doctrines that we consider evil.

There is a "strain toward consistency" which leads a country, once it has decided that another country is good or bad, peaceful or aggressive, to interpret every bit of information to fit that preconception, so much so that even a genuine concession offered by one is likely to be viewed by the other as a trick to gain some illicit advantage. A possible manifestation of this tendency is the North Vietnamese view of American proposals to negotiate peace as fraudulent plots. Having been betrayed after previous negotiations—by the French in 1946 and by Ngo Dinh Diem in 1955 when, with

American complicity, he refused to allow the elections called for in the Geneva Accords to take place—the Hanoi government may now feel that American offers to negotiate peace, which Americans believe to be genuine, are in reality plots to trick them into yielding through diplomacy what we have been unable to make them yield by force.

The gap between perceptions of a situation by antagonists is widened by their tendency to break off communications with each other, which is caused in part by the fear of inadvertently "giving something away" and by fear of being thought disloyal at home—the Johns Hopkins psychiatrist Dr. Jerome Frank calls this the "traitor trap." The result of the breakoff of communications and the refusal to renew them is that hostile images are then the only ones available and hostility is perpetuated accordingly. Dr. Frank points out that one of the principal values of group therapy is that the individual patient cannot easily break off communication and is thus encouraged to persevere in his treatment. I wish that Dr. Frank and his colleagues could be engaged to conduct group therapy for the leaders of China and the United States.

Of and by itself, however, communication is of limited value; in a hostile atmosphere it may even make things worse. One psychologist, Muzafer Sherif, conducted an experiment in conflict and cooperation among eleven-year-old boys in an experimental camp. The boys were divided into two groups, the "Eagles" and the "Rattlers" and kept apart while they developed separate and cohesive customs, leadership, and organization. They were then brought together in a series of competitive activities in which victory for one side inevitably meant defeat for the other. These activities generated a high level of mutual hostility, with each group attributing self-glorifying qualities to itself and assigning traits to the other which warranted treating it as an enemy. In the next stage of the experiment an effort was made to restore peace simply by bringing the two groups together in social events. This did no good, however, because the boys used the social occasions to engage in accusations and recriminations. In the next step of the experiment, problems and crises were contrived in such a way as to affect both groups and to require collaboration between them. These "crises" included interruption of the camp water supply, the running of a food-carrying truck into a ditch and other situations which could only be dealt with by cooperative action between the two groups. The effect of these invoked collaborations was striking: hostilities soon diminished to a point where boys in each group were again choosing friends from the other.[2]

One cannot make major inferences for international relations from an experiment involving well-adjusted middle-class American boys. The experiment suggests, however, that there may be promise in such enterprises as Soviet-American cooperation in the International Geophysical Year and in a whole spectrum of possible activities (some to be suggested in Chapter 10) associated with the "building of bridges" between East and West.

Dr. Brock Chisholm suggests that "What we the people of the world need, perhaps most, is to exercise our imaginations, to develop our ability to look at things from outside our accidental area of being." Most of us, he says, "have never taken out our imaginations for any kind of run in all our lives," but rather have kept them tightly locked up within the limits of our own national, and ideological, perspective.[3]

The obvious value of liberating the imagination is that it might enable us to acquire some understanding of the world-view held by people whose past experiences and present circumstances and beliefs are radically different from our own. It might enable us to understand, for example, what it feels like to be hungry, not hungry in the way that a middle-class American feels after a golf game or a fast tennis match, but hungry as an Asian might be hungry, with a hunger that has never been satisfied, with one's children having stunted limbs and swollen bellies, with a desire to

change things that has little regard for due process of the
law because the desire for change has an urgency and
desperation about it that few Americans have ever experienced. Could we but liberate our imagination in this way,
we might be able to see why so many people in the world
are making revolutions; we might even be able to see why
some of them are communists.

Practicing Psychology
in International Relations

Having suggested, as best an amateur can, some psychological principles that might be pertinent to international
relations, I now venture to suggest some applications.

The experiment in the boys' camp suggests that between
two such antagonists as the Soviet Union and the United
States, who have already engaged in limited cooperative
activities and who have grown reasonably familiar with if
not especially fond of each other, there may be great promise for strengthening world peace in limited, practical
projects of cooperation. Acting on the premise that the
experience of cooperation is probably more important than
the matter on which we are cooperating, we would do well
in our relations with the Russians to concentrate on the
most tractable issues rather than the most important. If
by a series of agreements on issues which in substance are
much less important than, say, the division of Germany and
the arms race—such agreements as the test ban treaty or
possible agreements for a reduction in the output of fis-
sionable materials, a new educational and cultural exchange
program, arrangements for the joint exploration of space,
or the opening of consulates and airline connections—we
succeeded in creating a *state of mind* in which neither side
considered war as a likely eventuality or as a real option for
itself except under radically changed conditions, then in

fact we would have progressed toward precisely the same objective which a German settlement or a general disarmament would help to achieve—a world substantially free of the threat of nuclear incineration.

It is probably too soon to contemplate practical programs of cooperation with China. In the wake of the historical trauma referred to in Chapter 7, China's fear and hatred of the West is probably still too deep, and likely to remain so for some time to come, to permit of positive cooperation, or indeed of anything beyond what we might call mutually respectful relations from a distance. Without being patronizing, we might do well to think of China in the terms suggested by United Nations Secretary-General U Thant who has referred to China as a nation which has had a kind of "nervous breakdown." "China," he said, "is going through a difficult stage of development and in such a delicate stage, countries will show certain emotions, certain strong reactions, certain rigidities, and even certain arrogance."[4] This suggests, to my mind, the importance of understanding, patience, and magnanimity on the part of the United States as the stronger and more secure nation. Americans must make a critical choice in their attitude toward China. On the one hand, we can treat her as persons with "nervous breakdowns" were treated in centuries past; we can throw her into the figurative snake pit of world politics, treating her as an insane and predatory creature with whom there can be no parlay or accommodation. On the other hand, we can treat China by the more civilized standards deriving from our modern understanding of human behavior; while resisting any aggressive act that she may commit, we can at the same time treat her as a respected member of the world community now going through a period of dangerous chauvinism and warranting our best efforts to rehabilitate her to the world community.

I hope that America will make the second choice. I hope that in her attitude toward China, America will act with the magnanimity that befits a great nation by following the advice of Pope Paul VI, who said in his address to the United Nations General Assembly on October 4, 1965:

> Your vocation is to make brothers not only of some, but of all peoples, a difficult undertaking, indeed; but this it is, your most noble undertaking. . . . We will go further, and say: strive to bring back among you any who have separated themselves, and study the right method of uniting to your pact of brotherhood, in honor and loyalty, those who do not yet share in it.

Paranoid fears are not entirely false fears; certainly, China's fear of American hostility, though distorted and exaggerated, is not pure invention. In dealing with paranoid individuals, Dr. Frank suggests, it is generally desirable to listen respectfully without agreeing but also without trying to break down or attack the patient's system of beliefs. It is also important not to get overfriendly lest the patient interpret effusive overtures as a hostile plot. Dr. Frank also suggests that the paranoid patient is certain to rebuff overtures of friendship many times before beginning to respond. Applying these principles to China, perhaps the best thing we can do for the time being is to reduce expressions of hostility, put forth only such limited proposals for friendship as might be credible, and otherwise leave her strictly alone.

Before China can accept the hand of Western friendship, she must first recover pride. She must recover that sense of herself as a great civilization which was so badly battered in the nineteenth century and with it the strength to open her door to the outside world. Having been all but destroyed as a nation by the forced intrusions of the West, China must first know that she has the strength to reject unwanted foreign influences before she can be expected to seek or accept friendly foreign associations. Or, to make the same point from the side of the United States, before we can extend the hand of friendship to China with any expectation of its being accepted, we must first persuade her that we respect her right to take what we offer or leave it as she thinks best. There is no better way to convey this message to China than by leaving her alone.

If we can give our imaginations a good "run," we are likely to learn that the "way of life" which we so eagerly commend to the world has little pertinence either to China's past experience or to her future needs. China, as John Fairbank points out, is a society in which the concept of "individualism" which we cherish is held in low esteem because it connotes a chaotic selfishness, the opposite of the commitment to the collective good which is highly valued by the Chinese. Similarly, the very word for "freedom" (*tzu-yu*) is said to connote a lack of discipline, even license, the very opposite of the Chinese ideal of disciplined cooperation. Even such basic Western ideas as "loyal opposition" and "self-determination," Professor Fairbank points out, are alien to the Chinese. The cultural gap is further illustrated by the difference in attitudes toward philanthropy: to Americans it is a Christian virtue; to the Chinese it is, unless reciprocal, insulting and degrading—something that we might keep in mind if relations ever thaw enough to make conceivable American economic aid or, more plausibly, disaster relief in the event of some natural calamity such as flood or famine.[5]

There are, I think, some limited positive steps which the United States might take toward improved relations with China. It would do the United States no harm in the short run and perhaps considerable good in the long run to end its embargo on trade in non-strategic items, to recognize the Peking Government *de facto*, to offer to establish formal diplomatic relations whenever the Chinese Communists care to reciprocate, and to end American opposition to the seating of Communist China in the United Nations while defending the right of the Chinese Nationalist government on Taiwan to a seat of its own in the United Nations. The United States has already proposed visits by scholars and newspapermen between China and the United States and, although these proposals have been rejected by the Chinese, it might be well, though not too often and not too eagerly, to remind them of the offer from time to time. In proposing such initiatives to the Senate Foreign Relations Committee as major components in a policy of "containment without isolation," Professor A. Doak Barnett made the point that "In taking these steps, we will have to do so in full recognition of the fact that Peking's initial reaction is almost certain to be negative and hostile and that any changes in our posture will create some new problems. But we should take them nevertheless, because initiatives on our part are clearly required if we are to work, however slowly, toward the long-term goal of a more stable, less explosive situation in Asia and to explore the possibilities of trying to moderate Peking's policies."[6]

The point of such a new approach to China, writes Professor Fairbank, is psychological: "Peking is, to say the least, maladjusted, rebellious against the whole world, Russia as well as America. We are Peking's principal enemy because we happen now to be the biggest outside power trying to foster world stability. But do we have to play Mao's game? Must we carry the whole burden of resisting Peking's pretensions? Why not let others in on the job? A Communist China seated in the UN," Fairbank continues, "could no longer pose as a martyr excluded by 'American imperialism.' She would have to face the self-interest of other countries, and learn to act as a full member of international society for the first time in history. This is the only way for China to grow up and eventually accept restraints on her revolutionary ardor."[7]

The most difficult and dangerous of issues between the United States and China is the confrontation of their power in Southeast Asia, an issue which, because of its explosive possibilities, cannot be consigned to the healing effects of time. The danger of war is real. It is real because an "open-ended" war in Vietnam can bring the two great powers into conflict with each other, by accident or by design, at almost any time. Some of our military experts are confident that China will not enter the war in Vietnam; their confidence would be more reassuring if it did not bring to mind the predictions of military experts in 1950 that China would not enter the Korean War, as well as more recent predictions about an early victory in Vietnam. In fact, it is the view of certain China experts in our government that the Chinese leaders themselves *expect* war with the United States, and some of our own officials also seem to expect a war with China.

How can we alter those fatal expectations, which, as we have noted, tend to influence behavior so as to make it likely that they will come true? Long-term efforts to break through hostile prejudices based on mutual ignorance will be valuable as a means of promoting the ultimate reconciliation of China and the West, but they are not likely to result in an early end to the war in Vietnam or to resolve the dangerous confrontation of Chinese and American power in Southeast Asia. These call for more urgent remedies, and in the next chapter I shall suggest what seems to me a responsible program for peace in Southeast Asia.

Perception and Perspective

We know so very much more about things than we do about people, so very much more about the workings of jet planes and nuclear missiles than about our own inner needs. We are exploring the mysteries of outer space while we remain puzzled and ignorant about the mysteries of our own minds. Far more than supersonic airplanes or rockets to the moon, we need objective perceptions of our own fears and hopes and a broader perspective about our own society, our relations with others and our place in the world.

Civilization is still a young and fragile thing on this earth.

Man has lived in some kind of civilized condition for no more than five thousand years; for hundreds of thousands of years before that he lived and fought and hunted for food in a manner not much superior to that of the other animals. The civilizing process is not only very recent; it has also been strikingly uneven. Until about two centuries ago there was no great disparity between progress in technology and progress in human relations, between man's understanding of *things* and his understanding of *himself;* both were progressing very slowly indeed. Then, with the Industrial Revolution, man achieved a gigantic breakthrough in his technology, a breakthrough which was followed by rapid and accelerating progress to which no end is yet in sight. There has been no comparable breakthrough in human relations; in the last two centuries our understanding of ourselves has progressed somewhat, perhaps a bit more rapidly than before, but not nearly as fast as our understanding of the physical world. The result of this disparity has been the development of an enormous gap between our facility with tools and our facility with ideas, between our control of the physical world and control of ourselves.

The acknowledgment of this disparity is the first step toward perception and perspective. Of and by itself, it will not give us complete understanding, but it may acquaint us with the limits of our understanding; it may help us to see that our judgments about ourselves and about others may be defective, that even our physical senses may deceive us. Applied to international relations, an awareness of the gap between technology and human relations must commend to us the advisability of skepticism in our judgments, restraint in our actions, and an effort to try to see the world as others may see it.

It is a curious thing, when you think of it, that people in different societies, in China and the United States say, would have minor differences if any at all on such matters as how to pave a road or build a tractor or a jet plane, but when it comes to such questions as how to organize a government or farm or factory, Chinese and Americans are not only unable to agree, they are not even able to credit each other with anything but the most dangerous and malicious intentions. Obviously, there are some problems of perception on one side or the other, or on both sides.

Erich Fromm writes: "The lack of objectivity, as far as foreign nations are concerned, is notorious. From one day to another, another nation is made out to be utterly depraved and fiendish, while one's own nation stands for everything that is good and noble. Every action of the enemy is judged by one standard—every action of oneself by another. Even good deeds by the enemy are considered a sign of particular devilishness, meant to deceive us and the world, while our bad deeds are necessary and justified by our noble goals which they serve. Indeed, if one examines the relationship between nations, as well as between individuals, one comes to the conclusion that objectivity is the exception, and a greater or lesser degree of narcissistic distortion is the rule."[8]

In 1955 a revered American commented on Soviet-American relations as follows: "The present tensions with their threat of national annihilation are kept alive by two great illusions. The one, a complete belief on the part of the Soviet world that the capitalist countries are preparing to attack it; that sooner or later we intend to strike. And the other, a complete belief on the part of the capitalist countries that the Soviets are preparing to attack us; that sooner or later they intend to strike. Both are wrong. Each side, so far as the masses are concerned, is equally desirous of peace. For either side, war with the other would mean nothing but disaster. Both equally dread it. But the constant acceleration of preparation may well, without specific intent, ultimately produce a spontaneous combustion."[9]

The speaker was General Douglas MacArthur, and his audience was made up of members of the American Legion. The point General MacArthur was making is one that has been made many times by psychologists and psychiatrists: people in different societies look at the same facts and "see" different things, that what they see, or think they see, is largely determined by what they *expect* to see.

The point is illustrated by an experiment in which a psychologist had two groups of schoolteachers, one Mexican, the other American, look into a device that simultaneously showed a picture of a bullfighter to one eye and a picture of a baseball player to the other. When asked what they had seen, most of the Mexicans said they had seen a bullfighter and most of the Americans said that they had seen a baseball player. Obviously, what each individual saw had a great deal to do with whether he was a Mexican or an American.

One day in the spring of 1966 both the Secretary of State of the United States and the Secretary-General of the United Nations made speeches about the war in Vietnam. Both are men of intelligence and high ideals. Both looked at the same situation but each saw a different picture. Dean Rusk saw the war as one of democracy versus communism, as a struggle for "the achievement of a peaceful world order that is safe for freedom." U Thant, on the other hand, saw a war of "national survival" for Vietnam, a war in which it had become "illusory" and "irrelevant" to refer to a contest between democracy and communism. Who is right and who is wrong? Who can say? The only thing that is very clear is that one Secretary's ballplayer is another's bullfighter.

We need to acquire some perspective on these matters which have so much to do with determining whether we will live or die in the nuclear age. We need to become cognizant of the varieties of human perception, of the gap between our understanding of the physical world and our understanding of ourselves and of the gap between our behavior and our needs. If we can do that, we will have taken an encouraging first step toward closing those gaps, because the acknowledgment of ignorance is the beginning of wisdom.

The development of some perspective about man and his

needs in different national environments is the principal purpose of such educational and cultural exchanges as the Fulbright program. No part of our foreign policy does more to make international relations *human* relations and to encourage attitudes of personal empathy, the rare and wonderful ability to perceive the world as others see it. Thus conceived, educational exchange is not a propaganda program designed to "improve the image" of the United States as some government officials seem to conceive it, but a program for the cultivation of perceptions and perspectives that transcend national boundaries. To put it another way, far from being a means of gaining some national advantage in the traditional game of international relations, international education purports to change the nature of the game, to civilize and humanize it in the nuclear age.

I would hope that psychologists and psychiatrists, who have already contributed so much to the understanding of individual and group behavior, will in the future devote a greater part of their scholarship to the understanding of political beliefs and behavior. It may be, as some psychologists and psychiatrists contend, that their field has little relevance to the study of politics. It may be, on the other hand, that psychology and psychiatry have a great deal to contribute. There is nothing to lose by trying. The insights provided by the established disciplines have by no means pre-empted the field, and their practitioners are not in a position to scorn a newcomer.

9

Toward Peace in Asia

As suggested in the preceding chapter, hostile relationships are not effectively dissolved by a complete reversal to sudden and overwhelming displays of friendliness. Such conversions, even if sincere, are not believable; they look like a plot. When an individual has long felt put upon by another, he does not want his antagonist to do a complete about-face and start showering him with gifts; he wants the other party to go away for a while, a good long while, and leave him alone. I think the same tendency applies to relations among nations. Between enmity and amity there must be a period of disengagement, a period in which passions cool, perceptions change, and new perspectives are formed.

I do not think America should be in a precipitate hurry to convert its present animosity toward the Viet Cong, North Vietnam, and China into warm friendship. It is interesting and instructive to note that France allowed a decade to elapse between her departure from Indochina in 1954 and her recent reassertion of interest, to which North Vietnam and Cambodia have been surprisingly receptive. I do not think it appropriate for the United States to be making promises of future economic aid to the North Vietnamese while American bombs are falling on their territory; if they have any pride at all—and they appear to have a great deal —the North Vietnamese must regard such offers as contemptuously insulting. Nor do I think we ought to make effusive offers of friendship to the Chinese if only they will stop supporting wars of "national liberation" and promise to uphold the principles of the United Nations Charter. After a long period of conflict nations, like individuals, are not only hostile; they are heartily sick of each other's company and what they most need is a long period of leaving each other strictly alone.

Applying these thoughts to the Vietnamese war and to the relations of the United States and China, it seems to me that the key to peace is mutual disengagement through political arrangements for the *neutralization* of Southeast Asia. I shall attempt in this chapter, as specifically as possible, to outline a possible plan for peace in Asia, a plan, I believe, which is sound in both psychological and traditional political terms and which could serve as a workable alternative to the current war policy of the United States.

Why Is an Alternative Needed?

I do not accept the view that criticism of the Vietnamese war is illegitimate in the absence of a foolproof plan for ending it; nor do I accept the view that because we are already deeply involved in Vietnam it is "academic" to debate the wisdom of that involvement. It is true that one cannot undo the past, but the assessment of past errors is absolutely indispensable to efforts to correct them and to avoiding their repetition. Far from being academic, the question of whether the United States should or should not have taken over the Vietnamese war in the first place is of the greatest pertinence in deciding whether we should now sustain the war indefinitely on its present scale, expand it, or try to bring it to an end. Criticism of present policy is therefore indispensable to and inseparable from the process of devising an alternative.

Why is an alternative needed? The general answer is the unwisdom of American involvement in the Vietnamese civil war for the reasons set forth in Chapter 5. More specifically, one can cite five major reasons why an alternative is needed.

First, the tactical premise underlying the large-scale American military involvement has proven to be unsound. In early 1965 it was hoped that the introduction of a large American force would not only blunt the anticipated monsoon offensive of the Viet Cong but would induce the enemy to enter peace negotiations in the fall of that year. That expectation proved to be a miscalculation; mounting American involvement and a steadily rising level of violence have inspired the Viet Cong and North Vietnam with determination to fight on, and as of the summer of 1966 the two sides were farther than ever from willingness to make the kind of concessions that might reasonably be expected to lead to peace negotiations, with the Saigon generals as obdurate as Hanoi in their refusal to negotiate.

Second, the level of violence has become so high as to negate the concept of "counter-insurgency," which purports to win the war by combining limited military activity with social, economic, and political reforms aimed at winning the support of the people and building a strong society and government. At the level of violence reached in 1966 American military operations, especially massive bombing raids within *South* Vietnam, were probably killing as many or more innocent villagers as Viet Cong soldiers. Such a conflict, with no end to it in sight, reduces social and economic measures to irrelevance and must raise doubts in the minds of both the South Vietnamese and other peoples whom the United States is pledged to defend as to whether the heavy price of being protected by the United States is worth paying.

Third, the war as now being fought is "open-ended." With little prospect of either negotiation or effective "counter-insurgency," the conflict is gradually expanding in scale and intensity, raising two exceedingly distasteful possibilities: either that it will remain a protracted endurance contest in which American lives are sacrificed in small but unlimited installments while China and Russia stand aside, or that it will explode into an all-out war with China and possibly the Soviet Union as well.

Fourth, insofar as it is based on strategic as distinguished from ideological considerations, the war is based on a misconceived strategy for the containment of China. South Vietnam, as Donald Zagoria, a leading China expert, has pointed out, is not the first of a series of "dominoes" before a Chinese tide; the success of the Viet Cong is closely related to the fact that communists have dominated the Vietnamese nationalist movement since World War II, a circumstance which does not obtain in other Southeast Asian countries. The successes of the Viet Cong, Dr. Zagoria points out, should not "obscure the more fundamental fact that the communists have been unable to seize control of a nationalist movement anywhere else in Asia, Africa or Latin America since the start of World War II."[1]

Fifth, as discussed in Chapter 6, the Vietnamese war is having a destructive "fallout" effect on American policy both at home and throughout the world. It has distracted both money and leadership from the Great Society program; it has damaged our relations with allies and neutrals; and it has put a virtual end to the "building of bridges" to the Soviet Union and Eastern Europe.

There is no alternative policy for Vietnam which is good and desirable in any positive sense because our choices are greatly limited by what has already been done. In retrospect it is clear that we should not have supported France's colonial war in Indochina from 1950 to 1954; we should not have supported Ngo Dinh Diem in his violations of the Geneva Accords of 1954; we should not have built up the unpopular Diem regime as our military and political protégé in the late fifties and early sixties; we should not have sent increasing numbers of military advisers to bolster the flagging South Vietnamese Army; and above all we should not have sent a large American army to take over the war when the South Vietnamese Army was on the verge of collapse in early 1965. All that is water over the dam; we cannot undo the past but we can hope to learn something from it, and perhaps also to retrieve something from it.

Mistakes are not liquidated without a price being paid. No responsible critic of the war—certainly no member of the Senate—advocates a disorderly withdrawal of American forces and the abandonment of South Vietnam to the Viet Cong, but many of us have pointed to the need for a peace short of victory, for a peace involving significant concessions by the United States. A concession, however, is not a humiliation and may indeed be turned to one's own advantage, as General de Gaulle demonstrated by giving independence to Algeria and as Khrushchev demonstrated by proclaiming himself a peacemaker while yielding to the American ultimatum in the Cuban missile crisis. The concessions we must make are necessary as an act of common sense in a tragic situation; as Walter Lippmann has written, "a display of common sense by a proud and imperious nation would be a good moral investment for the future."[2]

Accommodation and Neutralization in History

History seldom if ever tells us exactly what we must do in specific situations, but it does provide guidance as to the kinds of policies that are likely to succeed and the kinds that are likely to fail. The experience of nations in the last hundred and fifty years leaves one in no doubt that, more often than not, peace settlements based on accommodation between unbeaten belligerents or on the magnanimity of the victor toward the vanquished have proven to be durable and have often led to reconciliation, whereas peace settlements dictated by one side to the other in the wake of total victory have proven to be unstable, making for renewed conflict and generating greater problems than they solved.

In 1815 the great powers of Europe, led by the great conservatives, Lord Castlereagh of England and Prince Metternich of Austria, granted terms of peace to a defeated and helpless France which can only be described by twentieth-century standards as astonishingly generous. They did so despite the fact that France had conquered most of Europe and kept it in turmoil for a quarter of a century. Under the terms of peace the French lost no territory at all that had been theirs before the revolution, were subjected to a limited occupation of only three years, and were compelled to make limited reparations and then were given assistance in paying them, with the result that France's financial obligations were liquidated within four years of the end of hostilities.

Three years after the end of the Napoleonic wars France was brought into the concert of Europe as a full and equal great power. The conservative statesmen who made this generous peace did not do so out of love for a revolutionary and aggressive France but out of respect for the power and dynamism of the French nation. Wanting above all things peace and stability, Castlereagh and Metternich gave France a peace that she could endure. Castlereagh said that he had come to Vienna not to collect trophies but "to bring the world back to peaceful habits." He was admirably successful: not only was France reconciled with the nations that defeated her but never again after 1815 did France engage in major aggression and never again did she pose a major threat to the peace of Europe. I have the strong feeling, parenthetically, that if Castlereagh—who had no love of revolutions but a highly developed sense of the wisdom of even the most powerful nation's minding its own business—were alive today, he would come much closer to being a "dove" than a "hawk" on the matter of Vietnam.

Another example of a highly successful peace based on accommodation came out of our own war of 1812. The Americans won an important victory over the British at New Orleans but the victory did not win the war because the Treaty of Ghent which ended the war had already been signed when the battle was fought. England at the time was at the peak of her power. Napoleon had already been defeated, the British fleet was unchallenged on the seas, and undoubtedly, had they wished to do so, the British could have defeated the young American nation militarily and might even have brought it back into the British Empire. They had the generosity—and the wisdom—not to do so. Had the British tried to use their overwhelming power to reconquer America, they would probably have encountered fierce national resistance by an aroused American people fighting for their own homes, their own towns, and their own farms. The British themselves had supported the Spanish in their successful guerrilla war against Napoleon and, powerful as they were, the British apparently knew how hopeless it would be to try to subjugate a patriotic people determined to defend their independence.

The Treaty of Ghent simply restored the status quo between America and England as it had existed before the war. There were no victor and no vanquished, and the issues that had set America against England remained unsolved. But what diplomacy did not resolve, history did. Never again did England and America go to war and in the twentieth century, confronted with new circumstances and new dangers, they have become each other's closest allies. It all began with the unpromising Treaty of Ghent.

By contrast with the conflicts of the nineteenth century, twentieth-century warfare has been marked by total victories and total defeats. The total victories of 1918 and 1945 both generated more problems than they solved, sowing the seeds

of new, unforeseen, and more serious conflicts. These conflicts were generated by the totality of things—by the totality
of violence in two world wars and the totality of the victories
that ended them.

The harshness of the Treaty of Versailles was more in its
implementation than in its provisions. For many and complex reasons, the vindictive provisions of the treaty, those
pertaining to reparations and the occupation of Germany,
rather than the promising parts of the treaty, those pertaining
to disarmament and the League of Nations, were most vigorously implemented in the 1920s. The failure of the belligerents of World War I to reconcile in the twenties was the
most important single factor behind the rise of Hitler in the
thirties. In short, the vindictiveness of World War I became
the major cause of World War II.

The cold war of the last twenty years was spawned by the
total victory of 1945. The total destruction of German and
Japanese power created a vacuum which was soon enough
filled, quickly and eagerly by Russia and belatedly and reluc-
tantly by America. Had the generals who tried to kill Hitler
in 1944 been successful at that time or earlier, a negotiated
peace might conceivably have saved Germany from partition.
It was the total defeat of Germany that resulted in her division, and that division, the product of a total victory, became
the paramount issue in a new, great, and still unresolved
conflict.

The debate between those who would accelerate the war in
Vietnam and those who would reduce its scale is as fateful
and significant as any we have had in the last two decades.
There is a deceptive appeal about proposals for expanded
military action; they are simple and clean-cut and seem to
promise quick and easy solutions to difficult problems. Proposals for accommodation, on the other hand, are complex,
ambiguous, and easily misunderstood. History, however, suggests that the military solution that seems so promising today
is likely to result in disaster tomorrow, whereas the course of

accommodation, which always seems so difficult, is the only course with demonstrated promise of being able to bring about a lasting and honorable peace.

The essential principle of an accommodation in Southeast Asia is that it must apply not just to Vietnam but to all of Southeast Asia. Vietnam, after all, is only one of many small and weak nations on the periphery of a powerful China and, as has been pointed out innumerable times, what happens in one such country may well happen in another.

This premise underlies the "domino" theory, which holds that if one country falls to the communists, so must another and then another. The inference we have drawn from this is that we must fight in one country in order to avoid having to fight in another, although we could with equal logic have inferred that it is useless to fight in one country when the same conditions of conflict are present in another, that the failure of subversion in one country might simply result in the transfer of subversion to another.

History and logic and common sense suggest that a viable settlement in Vietnam must be part of a general settlement in Southeast Asia. Unless we are prepared to fight a general war to eliminate the effects of Chinese power in all of Southeast Asia, we have no alternative but to seek a general accommodation. The central issue is the contest between Chinese and American power and the prospect for a lasting peace depends far more upon the resolution of that issue than it does on the matter of who is to participate in a South Vietnamese government and by what means it shall be formed. If the issue between Chinese and American power in Southeast Asia can be resolved, the future of Vietnam should not be too difficult to arrange; but if the issue of Chinese and American power is left unresolved, any settlement in Vietnam, even one based on a total American military victory, would be in continuing jeopardy. As long as China and America are competitors for predominance in Southeast Asia, there is unlikely to be a secure peace in that part of the world.

Just as history suggests the advisability of accommodation, it also offers guidance as to the kind of accommodation which might make for lasting peace in Southeast Asia. In the past when great powers have competed for predominance over smaller and weaker nations, the one workable alternative to the victory of one or the other has been neutralization. In such arrangements, it is the fact of neutralization rather than the political or ideological complexion of the small countries concerned that has made for stability and peace. Neutralization is not a foolproof method of resolving great power conflicts, but it is a demonstrably more successful one than total victory.

Switzerland is an example. The Swiss Federation was established by the Congress of Vienna in 1815 as a perpetually neutral state. To this day, despite the fact that she is surrounded by great powers, Switzerland remains both neutral and at peace.

Belgium was established as a perpetually neutral state under the guarantee of the great powers by a treaty signed in 1839. The treaty was violated in 1914, but the more astonishing fact is that for seventy-five years Belgium remained both neutral and at peace despite the ambitions of the great powers and despite her strategic location between France and Germany. Belgium might well have been the victim of great-power ambitions but neutralization made her instead the beneficiary of great-power rivalry. The solution lay quite simply in the fact that, hopeful as each great power was for its own hegemony, it was no less fearful of the hegemony of the other and neutralization was judged to be the acceptable price of its prevention.

Austria is the outstanding contemporary example of accommodation by neutralization. Ten years after World War II Austria was divided and occupied by the great powers. The State Treaty of 1955 laid the basis for the independent and prosperous national existence that Austria now enjoys, and at the same time resolved a major issue between Russia and the West without upsetting the European balance of power.

Applying historical experience, the crisis in Southeast Asia might be resolved on a lasting basis by the neutralization of the entire region as between China and the United States. China is said by most experts to be deeply fearful of American bases on her periphery; indeed, she demonstrated that by intervening in the Korean War only when American troops approached her Manchurian frontier in November 1950. Fearful as she is of American military power in Southeast Asia, China might be willing—if not immediately then eventually—to purchase its removal by agreeing to the continued exclusion of her own. It would seem highly advisable that the United States indicate that it is prepared to remove American military power from Southeast Asia by carefully planned stages in return for a Chinese commitment to respect the independence of China's neighbors—an independence which in fact has not yet been violated by China in anything approaching a clear and consistent design of aggression.

An Alternative for Vietnam

With these historical considerations about accommodation and neutralization in mind, and with regard as well to some of the general tendencies of human behavior discussed in Chapter 8, I propose the following eight-point program for the eventual restoration of peace in Vietnam.

(1) The South Vietnamese government should seek peace negotiations with the National Liberation Front.

It is suggested that the Saigon government, the Buddhists, and other major groups be advised that the United States wishes the South Vietnamese government to take steps immediately to initiate peace negotiations with the National Liberation Front; it is further suggested that it be made clear that continued American support for the Saigon government will depend upon the energy and good faith with which it undertakes to negotiate a cease-fire with the National Liberation Front.

At present there is an apparent discrepancy between the attitudes of Washington and Saigon on peace negotiations. The United States is officially committed to unconditional negotiations whenever the other side is willing to negotiate but it is reported that in South Vietnam the mere advocacy of a negotiated peace is a criminal offense; indeed, in the election held in September 1966 in South Vietnam "neutralists" as well as communists were legally excluded from candidacy for the constituent assembly.

An effort should be made to bring the Saigon government's position on peace negotiations in line with that of President Johnson. To this end, it is recommended that the United States government remind the government in Saigon, clearly and forcefully, that the United States is committed to a policy of unconditional negotiations, and that this means that the United States is not now committed and does not intend to become committed to the objective of complete military victory for the present South Vietnamese government or any successor government. The South Vietnamese should be left in no doubt that the United States seeks and will continue to seek a negotiated peace and that it will not permit the Saigon government to exercise a veto on American policy.

(2) At the same time as the Saigon government makes direct overtures to the National Liberation Front the United States and South Vietnam together should propose negotiaions for a cease-fire among military representatives of four separate negotiating parties: the United States and South Vietnam, North Vietnam and the National Liberation Front.

Such a negotiation would reflect the military realities. Whatever the degree of the National Liberation Front's dependence on North Vietnam, there are four distinct principal belligerents in the Vietnamese war, and it seems reasonable that they should be the principal parties to negotiations for a cease-fire.

Despite the fact that the National Liberation Front is powerfully influenced if not actually dominated by the North Vietnamese government, it is recommended that it be accepted as a separate negotiating party and not merely as a part of a North Vietnamese delegation. This recommendation is made in the belief that it is in the interests of the United States to encourage the maximum degree of independence from North Vietnam on the part of the National Liberation Front and that this purpose is more likely to be advanced by offering to deal with the National Liberation Front as a separate party than by treating it as an instrument of Hanoi, which can have the effect of driving it to greater dependency on North Vietnam.

(3) The United States should terminate its bombing of North Vietnam, add no additional forces in South Vietnam, and reduce the scale of military operations to the maximum extent consistent with the security of American forces while peace initiatives are under way.

Peace initiatives would be more likely to be persuasive to the enemy, and more likely to enlist the support of non-belligerents who have influence with the enemy such as the Soviet Union and France, if they were accompanied by a general and sustained reduction in the scale of hostilities. Conversely, the continuation of hostilities without abatement while initiatives for peace were being taken would permit Hanoi and the National Liberation Front to believe that American military actions rather than American proposals for peace represented the true intentions of the United States. This would seem all the more likely in light of the fact that North Vietnam and the National Liberation Front have repeatedly shown themselves to be deeply suspicious of American objectives in Southeast Asia.

(4) The United States should pledge the eventual removal of American military forces from Vietnam.

The date and conditions for the removal of American military forces from Vietnam could be determined only in connection with an international agreement defining the status of a neutralized South Vietnam and establishing certain international guarantees as proposed in Point 6 below. It is important nonetheless that the United States state, in advance of peace negotiations, that it is prepared, as part of a multilateral agreement on Vietnam, to pledge the removal of all American forces on a fixed date or upon the realization of certain specified conditions such as the reassertion of authority by a revived International Control Commission. A forthright pledge to remove American forces is of great importance for the persuasiveness of peace initiatives because of the well-known Chinese and North Vietnamese fear that, despite assurances to the contrary, the United States wishes to maintain permanent military bases in South Vietnam.

(5) Negotiations among the four principal belligerents— the United States and South Vietnam, North Vietnam and the National Liberation Front—should be directed toward a cease-fire and plans for self-determination in South Vietnam.

The primary purpose of negotiations among the principals would be the drawing up of plans for a national referendum acceptable both to the government of South Vietnam and to the National Liberation Front. The American negotiators would do well to stay somewhat in the background in these discussions and to indicate American willingness to support any arrangements for self-determination on which the Saigon government and the National Liberation Front could agree. It might be that the two South Vietnamese parties would wish international supervision of the projected referendum; or it might be that they would wish to conduct it entirely on their own or essentially on their own but with international observers. It might be that they would wish to elect a permanent national legislative body or it might be that they would wish to elect a constituent assembly to draw up a permanent constitution for South Vietnam. In any case, it is suggested that the United States should be prepared to accept and support any arrangements agreed upon by the Saigon government and the National Liberation Front.

It would seem reasonable and necessary to concede to the National Liberation Front an important role in the conduct of a national referendum. The nature and extent of that role would depend upon many factors to be taken up in the negotiations, such as whether the election was to be conducted under international or exclusively South Vietnamese auspices. In any case the role of the National Liberation Front in the conduct of an election would have to be great enough to assure it against fraud but circumscribed enough to deny it the opportunity itself to engage in fraud or terror. Whether these conditions might require the participation of the National Liberation Front in a pre-election provisional government would be an appropriate subject of negotiation.

The United States should commit itself explicitly, and repeatedly if necessary, to accept and support the outcome of a national referendum in South Vietnam, whatever that outcome might be. Such a commitment will be more likely to allay suspicions deriving from the cancellation of the Vietnamese election scheduled for 1956 under the Geneva Agreements if it is forcefully stated at the highest level of the American government than if it is merely conceded in response to public or Congressional inquiry.

The outcome of a referendum in South Vietnam cannot be predicted. Qualified observers of Vietnamese affairs suggest that a free election would reveal the full diversity of South Vietnamese society, with the National Liberation Front emerging as a major political force in the country but with the Buddhists and Catholics, the Cao Dai and the Hoa Hao also showing themselves to be important forces in their respective zones of influence.

The belligerents might also wish to discuss plans for the reunification of North and South Vietnam. They might prefer to leave this to be negotiated between the Hanoi and Saigon governments or they might wish to make more specific plans, such as an internationally supervised referendum at an agreed time in the future as originally called for under the Geneva Agreements of 1954.

(6) After the principal belligerents have agreed on a cease-fire and plans for self-determination in South Vietnam, an international conference of all interested states should be convened to guarantee the arrangements made by the belligerents and to plan a future referendum on the reunification of North Vietnam and South Vietnam.

In addition to the Saigon and Hanoi governments and the National Liberation Front, all of whom should be represented at an international conference, it is suggested that the following countries should be invited to participate in the negotiations: the United States, China, the Soviet Union, France, Great Britain, Japan, India, Pakistan, and the countries of the Southeast Asian mainland: Cambodia, Laos, Thailand, Burma, and Malaysia. The larger nations—that is, the United States, China, the Soviet Union, France, Great Britain, Japan, India, and Pakistan—could be expected to act as guarantors of a final settlement.

Guaranteeing the arrangements for self-determination in South Vietnam already agreed upon by the belligerents would be the first and most essential business of the international conference. Unless certain problems relating to the projected referendum, such as possible arrangements for international supervision, had been referred to the international conference to be resolved, the work of the conference in this connection would consist mainly in the drawing up of an agreement for collective action, if requested by any of the Vietnamese parties, against any violation of the agreed conditions of the South Vietnamese referendum or any attempt to overthrow the government resulting from the referendum.

The second task of the international conference would be to make plans for a referendum at an agreed time for the possible reunification of North and South Vietnam. If the belligerents had already agreed on the time and conditions of a popular vote on reunification, the conference would have only to give its endorsement and collective guarantee to that agreement. If the belligerents had not settled the matter, the conference could devise a plan for an internationally supervised election and submit it to the Hanoi and Saigon governments and the National Liberation Front for their approval. Once the Vietnamese parties agreed on a plan, the conference could then give its collective guarantee. If the Vietnamese parties were unable to agree on a time and conditions for a referendum on reunification, the international conference would be well advised not to try to force a plan upon them but simply to give its collective guarantee in advance to any arrangement the North and South Vietnamese might work out later.

The oversight or, if desired by the Vietnamese parties, the execution of these arrangements for self-determination in South Vietnam and the possible reunification of North and South Vietnam should be vested in an appropriate international organ. The conference might find it desirable to revive and strengthen the existing International Control Commission composed of Canada, India, and Poland.

(7) In addition to guaranteeing arrangements for self-determination in South Vietnam and planning a referendum on the reunification of North and South Vietnam, the international conference should neutralize South Vietnam and undertake to negotiate a multilateral agreement for the general neutralization of Southeast Asia.

The neutralization of South Vietnam would seem to be essential; the neutralization of North Vietnam as well would be highly desirable. South Vietnam, or preferably the two Vietnamese states, should be prohibited from participation in military alliances with other powers, and foreign troops and military bases should be excluded from the territory of both North and South Vietnam. In addition the conference might specify that the conditions of neutrality applied to South Vietnam would be extended automatically to a reunified Vietnamese state. These conditions of neutrality should be collectively guaranteed by the states participating in the conference and overseen by the international organ referred to above in Point 6.

It would be highly desirable if an agreement on neutralization could be extended to cover all of Southeast Asia, making a Vietnamese settlement more viable by incorporating it into a general arrangement for the neutralization of all of Southeast Asia. The essential features of such an arrangement would be the exclusion of American, Chinese, and all other foreign troops and bases from the territory of the Southeast Asian countries, the formal commitment of these countries to abstain from military alliances, and the collective guarantee of these arrangements by the nations designated in Point 6 as prospective guarantors of a Vietnamese settlement.

A general neutralization agreement for Southeast Asia could be enforced in three ways. First, a degree of automatic enforcement would arise from the prospect that the introduction of Chinese military power would be followed by the reintroduction of American military power. Second, the United States, without stationing forces or establishing bases on the Asian mainland, could and should retain its sea and air power around the periphery of Asia. Third, a neutralization agreement could and should be placed under the collective guarantee of the major powers participating in the international conference, that is, the United States, China, the Soviet Union, France, Great Britain, Japan, India, and Pakistan.

Whether such far-reaching arrangements could be worked out at a Vietnamese peace conference is very doubtful. Certainly proposals for the general neutralization of Southeast Asia should not be allowed to jeopardize more limited arrangements for peace, neutrality, and self-determination in Vietnam. Nonetheless, nothing would be lost, and something might be gained, by introducing the idea of general neutralization in Southeast Asia at an international conference on Vietnam.

(8) If for any reason an agreement ending the Vietnamese war cannot be reached, the United States should consolidate its forces in highly fortified defensible areas in South Vietnam and keep them there indefinitely.

Such action, in the wake of an unsuccessful effort to end the war, would represent an accommodation to two fundamental realities: first, that the United States, as the nation with principal, though not exclusive, responsibility for world peace and stability, cannot accept defeat or a disorderly withdrawal from South Vietnam; second, that it now seems likely that a complete military victory can be accomplished only by sacrifices disproportionate to American security interests in South Vietnam and by raising the level of violence to a degree that would impose greatly increased suffering on South Vietnamese civilians and would also greatly increase the danger of war with China.

As long as the United States is expending increasing numbers of lives and increasing sums of money on the Vietnamese war, China, North Vietnam, and the National Liberation Front can logically, if erroneously, hope that the American people will sooner or later find the effort intolerable and force the withdrawal of United States forces from Southeast Asia. They may believe that the drain on American lives and resources in Southeast Asia will sap the will and ability of the United States successfully to oppose future wars of national liberation. Powerful evidence that the Chinese subscribe exactly to this view is contained in an editorial which appeared in the *People's Daily* of Peking on August 30, 1966, which stated:

> . . . To be quite frank, if United States imperialism kept its forces in Europe and America, the Asian people would have no way of wiping them out. Now, as it is so obliging as to deliver its goods to the customer's door, the Asian

people cannot but express welcome. The more forces United States imperialism throws into Asia, the more will it be bogged down there and the deeper will be the grave it digs for itself.

. . . The tying down of large numbers of United States troops by the Asian people creates a favorable condition for the further growth of the anti-United States struggle of the people in other parts of the world. With all the people rising to attack it, one hitting at its head and the other at its feet, United States imperialism can be nibbled up bit by bit.[3]

If instead of committing more and more men and resources to the Vietnamese war, we were to reduce our commitment to a level which our enemies knew we could sustain indefinitely at moderate cost, we would then be confronting them with the perfectly credible prospect of permanent American military bases on their borders—a prospect which China has shown herself to fear greatly. Knowing that we could remain in these bases indefinitely, the National Liberation Front and the North Vietnamese would have a powerful inducement to negotiate peace and China would have a powerful inducement to enter an agreement for the neutralization of Southeast Asia. At the very least, such a policy would convert a situation in which our enemies believe themselves to be wearing us down to one in which we, at supportable cost, would be wearing them down.

On Greatness and Magnanimity

In her relations with Asian nations, as indeed in her relations with all of the revolutionary or potentially revolutionary societies of the world, America has an opportunity to perform services of which no great nation has ever before been capable. To do so we must acquire wisdom to match our power and humility to match our pride. Perhaps the single word above all others that expresses America's need is "empathy," which Webster defines as the "imaginative projection of one's own consciousness into another being."

Should it be possible to end the Vietnamese war on the basis of an agreement for the neutralization of Southeast Asia, it would then be possible to concentrate with real hope of success on the long and difficult task of introducing some trust into relations between China and the West, of repairing history's ravages, and bringing the great Chinese nation into its proper role as a respected member of the international community. In time it might even be possible for the Chinese and Taiwanese on their own to work out some arrangement for Taiwan that would not do too much damage either to the concept of self-determination or to the Chinese concept of China's cultural indivisibility—perhaps some sort of an arrangement for Taiwanese self-government under nominal Chinese suzerainty. But that would be for them to decide.

All this is not, as has been suggested, a matter of "being kind to China." It is a matter of altering that fatal expectancy which is leading two great nations toward a tragic and unnecessary war. If it involves "being kind to China," those who are repelled by that thought may take some small comfort in the fact that it also involves "being kind to America."

America is a great and powerful and fundamentally decent nation; we know it—or ought to—and the world knows it. At times, however, we act as though we did not believe in our own greatness; we act as though our prestige as a great nation were constantly at issue, constantly in danger of being irretrievably lost, as if our greatness were something that had endlessly to be repurchased, requiring unending exertions to prove to the world that we are indeed an important and powerful nation.

We have been told that we must beat the Russians to the moon, that we cannot relent in our pressures against Castro, that we had no choice but to intervene against the Dominican Revolution, not primarily because these actions were consid-

ered of and by themselves to be essential but because if we did
not do these things, our prestige, which is to say, our reputation for greatness, would be hopelessly compromised. In the
case of Vietnam, we have been told that our massive military
commitment is essential less because of the strategic importance of Vietnam itself than for the purpose of proving to
the communists that America is not a "paper tiger" and
proving to the world that America cannot be pushed around.
Again and again, in many parts of the world, we have engaged in enormous exertions at enormous cost, not so much
for the sake of our greatness as for its shadow.

I do not think that America's greatness is questioned in the
world, and I certainly do not think that strident behavior is
the best way for a nation to prove its greatness. Indeed, in
nations as in individuals bellicosity is a mark of weakness
and self-doubt rather than of strength and self-assurance.
There is something appropriate and admirable about a small
country standing up defiantly to a big country; such behavior
confers upon the small country a strength and a dignity that
it would not otherwise possess. The same behavior on the
part of a big nation is grotesque, marking it as a bully. The
true mark of greatness is not stridency but magnanimity.

It is precisely because of America's enormous strength and
prestige that we can afford to be magnanimous in Vietnam.
If the Viet Cong or North Vietnam were to take the initiative
in offering substantive concessions, they could plausibly be
regarded as having been intimidated by American power. If
the United States were to take the lead in suggesting peace
terms involving significant concessions to the Viet Cong,
many people would suppose that the American people had
grown weary of the war—which is probably true; but no
one could seriously believe that the United States had been
frightened into submission by a small undeveloped country
in Southeast Asia.

On September 1, 1966, President de Gaulle of France made
a speech in Cambodia. Speaking of America and of the prob-

able effects of an American policy of accommodation and
neutralization in Southeast Asia, he said:

> . . . in view of the power, wealth and influence at present
> attained by the United States, the act of renouncing, in
> its turn, a distant expedition once it appears unprofitable
> and unjustifiable and of substituting for it an international
> arrangement organizing the peace and development of
> an important region of the world, will not, in the final
> analysis, involve anything that could injure its pride, inter-
> fere with its ideals and jeopardize its interests.
>
> On the contrary, in taking a path so true to the Western
> genius, what an audience would the United States recap-
> ture from one end of the world to the other, and what an
> opportunity would peace find on the scene and everywhere
> else.[4]

10

Rebuilding
Bridges

SO PREOCCUPIED have we Americans become with the war in Vietnam that we are not thinking much about the things America could be doing if there were no war; we are not thinking about the bright opportunities that will still be ours if the war can be ended before it explodes into a general Asian war or before its fallout utterly disrupts our domestic affairs and corrodes our relations with most of the world. Assuming that the war can be ended by negotiation within a reasonable time—and I do so more in hope than in confidence—America will have the opportunity to recapture that world audience of which General de Gaulle spoke in Cambodia; she will have the opportunity to rebuild those bridges to the East which were coming along so hopefully before Vietnam, to reconstruct her partnership with Western Europe and to resume the hopeful work of domestic reconstruction begun by Presidents Kennedy and Johnson but now interrupted by the war.

Reconciling with the East

The possibility for a degree of reconciliation in East-West relations derives in great part from enormously important changes which have been taking place within the Communist world. Communism has ceased to be the monolith it seemed to be in Stalin's time; its practice is increasingly being nationalized to fit the conditions of particular countries. What is more important, the communism of Eastern Europe and the Soviet Union is slowly but steadily being humanized. The terror of Stalin's time has largely disappeared from Russia; the Hungarian government now tolerates a degree of individual liberty; Rumania practices a defiantly independent national communism; Yugoslavia seems slowly and hesitatingly to be coming to accept the legitimacy of open expressions of doubt about communism itself.

The architect, or executor, of these extraordinary developments was Nikita Khrushchev. Whether Khrushchev actually intended to preside over the liquidation of Stalin's empire may well be questioned, but that has clearly been the major result of his ten years of leadership. Starting with his famous secret speech of February 1956 in which he denounced Stalin, Khrushchev initiated a process which is beginning to undermine the bases of communist totalitarianism. Heretofore the judgments and the words of Soviet dictators had been deemed infallible; by denouncing his predecessor, Khrushchev admitted the fallibility of Soviet communism and set an enormously important precedent for future doubts, future questions and future criticism, in Russia, in other communist societies, and insofar as there can still be said to be one, in the international communist movement.

The most striking results of this new ferment in the communist world have been in the countries of Eastern Europe, but important changes have taken place and continue to take place in the Soviet Union itself. The very manner of Khrushchev's removal from power is illustrative of the new atmosphere in the Soviet Union. By Western standards it was crudely done, to be sure, but by previous Soviet standards the removal of Khrushchev and his subsequent reappearance as a private citizen were notable steps forward toward the development of civilized political methods.

Rebuilding Bridges

Khrushchev's most important contribution was the practice of "peaceful coexistence." I believe that both he and his successors have been earnest in their declared desire to avoid nuclear war with the West. I believe they have been sincere in their stated belief that ideological warfare should be conducted by peaceful economic competition. Many Americans have pointed to Khrushchev's unfortunate declaration, "we will bury you," as evidence of the Soviet Union's warlike intent. I am much inclined to the view that Khrushchev was talking about peaceful competition in the production of goods and services and in efforts to raise popular living standards. I think that he genuinely believed that communism could win a global victory by "putting more meat in the goulash" and "more rice in the worker's bowl."

Such a challenge should be most welcome to the United States, for two reasons: first, because the United States, with an economy that is not only the world's greatest by far but also one of the fastest growing, has every prospect of winning an economic competition with the Russians; second, because no one can really lose a creative competition in efforts to make a better life for millions of people. It would be a great blessing for humanity if both sides in the cold war would expend less energy on preaching their doctrines abroad and more energy on making them work at home. If they did this, I feel confident, they would discover one day that the doctrinal differences that more than once have brought them to the brink of war are differences of doctrine and not much more, having little to do with the welfare and happiness of mankind.

Constructive competition can have a beneficial effect on Soviet-American relations; there is also a great deal that can be done to advance the reconciliation of East and West through projects of direct cooperation. We spoke in Chapter 8 of the psychological consequences of putting hostile groups into a relationship of interdependence;* contact alone served

---

* See Chapter 8, pp. 166–167.

only as the occasion for recrimination, but the necessity of working together for some common purpose had the effect of dissolving animosities and generating friendliness between members of the two groups.

The reconciliation of East and West is primarily a psychological problem, having to do with the cultivation of cooperative attitudes and of a sense of having practical common objectives. A grand design for ending the cold war in a single stroke of statesmanship is not even remotely feasible. What is feasible in East-West relations is the advancement of a great many projects of practical cooperation, projects which, taken by themselves, may be of little importance, but which, taken together, may have the effect of shaping revolutionary new attitudes in the world.

The shaping of such attitudes is, or ought to be, the primary objective of our foreign policy. It is not simply a question of learning to value peace over war. Virtually everybody wants peace but most nations want something else even more, be it conquest or glory or prestige or some objective or other that is taken to be essential for their honor. The problem, then, is not merely to persuade people to want peace but to persuade them to want it more than all those other things for which they are usually ready to sacrifice it. If there is any key to survival and security in the nuclear age, it probably does not lie in new and improved international peace-keeping organizations, nor in elaborate schemes for disarmament, which has proven historically to be one of the most intractable of international problems, but in the personal attitudes of peoples and their leaders, in their willingness to place at least some of the common requirements of humanity over the conflicting aspirations of nations and ideologies.

If attitudes rather than formal arrangements are the critical factor in international relations, then a somewhat different set of priorities is indicated for foreign policy from those which we generally profess. Formal East-West security arrangements may seem no more important than an increasing flow of East-West trade; phased disarmament, important and desirable though it is, may seem no more important for world peace than a widening exchange of persons and ideas.

Such objectives as the reunification of Germany and "general and complete disarmament" as it is called are important not only because the German people should have the right of self-determination—as they should—and because nuclear weapons are expensive and might accidentally go off— as indeed they might—but because these issues are the cause of tensions that increase the danger of war. This of course is a very commonplace observation but it points up a distinction that is easily overlooked, namely, that it is not the reunification of Germany and the termination of the arms race in themselves that are absolutely essential to world peace but the curbing of the tensions and the animosities to which they give rise.

The distinction is more than academic. Its implication in operational terms is that there can be many means to the same end. It means that when we fail to make progress on German unification and disarmament it is still possible to seek other means of reducing international tensions. It means that trade and cultural exchanges and other forms of limited cooperation that represent available options can advance exactly the same objectives, albeit much more slowly, than would be advanced by German reunification or general disarmament if these were available options.

If our concern is with the attitudes that govern human behavior rather than with formal political arrangements, it follows that the most rewarding initiatives we can take toward the improvement of East-West relations may be in fields that seem irrelevant to the major political issues of our time but which may in fact be highly pertinent because of their prospective psychological effect in reducing tensions and helping to build the *habit* of cooperation. Indeed, under existing world conditions there is likely to be far more profit in the resolution of peripheral issues than in efforts to resolve the central issues, which, with their highly emotional content and their history of intractability, are as likely to aggravate tensions as to allay them.

In foreign relations as in our individual lives we must strike a balance between our aspirations and our limitations. Our aspiration is toward a peaceful community of nations, but we must seek it within the limitations of a world divided by ideology and nationalism and by the enormous gap between the rich and the poor. In a world so divided there is little promise and considerable risk in great and sweeping designs, whether in the field of international organization or disarmament or general territorial settlements. The major risk of such designs, apart from the probability of failure, is that in the course of failing they are likely to heighten the very animosities they are meant to reduce and to distract us from the modest and practical measures of cooperation which offer the only real prospect of carrying a divided world toward a measure of genuine community.

What are some of the modest and practical measures that might be taken, in the wake of—or wherever possible in advance of—an Asian peace settlement, to advance the gradual reconciliation of East and West? The agreement in November 1966 to open up direct air service between New York and Moscow after years of delay is a modest but valuable step in the right direction. In addition, we would do well to pick up those projects which have been frozen by the Vietnam fallout, notably the Soviet-American consular treaty, which languishes unratified in the United States Senate, and President Johnson's legislative proposal for expanded trade with the communist countries, on which the House of Representatives has declined to act.*

In a book published in 1964 I suggested, in connection with a proposal for an international consortium to build and

---

* See Chapter 6, pp. 123–125.

operate a new Central American canal as an international utility, that it would be desirable for the Soviet Union, as a user of the canal, to participate in the consortium. Noting that under a reasonable consortium agreement no single member would have the authority or the means to close the canal or disrupt its operations, I raised, rhetorically, certain questions regarding Soviet participation:

> Would not Soviet participation in a canal consortium tend to strengthen their commitment to a peaceful status quo, just as their adherence to the Antarctic Treaty has made them cooperative associates in keeping the cold war away from the Antarctic continent? Is there not something to be gained for world peace and stability from an arrangement which would bring the Russians into close cooperation with nations they regard as "imperialists" in a kind of enterprise which they have hitherto denounced as "imperialist exploitation"? Would there not be significant psychological symbolism in the Soviet Union sharing responsibility for the construction and maintenance of a vital international facility, if only because of the striking contrast with the more disruptive activities of their revolutionary past? In summary, is there not something to be gained for world peace from bringing a difficult and dangerous nation into one more enterprise in which cooperation in the performance of practical tasks would be permitted to do its eroding work on the ideological passions that divide us?[1]

Important opportunities for encouraging habits of practical cooperation can also be found through international trade, business arrangements, and the settlement of financial claims —to say nothing of cultural and educational exchanges, which to my mind are probably the most rewarding of all forms of international cooperation.

In 1965 the Senate Foreign Relations Committee held hearings on the prospects and desirability of expanded East-West trade. The testimony showed a consensus, although not unanimity, among the experts and scholars who testified, including representatives of the business community, that the relaxation of existing restrictions and the expansion of trade between the United States and communist countries could have modest economic benefits for both sides and could also have political and psychological effects in reducing tensions and improving the general atmosphere of East-West relations.

Even if existing restrictions were substantially relaxed, the volume of trade that might develop between the Soviet Union and the United States would be very limited. Because the Soviet economy is heavily oriented to the production of capital goods, export industries have been neglected, with the result that the Soviet Union has neither the desired goods nor the hard currency reserves to finance a major expansion of trade with the United States.

The value of trade as a positive vehicle of Soviet-Western détente can in any case be exaggerated. Normal trade relations would not of themselves be likely to result in greatly improved political relations but discrimination in trade is certainly an obstacle to good relations. The establishment of normal trade with the Soviet Union in non-strategic goods, involving no special favors but no special discrimination either, should be regarded as a clearing of the decks, as a way of helping to establish the preconditions for active forms of cooperation.

In the case of the communist countries of Eastern Europe the removal of trade restrictions might have more positive effects. These countries by and large have a strong affinity for the West, and trade could go a long way to help satisfy this affinity and also to advance their aspirations toward greater independence of the Soviet Union. This relative economic independence in turn might give them additional leverage on Soviet policy, a leverage which might be used to encourage more friendly attitudes toward the West on the part of the Soviet Union itself.

The political and psychological benefits of East-West trade would probably prove to be considerably more important than the economic benefits. As Professor Isaiah Frank of the Johns Hopkins University School of Advanced International Studies has said: "Because the Soviet Union values acceptance in the world arena, our discrimination produces a psychological scar far out of proportion to the physical wound inflicted. Whenever the occasion presents itself, the Soviets call for an end to trade discrimination and for 'normalization' of trade relations with all countries. A willingness on our part to loosen up commercial relations could conceivably serve as a prelude to negotiations on broader political issues."[2]

In a practical way Western businesses, mostly European, are already helping to build bridges of cooperation between East and West. One recent example is the arrangement between the Soviet government and Fiat of Italy for the construction of an automobile plant in the Soviet Union.

A more limited, related matter that might profitably be pursued is the possibility of a Soviet-American settlement of the Lend-Lease debt from World War II, which the United States has offered to reduce to about $800 million. The existence of this debt is an obstacle to trade because the Johnson Act of 1934 prohibits the extension of long-term private credits to nations in default on their financial obligations to the United States. One proposal which might prove practicable calls for a settlement, or partial settlement, under which a lend-lease ruble account would be established in the Soviet Union from which American firms would be authorized to draw in order to undertake joint enterprises with the Russians within the Soviet Union; the American companies would then convert a part of their earnings from the joint ventures into dollars which would be used to compensate the United States government. Alternately, the two countries might use the funds accruing from a lend-lease settlement to finance joint development projects in underdeveloped countries.

Aside from its primary purpose as a means of financing

development, foreign aid has potential value as an instrument of East-West cooperation. For twenty years we have thought of foreign aid as a weapon in the cold war—a humane and intelligent one for the most part but nonetheless a weapon in a global struggle against communism. Looking beyond the Vietnamese war to the time when one hopes the Western and communist nations will have resumed the building of bridges, it may be that we shall find it possible to convert assistance to the underdeveloped countries from an instrument of rivalry to an instrument of reconciliation.

We are coming to discover that all Soviet aid programs are not detrimental to our interests, that some, indeed, may advance objectives, such as the development of India, that we ourselves favor. Why then could not the United States propose to the Soviet Union that the two countries cooperate, under the auspices of an international agency, in a particular development project that both favor—such as the construction of a canal or fertilizer plant in India or another country? If a project could be found that both countries considered to be in their interests—and I am sure a specific project could be found—a modest gain for economic development and a considerable gain for world peace could be achieved by a joint Soviet-American venture or, better still, by a joint venture involving several communist countries and several Western countries.

Cooperation, like conflict, tends to feed on itself. An initial, tentative venture in East-West cooperation in economic aid could lead to another, bolder venture and to a genuine broadening of the area of common interests, which in turn might lead to Soviet membership in the international lending agencies and a general multilateralization, indeed internationalization, of aid along the lines to be developed in the next chapter.

It is through such enterprises as the foregoing, some bigger, some smaller, but none very sweeping or decisive in themselves, that bridges can be built across the chasm of ideology.

All have the advantage that they can contribute to the shaping of new attitudes and new expectations. As we have noted, men tend to act on their expectations, and prophecies, firmly believed, have a way of fulfilling themselves. Perhaps the best that we can do in this imperfect world is to work hard and patiently, in our daily lives and in all the diverse pursuits of men and nations, to cultivate new and more hopeful expectations on which to act and prophecies whose fulfillment will benefit the human race.

Reuniting Europe

In Europe the tide of change in relations within and between the two blocs has profoundly altered the meaning of the cold war. Each side is now convinced—although neither is likely to admit it—that the other is in secure possession of the territories under its control. One hears little indeed these days of communist subversion in Western Europe or of the forcible liberation of Eastern Europe. Europe remains unnaturally divided but no serious observer expects war and it is now generally agreed on both sides that if the two Europes are to come together it can only be through a process of gradual change and accommodation.

I do not believe reunification of Eastern and Western Europe requires the severance of the latter's bonds with the United States. Both America and the Soviet Union, as the leaders of the two coalitions, should play leading roles in the task of reconciliation. Much of the hope for an improvement of relations leading to the ultimate reunification of Europe derives from the approximate balance of power between the two sides. Were Western Europe to be detached from America, an imbalance would come into existence, one which might tempt the Russians once again with the possibility of dominating Western Europe. As Raymond Aron has pointed out. "The reunification of Eastern and Western Europe requires a détente between the two blocs rather than a loosening of the ties between the two segments of the Atlantic alliance."[3]

If, however, the United States fails to lead the West in the building of bridges to the East, then Western Europe will almost certainly continue to build bridges of its own, drawing away from the United States in the process. That indeed is happening already: General de Gaulle, with some success, has taken the leadership in a long-term effort to reconcile the two European coalitions. Whatever the effects of the virtual withdrawal of France from NATO, de Gaulle's policy toward the Soviet Union and Eastern Europe is consistent with America's declared policy of building bridges to the East. If, nonetheless, French initiatives toward the Soviet Union are having the effect of separating France from the United States, it is primarily because the United States is not leading the West in the great task of reconciliation with the East. Whether or not President de Gaulle wishes to detach Europe from America—my own feeling is that he does—his policies are unlikely to have that result unless America, by a default of leadership, detaches herself from Europe.

The reason for America's unwillingness, or inability, to lead in the reconciliation of the two halves of Europe is of course the Vietnam fallout. While the war continues, the Soviet Union regards its relations with the United States as "frozen," and while they are proceeding with the improvement of their relations with Western Europe, the Russians are showing little interest in such arrangements with the United States as those suggested in the previous section. The leaders of the United States, moreover, preoccupied as they are with their Asian war, have little time or energy for leadership in Europe; their initiatives are half-hearted and desultory, put forward, it would seem, in ritualistic deference to the professed policy of bridge building, but without energy, conviction, persistence, or serious expectation of result.

Insofar as the United States is concerned with Europe, it

is additionally handicapped by an ambivalent attitude toward détente with the East. We want it no doubt but we also want to maintain the Western alliance as nearly as possible in its original form. We want to allay the genuine fear which the Russians and all other Eastern Europeans have of Germany but we do not wish to say or do anything that would displease the West German government. Specifically, we have been unwilling thus far either to allay Soviet anxiety by agreeing to deny West Germany direct access to nuclear weapons or to enter an arrangement with West Germany that would give her such access. So marked is the ambivalence that it is impossible to say whether the ill-starred plan for a multi-lateral nuclear force which would include West Germany has been officially abandoned or is still an official objective of American policy.

The United States is unlikely to be able to exercise effective leadership in European affairs until the Vietnamese war has been brought to an end. It is also unlikely to be able to lead effectively until it resolves the ambivalence in its European policy, by deciding once and for all whether it wishes to make West Germany a nuclear power in the hope of keeping her loyal to the West or to advance the reconciliation of the two blocs by abandoning the proposed multilateral force or any other scheme that would give West Germany access to nuclear weapons.

The choice, I think, is as stark as that because the Soviet Union and the Eastern European countries retain an over-riding fear of Germany. I am convinced that that fear, rooted in the Second World War, is genuinely felt, however ill founded it may be in fact. Above all, the Eastern Europeans fear the prospect of a Germany armed with nuclear weapons. They are persuaded, quite wrongly perhaps, that the creation of a multilateral force in any form would constitute the nuclear armament of Germany, and no amount of reassurance is likely to dissuade them from this view. It is rooted more in fear than fact but their fear itself is a fact, and a most important one, of which we must take due cognizance in the shaping of our own policy.

In the fall of 1964, when the proposed multilateral force was under active discussion, I visited Yugoslavia. Virtually every Yugoslav to whom I spoke raised the question, expressing alarm and fear at the possibility of a German role, however circumscribed, in the disposition of nuclear weapons. I explained repeatedly, and I am sure vainly, that under the proposed multilateral force arrangement Germany would have no independent authority whatever to dispose of nuclear weapons, that, indeed, Germany would be so firmly locked into a multilateral system as to preclude the possibility of a German national nuclear force in the future. As these discussions progressed, I became equally convinced of the logic of my position and of the impossibility of making it persuasive to the Yugoslavs.

The Eastern European fear of Germany is irrational and exaggerated but wholly understandable. It is the product of tragic and shocking experience, and only the healing effects of time, a great deal of time, will alleviate it. No matter what safeguards surrounded a German role in a Western nuclear deterrent system, neither the Russians nor any other people in Eastern Europe would feel safe with them. Their fear of Germany is an unalterable fact of our time; it exists— and must be taken due account of—despite the fact, which is evident to a fair-minded observer, that the German Federal Republic has become a decent, democratic, and peaceful society.

The Eastern Europeans have not understood, and perhaps cannot be expected to understand, the extent of the changes which have taken place in the new Germany. One may hope, however, that the coming of age of a new generation and continuing evidences of the decency and democracy of the Federal Republic will ultimately dispel Eastern Europe's fear of Germany. I am convinced that nothing we can do in the meantime will dispel that fear.

Rebuilding Bridges

The gradual breaking down of the fears of the Eastern Europeans is Germany's best hope, probably her only hope, for reunification. Only when the Eastern Europeans are convinced that it is safe and profitable to do business with Germany can they be expected to relent from their insistence upon the continued survival of the East German regime. The very core of the problem is to persuade the Eastern Europeans, who have suffered so grievously from past German aggression, that the new Germany of the Federal Republic is a respectable and reliable nation, committed to maintaining the peace of Europe and committed specifically to pursuing its own national aims by peaceful means.

For these reasons, the German Federal Republic has a high stake in the improvement of relations between Eastern and Western Europe. It would be very helpful indeed, to this end, if the Germans themselves cared to renounce the various schemes which might give them access to nuclear weapons. I would think it desirable, in addition, for West Germany to take a vigorous lead in the expansion of economic and cultural relations with Eastern Europe.

A degree of practical reconciliation between West Germany and Poland would be of particular value, not only to help heal the lingering wounds of World War II but also to allay the Polish fear that Germany may someday seek to recover the territories lost to Poland in 1945. A general expansion of cultural relations between Germany and Poland, even joint commercial ventures, would go far to allay old grievances and to build a foundation for future agreements.

The building of economic and cultural bridges could pave the way for the reunification of Europe. As it became clear to each side that it was safe and profitable to do business with the other, ideological barriers could be expected to erode. As the barriers of ideology gave way to friendly relations based on mutual interests, and as it became clear to Eastern Europeans that the German Federal Republic was a decent, honorable, and peaceful nation, the foundations of the East German puppet state could also be expected to erode. Given such an evolution, the Eastern nations and ultimately the Soviet Union itself might eventually come to the conclusion that they had no vital interest in the continued division of Germany. At that time it would be realistically possible for the first time since the end of World War II to negotiate the reunification of Germany.

On the evening of August 4, 1914, the British Foreign Secretary, Sir Edward Grey, stood at his window in the Foreign Office in London watching the lamplighters turning off the lights in St. James' Park. "The lamps are going out all over Europe," he said; "we shall not see them lit again in our lifetime." It is doubtful that even Lord Grey foresaw the dimensions of the catastrophe he prophesied that day. The lamps of Europe were not lit again in his lifetime, nor have they been restored yet. A whole world collapsed during those August days over fifty years ago—an imperfect world, to be sure, but a civilized and sane one, a world in which there was order and continuity and security. When it collapsed, the world fell into an era of violence and crisis and revolution which has not yet come to an end.

Now, for the first time since the end of World War II, we may be approaching a point from which it will be possible to see the shape of a new European order to replace the system that was destroyed so blindly fifty years ago; it is perhaps not too much to say that the lights which went out for Sir Edward Grey in 1914 are flickering on again. At present the process of reconciliation between the two Europes is proceeding without effective American participation because of America's preoccupation with the Vietnamese war; the result of course is that the United States is being left behind and Western Europe's developing friendliness with Eastern Europe is beginning to separate Europe from America. It is to be hoped that America will soon resume her proper role of leadership in the creative task of reconciling hostile worlds.

Putting Our Own House in Order

We spoke in Chapter 6 of the disruptive effect of the Vietnamese war on the internal life of the United States; I return now to that theme in order to suggest that there is one more bridge waiting to be rebuilt, at least as important as those to the communist world and to our allies, the bridge between the American people and their government which is absolutely critical for the strength and health of our society.

The human and material resources that make a great society are produced at home, not abroad. An ambitious foreign policy built on a deteriorating domestic base is possible only for a limited time; like the light cast by an extinct star, it is predestined to come to an end. Such, approximately, was the experience of France before the war of 1870 and of Austria before the war of 1914. America is nowhere near that extremity but she will come to it eventually if we do not stop to put our own house in order or, more exactly, if we do not resume the work of educating our children, combating poverty, renewing our cities, and purifying our physical environment begun so hopefully by Presidents Kennedy and Johnson.

There has been a great deal of talk about "neo-isolationism." It is true that a growing number of Americans— I am one of them—are expressing concern with what they regard as the overinvolvement of the United States in certain parts of the world with the consequent neglect of important problems here at home. It is not true that this concern indicates a willingness to abandon vital American interests abroad and to let the world go its way while we retreat into an illusory isolationism.

The charge of "neo-isolationism" is defective on at least two counts. First, it is based on the premise that the United States has a vital interest in just about every country in the world, when in fact many things happen in many places that are either none of our business or in any case are beyond the range of our power, resources, and wisdom. Second, those who worry about "neo-isolationism" seem to assume that we must *either* meet our foreign responsibilities while neglecting our own society *or* meet domestic needs while turning our backs on the outside world. In fact it is a problem of striking a balance. It is perfectly clear that we cannot spend all our time and all our mental energy on domestic problems, but the balance is now so heavily weighted on the other side and foreign problems have so unerring a way of calling themselves to our attention that worrying about overconcentration on domestic affairs is a little like worrying about overpopulation of the moon: it is one of those things that conceivably could happen but does not seem likely to happen very soon. It is obvious that we must meet both foreign and domestic responsibilities.

What is called for now is a redressing of the balance toward domestic affairs after twenty-five years of almost total preoccupation with wars and crises abroad. At the Yalta Conference in 1945 Winston Churchill asked President Roosevelt how long American troops could be expected to remain in Europe; "a maximum of two years," replied the President. That was over twenty years ago and there are still a quarter of a million American soldiers in Europe, and many more than that in Vietnam. It is not out of a desire to renounce America's foreign obligations that many of us are calling for renewed attention to domestic affairs, but out of an awareness that our commitments abroad are about as permanent as anything can be in human life and that the postponement of domestic action until foreign needs subside probably would mean its postponement forever.

America has not stood still in the years of her preoccupation with foreign wars and crises. Our population has grown since the Second World War from 137 million to almost 200 million—an increase approaching 60 million people, which is more than the population of either Britain or France. This population explosion has precipitated crises in education, employment, and transportation, and in the whole structure of life in our cities. These changes have been accompanied by revolutionary changes in our economy and by the upsurge of powerful new social movements such as the drive of American Negroes for a better life. Clearly, the time has come to divert some portion of our material and intellectual energies from the challenge of communism abroad to the challenge of improvement at home.

Much of the alarm over "neo-isolationism" is related to a problem of generations. Our former Ambassador to India, Professor John Kenneth Galbraith, suggests that there have been three generations of American foreign policy since World War II, each with a special point of view toward the world.[4] The first generation came out of the war with a vision of world order and high hopes for peaceful cooperation with the Soviet Union. When these hopes were shattered by Stalin's expansionist policies, the reputations of more than a few men of good will were tarnished and a new generation emerged, a generation dedicated to relentless conflict against communist imperialism. The second generation, arising after the Czech coup, the collapse of Chiang Kai-shek, and the Korean War, prided itself on being hard-boiled and devised policies on the assumption that anything that was bad for the Russians was good for us. Included in the ranks of the second generation is a new breed of university professor who sneers at proposals for the relaxation of tensions and occupies himself with more "realistic" matters such as calculating "acceptable" levels of "megadeaths" in the event of nuclear war.

A third generation has now emerged which recognizes that, largely because of the success of America's postwar policies, the character of the cold war has been altered. The communist world has ceased to be a unified bloc and now consists of diverse nations, ranging from China, which is hostile to the West, to the Soviet Union, whose unfriendliness is much less virulent, to Yugoslavia, which is friendly to the West. The third generation recognizes that the misfortunes of the Soviet Union are not necessarily blessings for the West, that in fact limited areas of common interest are developing between us and, above all, that the survival of civilization requires at least a tacit understanding among the nuclear powers.

The third generation has recognized the desirability and feasibility of both limited cooperation and a new and constructive kind of competition between the communist countries and the West. Instead of the hostile rivalries of the cold war in which each side tries to undermine the strength of the other, the new generation advocates a creative competition to see who can build the stronger and more prosperous society at home, who can more effectively help the world's less developed nations, who can build better schools and raise healthier children, who, in Khrushchev's colorful phrase, can provide more and better goulash. I think that America can win this kind of competition but, what is more to the point, no one can really lose it because everyone will end up with better schools, healthier children, and more goulash. It is this emphasis on domestic needs that has led the second generation to level the inaccurate charge of "neo-isolationism" against the third.

At exactly the moment when the third generation seemed about to take full control of America's affairs, events and misjudgments caused a regression. The Vietnamese war is a manifestation of second-generation attitudes toward communism. It is basically an ideological war, which is being fought because the Viet Cong is regarded as an instrument of North Vietnam and North Vietnam is regarded as an instrument of China. Underlying the American intervention is the old and discredited idea of a centrally directed global communist monolith.

Another hangover from the second generation is the space race, as an enterprise in itself and as a symbol and manifestation of the arrogance of power. The commitment to land an American on the moon by 1970—and ahead of the Russians —was unwisely made by President Kennedy in the wake of the Bay of Pigs fiasco in 1961. It was a dramatic gesture, designed to recover pride at a moment of national embarrassment. It was a very expensive gesture; the embarrassment of that moment has long since passed but we are left with the enormous expense of an ill-conceived project. There is nothing wrong with going to the moon if we do it under a program whose cost and priority are carefully weighed against other national needs; there is everything wrong with a crash program aimed at landing on the moon by 1970 at a cost of $20 to $30 billion for the sole and express purpose of getting there ahead of the Russians.

It is a fine thing to win a spirited contest and I am all in favor of beating the Russians to the moon, in principle. In practice, however, I am much less enthusiastic if it means the slowing down of the Arkansas River development program, which is bringing great benefits to the people of my state, or if it means the postponement of housing and school construction and urban renewal, which are essential to the welfare of the entire nation. If that is the price of beating the Russians to the moon, then it strikes me that the price of glory is too high.

I think it would be far more mature, and far more considerate of the needs of our own people, if we would orient our space program to our own needs instead of letting the Russians determine for us what we will do and how much we will spend. We are perfectly capable of conducting a reasonably paced space program while also giving necessary attention and resources to domestic needs. The fact of the matter is that the Soviet Union and the United States have different stakes in the space race. Russia suffers from a profound inferiority complex: she is painfully aware of being behind the United States in power and productivity and far behind the United States in the standard of living of her people.

Space is one of the few areas in which, by enormous concentration of resources, the Russians have been able to surpass us in certain respects and this success, hopefully, will ease their feeling of inferiority.

The United States, on the other hand, is the richest, most powerful, and generally most successful nation in the world, and everyone knows it. It is simply not necessary for us to go around forever proclaiming: "I am the greatest!" The more one does that sort of thing, in fact, the more people doubt it, and if the world is not persuaded of our pre-eminence now it probably never will be. Would it not be more dignified, more sensible, and more realistic if we responded to Soviet space achievements by offering our own sincere congratulations while continuing to go about our business in a way that meets our own needs and our own national priorities? I think it would be a heartening sign that America has truly come of age if we could take the attitude that the Russians are free to concentrate their resources on going to the moon if that is what they think they most need and we wish them well, but that, as for ourselves, the moon is only one of our aspirations, a distant one at that, and in the meantime we have children to educate and cities to rebuild.

A concluding point, which political "realists" may consider extraneous, is that, insofar as the satisfactions of life have anything to do with politics at all, they have to do with domestic not foreign politics, with projects of education, culture, employment, renewal, and beautification rather than with foreign wars and alliances, to say nothing of crash projects for going to the moon and the development, at immense cost, of airplanes that will fly two thousand miles an hour—which is much faster than anybody needs to go. As Thomas Huxley said of the inventions of the nineteenth century—the dynamos, the open-hearth furnaces, and the locomotives—"The great issue about which hangs a true sublimity and the terror of overhanging fate is, what are you going to do with all these things?"[5]

11

A New Concept
of Foreign Aid

I HAVE GREAT MISGIVINGS about the foreign-aid program of the United States. My misgivings are neither about foreign aid as such nor about our Agency for International Development, its personnel, and their administration of the program. My misgivings have to do with the basic character of the program and the need, as I see it, for a new concept of foreign aid. In its present bilateral form foreign aid, though composed principally of interest-bearing loans, is run as a kind of charity, demeaning to both recipient and donor. In addition, it is becoming a vehicle for deep American involvement in areas and issues which lie beyond both our vital interests and our competence. For these two essential reasons, on which I shall elaborate, I propose the transformation of aid, through internationalization, from private charity to community responsibility, from a dubious instrument of national policy to a stable program for international development.

The obligation of the rich to help the poor is recognized, so far as I know, by every major religion, by every formal system of ethics, and by individuals who claim no moral code beyond a simple sense of human decency. Unless national borders are regarded as the limits of human loyalty and compassion as well as of political authority, the obligation of the rich to the poor clearly encompasses an obligation on the part of rich nations to poor nations. Indeed, it is no more than common sense to recognize that, among nations as within them, the security of the rich is best assured by providing hope and opportunity for the poor.

Neither we nor any other nation, however, has yet accepted an obligation to the poor nations in any way analogous to that which we accept toward the individual poor and the poorer states and regions within our own country. In America and other democratic societies higher income people provide the bulk of the tax money to finance public services of which the poor are the principal beneficiaries; the redistribution of wealth has become a normal and accepted function of democratic government. The rich pay not as a private act of *noblesse oblige* but in fulfillment of a social responsibility; the poor receive benefits not as a lucky gratuity but as the right of citizens. The effect of the great social reforms in our country from the time of Theodore Roosevelt to the Great Society has been the virtual displacement of private philanthropy by public responsibility. The Salvation Army has just about been put out of business by social security and, with due respect for the humanity and kindness of the Salvation Army, who can deny that unemployment compensation is a major improvement?

With no less respect for the competence and dedication of our Agency for International Development, I suggest that we begin to replace bilateral foreign aid, which is analogous to private philanthropy, with an internationalized program based on the same principle of public responsibility which underlies progressive taxation and the social services we provide for our own people. I suggest that we extend the frontiers of our loyalty and compassion in order to transform our aid to the world's poorer nations from something resembling a private gratuity to a community responsibility.

It is with such thoughts in mind that I have decided, after almost twenty years of American foreign aid, that I for one can no longer actively support an aid program that is primarily bilateral. I would, however, support and do all within my power to secure an expanded program of economic aid—a greatly expanded program of economic aid—provided that it were conducted as a community enterprise, that is, through such international channels as the United Nations, the International Development Association of the World Bank, and the regional development banks.

The Consequences of Bilateralism

The crucial difference between bilateral and international aid is the basic incompatibility of bilateralism with individual and national dignity. Charity corrodes both the rich and the poor, breeding an exaggerated sense of authority on the part of the donor and a destructive loss of self-esteem on the part of the recipient. Whatever the material benefits of our aid—and they have been considerable in some countries —I am increasingly inclined to the view that they have been purchased at an excessive political and psychological cost to both lenders and borrowers. The critical question is whether the transfer of wealth between nations can be made compatible with human dignity as has been done within our own country.

Difficult as the effort might be, it would be salutary for Americans to try to imagine exactly how they might feel as recipients of economic aid—and all that goes with it—from foreign countries.

How, for example, would the management and employees of the New Haven Railroad feel if they were placed under the tutelage of a mission of, say, German transportation experts—not just transportation experts but *German* experts, who, for all they might do to show us how to run a railroad, would also be living purveyors of a message to the effect that "we Germans know how to do something that you Americans don't know how to do"?

Or consider how a Texas rancher might feel as the pupil of a group of agronomists from Colombia assigned to teach him how to grow coffee. Would he be humbly and touchingly grateful? Or would his gratitude be tinged with a touch of rancor toward his benefactors because his pride was injured by the feeling of being a recipient and a suppliant?

Imagine, to take another example, how the victims of a flood in California or an earthquake in Alaska might feel if, having lost their homes and possessions and perhaps members of their families, they were then asked to participate in little picture-taking ceremonies with beaming foreign ambassadors dispensing food and blankets labeled "gift of the French people" or "gift of the Russian people." If we can imagine ourselves in this position, I think we might agree that it is not an altogether heartwarming experience to be confronted with a gift of food whose label seems to convey the message that "the soup which you are about to consume is a charity from the great and generous and affluent people of some-place or other."

Several years ago, in the course of a visit to a country which was then receiving American aid, I attended an informal supper with some local officials and American diplomats. One of the Americans favored us with an explanation of the costs and logistics of an impending disaster-relief mission in which American supplies were involved. As he warmed to his subject, I noticed our hosts becoming increasingly preoccupied with their soup. The American official was clearly well-informed on all the details of our mission of mercy but the local officials did not seem to appreciate it. I do not think they were ungrateful for American relief supplies. I think what they failed to appreciate was the strong and clear suggestion that they were our wards and we their patrons, that they were benighted and we were blessed, that they were incompetent and needy while we were rich and happy and very tenderhearted besides. They did not seem to appreciate this at all, and I did not appreciate it either.

These are extreme examples of what might be called extreme bilateralism in relations between a rich country and a poor country. They are by no means representative of how most American aid is extended and received but they do, I think, illustrate the psychological problem that is inherent in every manifestation of *direct* American assistance to under-developed countries.

The disruptive effects of bilateral American aid have been referred to by some prominent individuals who know something about it. They emphasize the importance of the way in which the gift, or loan, is provided. There is wisdom if also malice in Prince Norodom Sihanouk's comparison of American and Chinese aid to Cambodia: "You will note the difference in the ways of giving," he has written. "On one side we are being humiliated, we are given a lecture, we are required to give something in return. On the other side, not only is our dignity as poor people being preserved, but our self-esteem is being flattered—and human beings have their weaknesses, and it would be futile to try to eradicate [them]."[1]

General Ne Win has all but ended foreign economic aid to Burma despite its great need of capital and technical assistance: "Unless we Burmans can learn to run our own country," he has said, "we will lose it. Of course, there are hardships. But we must put our house in order." Noting the effects of vast American military and economic assistance on such countries as South Vietnam and Thailand, Ne Win said: "This kind of aid does not help. It cripples. It paralyzes. The recipients never learn to do for themselves. They rely more and more on foreign experts and foreign money. In the end they lost control of their country."[2]

Extended in the wrong way, generosity can be perceived by its intended beneficiary as insulting and contemptuous. I rather suspect, in this connection, that the well-intentioned public American offer to include North Vietnam in a Southeast Asian development program may have been interpreted by the North Vietnamese as an attempt to buy them off from the war and make them an American dependency. Coming as it did from a nation with which North Vietnam was at war, a nation which was bombing its territory, the American offer, though sincere, was perhaps too generous to be credible, and that may explain why it was rejected as another "peace plot," as an effort on the part of the United States to win by bribery what it had been unable to win on the battlefield. If the same offer of aid were made privately to the North Vietnamese by the representatives of an international agency, it is possible that it would elicit a different kind of reaction.

The problem of bilateralism is psychological and political rather than managerial. It is a problem of pride, self-respect, and independence, which have everything to do with a country's will and capacity to foster its own development. There is an inescapable element of charity and paternalism in bilateral aid—even when it is aid in the form of loans at high interest rates—and charity, over a long period of time, has a debilitating effect on both its intended beneficiary and its provider; it fosters attitudes of cranky dependency or simple anger on the part of the recipient and of self-righteous frustration on the part of the donor, attitudes which, once formed, feed destructively upon each other. International aid, on the other hand, has the more dignified connotation of a community organized to meet its common and rightful responsibilities toward its less fortunate members. Bilateralism is appropriate to a world of nations with unlimited sovereignty, multilateralism to a world that is at least groping toward a broader community.

Military Assistance

When economic assistance fails, the result is a breakdown or delay in some aspect of development; when military assistance goes wrong, the consequences are much more spectacular.

A New Concept of Foreign Aid

Former Ambassador John Kenneth Galbraith believes that American military aid to Pakistan actually *caused* the war between India and Pakistan in 1965, simply because, quite apart from the merits of the Kashmir dispute, if the United States had not provided the arms, Pakistan would not have been able to seek a military solution.

These arms of course were meant to be used for defense against China and the Soviet Union, not against India. The trouble was that Pakistan did not and does not share the American view of Kashmir as a secondary issue and therefore regards India, not China or Russia, as her principal enemy. American military assistance had been provided on the condition and in the expectation that it would be used only against communist aggression, but as might have been expected these pledges were cast aside in the summer of 1965.

Should this have come as a great surprise? I do not think so. President Ayub Khan said with perfect candor in 1961 that the United States should be "mindful of the fact that if our territory was violated, we would spend our time dealing with the enemy rather than putting the American weapons in cotton wool."[3]

The mistake the United States made was the common one of assuming that its preoccupations were everybody's preoccupations. It seemed to us perfectly obvious that the only real threats in South Asia were the Soviet Union and Communist China and that it was absurd for India and Pakistan to be in conflict with each other over a secondary issue like Kashmir. It seemed to us that anyone with sense would share our view that there was only one truly crucial issue in world affairs, the threat of communism, be it in India or Vietnam, in Cuba or the Dominican Republic. The crowning irony of the affair was that this war, which could not have been fought without American military aid, was settled primarily through the mediation of the Soviet Union, one of the two countries against which American arms were meant to be directed.

Administration witnesses tell the Senate Foreign Relations

Committee every year that military assistance to the countries bordering on the Soviet Union and China is vital to America's "forward strategy," sustaining some three and a half million men under arms at far lower cost than would be required to sustain comparable American forces. This of course is an example of the ancient and sound practice of great military powers, developed by the Romans, of maintaining foreign mercenaries to do their peripheral fighting while keeping their own main forces as strategic reserves.

The variation introduced by the Americans is that our mercenaries usually remain neutral while *we* fight brushfire wars with our own soldiers. Among the countries bordering on Russia and China which receive American military assistance are Greece, Turkey, Iran, Thailand, Laos, Taiwan, and Korea. Of these only the Koreans have men fighting in Vietnam and they are receiving a handsome subsidy for their effort. The Greeks and the Turks are too busy menacing Russia with their military power, to say nothing of each other, while we do not dare to use Chiang Kai-shek's large and well-financed force lest it bring the Chinese Communist Army swarming into Vietnam. The result is that we are sustaining over three million non-fighting men along the borders of Russia and China who do guard duty while American soldiers fight in Vietnam. One wonders whether some of the countries which maintain these forces would not be more stable and secure today if much of the money spent on armaments over the years had been used instead for development and social reform.

America's modest military aid in Latin America is decidedly more effective than its mercenary forces in Europe and Asia, not, however, in holding back communists but in holding *up* military oligarchies.

Mr. John Duncan Powell, a political scientist who had studied the impact of American military assistance in Latin America, has pointed out that the smallness of the sums involved is deceptive, and that, measured in terms of their effect on the ability of military forces to apply violence against civilian groups, American arms are very significant indeed.[4] In countries where per-capita income is low, where political institutions are fragile, where great numbers of people are uneducated, unorganized, and often demoralized, even a small amount of military equipment and training, say $10 worth, can give a soldier an overwhelming advantage over a civilian in a conflict situation. Taking AID figures on cumulative United States military assistance per soldier as of 1962 and matching these against per-capita income, Mr. Powell points out that as of 1962 each member of Nicaragua's armed forces represented $930 worth of United States arms and training available for use in possible street fighting against students and workers with a total annual per-capita income of only $205, while each member of Guatemala's armed forces represented $538 worth of United States arms and training as against students and workers with a per-capita income of only $185.

Viewed in the physical and economic context of a poor country in Central America, United States military assistance no longer appears small and innocent; it contributes in an important way to the perpetuation of military oligarchies. It is not a large program but, as Mercutio said of his fatal wound, "No, 'tis not so deep as a well, nor so wide as a church door, but 'tis enough, 'twill serve."[5]

Mr. Powell concludes that, small as it is, the American military assistance program is "a contributory cause of militarism in Latin America" and that "the shift in emphasis from hemispheric security to internal security capabilities will make the Latin American military better trained and equipped than ever to intervene in the political systems of their nations." "This," says Powell, "may be the hidden price tag on the anti-communist security which the United States seeks in the western hemisphere through the military assistance program." Events in Brazil and Argentina have certainly borne him out.

On an evening in the summer of 1966 an American jour-
nalist's interview with rebels in the Guatemalan jungle was
shown on television. A young rebel leader said he was a
Marxist because Marxism, as he understood it, called for
giving the land to the peasants; he thought of the United
States as an enemy, because, he thought, American arms and
power were always placed at the disposal of the oppressors
of his people. This view of America is not unknown in other
parts of the world; it is one of the rewards of the "forward
strategy" of American military assistance.

Foreign Aid and American Overcommitment

At the same time as it has had disruptive effects on its
recipients, bilateral American military and economic assistance has also had some unforeseen effects on the United
States: it has become a vehicle toward commitments which
exceed both American interests and American material and
intellectual resources.

Foreign aid is not in a literal sense the cause of or the reason for American military involvement in Vietnam. It was,
however, an important factor contributing to the *state of
mind* of policy-makers who committed the United States to
a major land war in Asia after having stated forcefully, repeatedly and, to many of us, quite convincingly that that was
exactly what they intended not to do. The relationship
between American aid and the Vietnamese war is no less significant for being psychological rather than juridical; indeed
it is probably more significant.

The idea of foreign aid as a source of American military
involvement is certainly not my own; on the contrary, such
a connection never even occurred to me or, I daresay, to other
members of the Foreign Relations Committee until Adminis-

tration officials began referring to the aid program as cause and evidence of what they judged to be an American military obligation in Vietnam. Nor, I think, can the connection between aid and military involvement be dismissed as mere excess of rhetoric by partisans of the Vietnamese war.

Although he has now disavowed aid as a source of military obligations, the Secretary of State on no fewer than three occasions referred to Congressional approval of aid programs as a basis of authority for the American military involvement in Vietnam. He did so at a Senate hearing in August 1964. He did so again in a hearing before the Senate Foreign Relations Committee on January 28, 1966, when, after citing the SEATO Treaty as authorizing American military action in Vietnam, he went on to say:

> In addition to that, we have bilateral assistance agreements to [*sic*] South Vietnam. We have had several actions of the Congress. We have had the annual aid appropriations in which the purposes of the aid have been fully set out before the Congress. . . .[6]

The Secretary made the same point most explicitly in a speech in Las Vegas on February 16, 1966. He said:

> We are committed to assist South Vietnam resist aggression by the SEATO Treaty, which was approved by the Senate with only one dissenting vote; by the pledges of three successive Presidents; *by the aid approved by bipartisan majorities in Congress over a period of twelve years;* by joint declarations with our allies in Southeast Asia and the Western Pacific; and by the Resolution which Congress adopted in August 1964, with only two dissenting votes [emphasis added].[7]

I very much doubt that any member of the Senate ever supposed that by voting for foreign aid, the Senate was authorizing or committing the United States to use its armed forces to sustain the ruling government of any recipient country against foreign attack, much less against internal insurrection. I rather doubt, too, that those who later cited such a connection thought of it *before* the United States took over the Vietnamese war.

What seems to have happened is that large-scale military and economic aid, along with our gradual assumption of the French role in Indochina and the adoption of Ngo Dinh Diem as an American protégé, created a *state of mind* among American policy-makers under which it was felt that the United States had a proprietary investment in Vietnam—an investment of prestige and money which those responsible were naturally unwilling to see go down the drain. A gambler is always tempted, once he has begun to lose, to keep raising the stakes in the hope of recouping his losses; since early 1965 American policy-makers have been steadily raising the stakes of a gamble which began in part with aid and which until the dispatch of a large American army to Vietnam in the first months of 1965 could have been liquidated with a fairly small loss. Once the stakes became high, however, explanations were called for and, apparently without awareness of the implications of what they were saying, our policy-makers began referring to foreign aid as one of the factors that committed the United States to war in Vietnam.

Explicit references to foreign aid as a legal basis for an American military obligation seem, therefore, to have been *ex post facto;* policy-makers who came to feel that the United States was obligated to take over the Vietnamese war, in part because aid programs authorized with no such intention had contributed to the sense of an American investment, later referred back to foreign-aid legislation as justifying and authorizing the American military commitment. Subsequent disavowals of aid as a source of military obligation cannot undo its prior contribution to that state of mind which made military involvement seem essential.

It is a little late to be locking the barn door after your prize herd has galloped off into the distance. Nonetheless, in order to disabuse the Administration of the view that the

Congress, by adopting aid legislation, is authorizing the President to go to war in defense of the beneficiaries, the Senate Foreign Relations Committee added language to the policy statement of the foreign-aid bill in 1966 stating that the authorization of military and economic aid "shall not be construed as creating a new commitment or as affecting any existing commitment to use armed forces of the United States for the defense of any foreign country."

Alerted by the experience of Vietnam, the Senate Foreign Relations Committee undertook a brief inquiry in the fall of 1966 into the implications of American military and economic assistance as well as other aspects of American policy toward Thailand. The inquiry was undertaken as a normal exercise of the Senate's advisory responsibility in foreign relations. Before it began, however, Mr. Joseph Alsop, in an obviously overexcited condition caused no doubt by the war, denounced it as a "plan for giving aid and comfort to the enemy."[8]

Until the purposes of foreign aid are clarified, I am disinclined to support long-term authorizations or other legislative provisions that would give the Executive greater latitude than it already has in the conduct of foreign aid. I would strongly favor the long-term authorization of an *internationalized* foreign-aid program; should the Congress ever be asked to approve such a program, I for one would not only support the principle of long-term authorization but would do all that I could to secure its adoption. In the meantime, I must state quite frankly that my attitude is influenced by a lack of confidence in the purposes for which bilateral aid is likely to be used. I have been particularly disturbed by the implications of the "Asian Doctrine," discussed in Chapter 2, under which the United States would accept unilateral responsibility for maintaining order and extending the Great Society to non-communist Asia. Until confidence in the uses to which our aid is likely to be put is restored—and I would hope although I do not really expect that it will be in the near future—I think it prudent for the Congress to retain its full authority to review the authorization as well as the appropriation of funds for foreign aid.

Many programs are justified by the Agency for International Development on the ground that they will maintain an "American presence." These programs are too small to have much effect on economic development but big enough to involve the United States in the affairs of the countries concerned. The underlying assumption of these programs is that the presence of some American aid officials is a blessing which no developing country, except for the benighted communist ones, should be denied.

I think this view of aid is a manifestation of the arrogance of power. Its basis, if not messianism, is certainly egotism. It assumes that the size, wealth, and power of the United States are evidence of wisdom and virtue as well; it assumes that just as the right-thinking, hard-working laborer in a Horatio Alger novel might have counted it a privilege to take counsel with the local tycoon, every right-thinking, hard-working underdeveloped country must consider it a privilege to have some resident Americans around to tell its leaders how to run their affairs.

It is a flattering idea but unfortunately it is an inaccurate idea. Experience has shown—and not just in our case but in that of other big countries as well—that affection is more likely to be won by an American "absence" than by a conspicuous American presence. In fact, the countries that are fondest of us often seem to be those who have had the Russians around for a long time, and I think the Russians have profited in the same way from some of our involvements. This is not because we lack good intentions but simply because people like to make their own decisions and their own mistakes in their own way, and our "presence" tells them that we do not think them qualified to do so. We can give them all the money and all the technique in the world, but what is their use if the very act of giving robs the recipients of dignity?

Bilateral foreign aid, like some of the other "instruments" of American foreign policy, has become a vehicle toward the involvement of the United States in matters lying far beyond its proper concern. Though by no means the sole cause, or even the major cause, of the developing role of the United States as ideological policeman for the world, bilateral aid has been a factor in that development. It has become a factor in a general tendency to go it alone, a tendency reflected in our neglect of the United Nations, in our neglect of the views and sensibilities of allies and other countries, and in the diversion of money and effort from those promising and essential domestic reforms which until recently bade fair to make the United States an example of progress and social justice for the world.

Foreign aid does not have to contribute to such results. It can indeed be a powerful means toward the renewal of strained partnerships, toward the reconciliation of national animosities, and above all toward the economic growth of the world's poor countries under conditions that foster dignity as well as development. To accomplish these ends we will have greatly to increase our aid program and to transform it from an instrument of national policy to a community program for international development.

The New Concept

I propose, therefore, the internationalization and expansion of foreign aid. I propose its conversion from an instrument of national foreign policy to an international program for the limited transfer of wealth from rich countries to poor countries in accordance with the same principle of community responsibility that in our own country underlies progressive taxation, social-welfare programs, and the effective transfer of wealth from the rich states to the poor states through programs of federal assistance. The time has come to start thinking of foreign aid as part of a limited international fiscal system through which the wealthy members of a world community would act sensibly and in their own interests to meet an obligation toward the poor members of the community.

So great a transformation in the character and conduct of aid cannot be made all at once. A significant advance would be achieved by a favorable American response to the request of Mr. George Woods, President of the World Bank, for greatly increased contributions to the International Development Association, the affiliate of the Bank which provides long-term loans at very low interest rates. At present, however, only slight progress is being made toward the internationalization of aid. Prior to 1966 the Congress repeatedly approved a modest amendment to the Foreign Assistance Act authorizing the President to channel 15 percent of the development-loan fund through the World Bank and its affiliated agencies, but in each instance the subsequent appropriations measure prohibited the use of foreign-aid funds for this purpose. In 1966 Congress adopted an amendment *requiring* the diversion of 10 percent of the development-loan fund to the international lending agencies; the appropriations bill altered this to give the President *permissive* authority to channel these funds through international agencies.

What steps can be taken toward the development of an international system for the limited redistribution of income between rich countries and poor countries? First, the aid-providing countries of the world should terminate bilateral programs and channel their development lending through the World Bank and its affiliated agencies, especially the International Development Association. Secondly, the Bank and its affiliates should be authorized to dispense the increased development funds that would be at their disposal as they now dispense limited amounts, that is, according to social needs and strict economic principles. Third, the Bank and its affiliates should execute aid programs through an expanded corps of highly trained international civil servants, encouraging objectivity by the assignment of field personnel, so far as possible, to countries and regions other than their own. Fourth, the Bank and its affiliates should be authorized to recommend amounts to be contributed each year by member countries to an international development pool; contributions should be progressive, with the main burden falling on the rich countries but, in keeping with the principle of a community responsibility, with even the poorest countries making token contributions.[9]

An internationalized system would provide a framework within which the great powers could convert their aid programs from cold war instruments of competition to cooperative ventures that would benefit their own relations as well as the economic needs of the developing countries. It would be a great thing indeed if the United States and the Soviet Union, the world's two most economically powerful nations, would join in endorsing the principle of an international fiscal system. In this connection, it would be highly desirable for the Soviet Union to join the World Bank, of which Yugoslavia at present is the only communist member. Perhaps the United States government could take the initiative of suggesting to the Russians that they join and of offering, if necessary, to sponsor amendments to the Bank's charter that might make membership more attractive to the Soviet Union.

There are many possibilities for Soviet-American cooperation through development aid. The advantages of joint development projects were cited in Chapter 10 (See pp. 209–10). Beyond these, it would be a boon to their own relations and a splendid example for other countries if the United States and the Soviet Union agreed to divert equivalent sums of money from armaments to the international development pool. Under an internationalized development program, one can envision Russian and American engineers and economists working together in many parts of the world as members of an international corps of civil servants. The internationalization of aid, by creating a framework for co-operation between the great powers, could thus provide a powerful impetus for world peace as well as for economic development.

The transformation of economic aid from a national charity, and an instrument of cold war competition, to an international responsibility would put an end to the peculiar and corrosive tyranny which donor and recipient seem to exercise over each other in bilateral relationships. Aid would be converted to a community responsibility characterized by continuity, predictability, and dignity for all parties. The economic development of the poor nations of the world would be treated for the first time as an end in itself, insulated from international political rivalries and internal political pressures. Instead of being a weapon in the ancient and discredited game of power politics, aid could become, like educational exchange, a means for changing the nature of the game, for civilizing it and for adapting it to the requirements of survival in the nuclear age.

It may be contended that such a program is unrealistic, that there are insuperable obstacles to its realization. There are indeed obstacles and they are formidable, but they are not insuperable; they are not natural obstacles, like man's inability to fly by flapping his arms, or technological, like his momentary inability to fly a rocket ship to Mars, but psychological. If the program I recommend is unrealistic, it is unrealistic because, and only because, people *think* it is unrealistic.

As with most important adjustments in human affairs, the first and most important requirement toward the formation of an international fiscal system is a change in our *thinking*. We must learn to think of the world as a community in which the privileged accept certain responsibilities toward the underprivileged just as they do in our own country. We must develop a new idea of generosity, one which purports to help people without humiliating them, one which accepts the general advancement of the community rather than cloying expressions of gratitude as its just and proper reward.

Much will be required to accomplish such a transformation in the meaning and purpose of foreign aid. For my own part, whenever the Administration is prepared to ask for legislation authorizing the United States to participate in a program of aid to developing countries involving significantly increased amounts of money, softer lending terms, and international management, I pledge to use all my resources as a Senator and as Chairman of the Foreign Relations Committee to secure its enactment.

THE
TWO AMERICAS

THERE ARE TWO AMERICAS. One is the America of Lincoln and Adlai Stevenson; the other is the America of Teddy Roosevelt and the modern superpatriots. One is generous and humane, the other narrowly egotistical; one is self-critical, the other self-righteous; one is sensible, the other romantic; one is good-humored, the other solemn; one is inquiring, the other pontificating; one is moderate, the other filled with passionate intensity; one is judicious and the other arrogant in the use of great power.

We have tended in the years of our great power to puzzle the world by presenting to it now the one face of America, now the other, and sometimes both at once. Many people all over the world have come to regard America as being capable of magnanimity and farsightedness but no less capable of pettiness and spite. The result is an inability to anticipate American actions which in turn makes for apprehension and a lack of confidence in American aims.

The inconstancy of American foreign policy is not an accident but an expression of two distinct sides of the American character. Both are characterized by a kind of moralism, but one is the morality of decent instincts tempered by the knowledge of human imperfection and the other is the morality of absolute self-assurance fired by the crusading spirit. The one is exemplified by Lincoln, who found it strange, in the words of his second Inaugural Address, "that any man should dare to ask for a just God's assistance in wringing their bread from the sweat of other men's faces," but then added: "let us judge not, that we be not judged." The other is exemplified by Theodore Roosevelt, who in his December 6, 1904, Annual Message to Congress, without question or doubt as to his own and his country's capacity to judge right and wrong, proclaimed the duty of the United States to exercise an "internal police power" in the hemisphere on the ground that "Chronic wrongdoing, or an impotence which results in a general loosening of the ties of civilized society, may in America . . . ultimately require intervention by some civilized nation. . . ." Roosevelt of course never questioned that the "wrongdoing" would be done by our Latin neighbors and we of course were the "civilized nation" with the duty to set things right.

After twenty-five years of world power the United States must decide which of the two sides of its national character is to predominate—the humanism of Lincoln or the arrogance of those who would make America the world's policeman. One or the other will help shape the spirit of the age —unless of course we refuse to choose, in which case America may come to play a less important role in the world, leaving the great decisions to others.

The current tendency is toward a more strident and aggressive American foreign policy, which is to say, toward a policy closer to the spirit of Theodore Roosevelt than of Lincoln. We are still trying to build bridges to the communist countries and we are still, in a small way, helping the poorer nations to make a better life for their people; but we are also involved in a growing war against Asian communism, a war which began and might have ended as a civil war if American intervention had not turned it into a contest of ideologies, a war whose fallout is disrupting our internal life and complicating our relations with most of the world.

The Two Americas

Our national vocabulary has changed with our policies. A few years ago we were talking of détente and building bridges, of five-year plans in India and Pakistan, or agricultural cooperatives in the Dominican Republic, and land and tax reform all over Latin America. Today these subjects are still discussed in a half-hearted and desultory way but the focus of power and interest has shifted to the politics of war. Diplomacy has become largely image-making, and instead of emphasizing plans for social change, the policy-planners and political scientists are conjuring up "scenarios" of escalation and nuclear confrontation and "models" of insurgency and counter-insurgency.

The change in words and values is no less important than the change in policy, because words *are* deeds and style *is* substance insofar as they influence men's minds and behavior. What seems to be happening, as Archibald MacLeish has put it, is that "the feel of America in the world's mind" has begun to change and faith in "the idea of America" has been shaken for the world and, what is more important, for our own people. MacLeish is suggesting—and I think he is right—that much of the idealism and inspiration is disappearing from American policy, but he also points out that they are not yet gone and by no means are they irretrievable:

> . . . if you look closely and listen well, there is a human warmth, a human meaning which nothing has killed in almost twenty years and which nothing is likely to kill. . . . What has always held this country together is an idea— a dream if you will—a large and abstract thought of the sort the realistic and the sophisticated may reject but mankind can hold to.[1]

The foremost need of American foreign policy is a renewal of dedication to an "idea that mankind can hold to"—not a missionary idea full of pretensions about being the world's policemen but a Lincolnian idea expressing that powerful strand of decency and humanity which is the true source of America's greatness.

Humanism and Puritanism

I am not prepared to argue that mankind is suffering from an excess of virtue but I think the world has endured about all it can of the crusades of high-minded men bent on the regeneration of the human race. Since the beginning of history men have been set upon by zealots and crusaders, who, far from wishing them harm, have wanted sincerely and fervently to raise them from benightedness to blessedness. The difficulty about all this doing of noble deeds has not been in its motives but in the perverseness of human nature, in the regrettable fact that most men are loutish and ungrateful when it comes to improving their souls and more often than not have to be forced into their own salvation. The result has been a great deal of bloodshed and violence committed not in malice but for the purest of motives. The victims may not always have appreciated the fact that their tormentors had noble motives but the fact remains that it was not wickedness that did them in but, in Thackeray's phrase, "the mischief which the very virtuous do."

Who are the self-appointed emissaries of God who have wrought so much violence in the world? They are men with doctrines, men of faith and idealism, men who confuse power with virtue, men who believe in some cause without doubt and practice their beliefs without scruple, men who cease to be human beings with normal preferences for work and fun and family and become instead living, breathing embodiments of some faith or ideology. From the religious wars to the two world wars they have been responsible for much or most of the violence in the world. From Robespierre to Stalin and Mao Tse-tung they have been the extreme practitioners of the arrogance of power—extreme, indeed, in a way that has never been known and, hopefully, never will be known in America.

There are elements of this kind of fanaticism in Western

societies but the essential strength of democracy and capitalism as they are practiced in the West is that they are relatively free of doctrine and dogma and largely free of illusions about man and his nature. Of all the intellectual achievements of Western civilization, the one, I think, that is most truly civilized is that by and large we have learned to deal with man as he is or, at most, as he seems capable of becoming, but not as we suppose in the abstract he ought to be. Our economy is geared to human acquisitiveness and our politics to human ambition. Accepting these qualities as part of human character, we have been able in substantial measure both to satisfy them and to civilize them. We have been able to civilize them because we have understood that a man's own satisfaction is more nearly a condition of than an obstacle to his decent behavior toward others. This realism about man may prove in the long run to be our greatest asset over communism, which can deny and denounce but, with all the "Red Guards" of China, cannot remake human nature.

Acceptance of his own nature would seem to be the most natural thing in the world for a man, but experience shows that it is not. Only at an advanced state of civilization do men become tolerant of human shortcomings. Only at an advanced level of civilization, it seems, do men acquire the wisdom and humility to acknowledge that they are not really cut out to play God. At all previous levels of culture men seem to be more interested in the enforced improvement of others than in voluntary fulfillment for themselves, more interested in forcing their fellow creatures to be virtuous than in helping them to be happy. Only under the conditions of material affluence and political democracy that prevail in much of the modern West have whole societies been able and willing to renounce the harsh asceticism of their own past, which still prevails in much of the East, and to embrace the philosophy that life after all is short and it is no sin to try to enjoy it.

Our hold on this philosophy is tenuous. There is a strand

in our history and in our national character which is all too congenial to the spirit of crusading ideology. The Puritans who came to New England in the seventeenth century did not establish their faith as a major religion in America but the Puritan way of thought—harsh, ascetic, intolerant, promising salvation for the few but damnation for the many—became a major intellectual force in American life. It introduced a discordant element into a society bred in the English heritage of tolerance, moderation, and experimentalism.

Throughout our history two strands have coexisted uneasily —a dominant strand of democratic humanism and a lesser but durable strand of intolerant puritanism. There has been a tendency through the years for reason and moderation to prevail as long as things are going tolerably well or as long as our problems seem clear and finite and manageable. But when things have gone badly for any length of time, or when the reasons for adversity have seemed obscure, or simply when some event or leader of opinion has aroused the people to a state of high emotion, our puritan spirit has tended to break through, leading us to look at the world through the distorting prism of a harsh and angry moralism.

Communism has aroused our latent puritanism as has no other movement in our history, causing us to see principles where there are only interests and conspiracy where there is only misfortune. And when this view of things prevails, conflicts become crusades and morality becomes delusion and hypocrisy. Thus, for example, when young hoodlums—the so-called "Red Guards"—terrorize and humiliate Chinese citizens who are suspected of a lack of fervor for the teachings of Mao Tse-tung, we may feel reconfirmed in our judgment that communism is a barbarous philosophy utterly devoid of redeeming features of humanity, but before going into transports of moral outrage over the offenses of the "Red Guards," we might recall that no fewer than two hundred thousand, and possibly half a million, people were murdered in the anti-communist terror that swept Indonesia in 1966 and scarcely a voice of protest was heard in America—from our leaders, from the press, or from the general public. One can only conclude that it is not man's inhumanity to man but communist manifestations of it that arouse the American conscience.

One of the most outrageous effects of the puritan spirit in America is the existence of that tyranny over what it is respectable to say and think of which we spoke in Part I. Those who try to look at the country with some objectivity are often the objects of scorn and abuse by professional patriots who believe that there is something illegitimate about national self-criticism, or who equate loyalty to our fighting men in Vietnam with loyalty to the policy that put them there.

Puritanism, fortunately, has not been the dominant strand in American thought. It had nothing to do with the intelligent and subtle diplomacy of the period of the American Revolution. It had nothing to do with the wise policy of remaining aloof from the conflicts of Europe, as long as we were permitted to do so, while we settled and developed the North American continent. It had nothing to do with the restraint shown by the United States at moments of supreme crisis in the cold war—at the time of the Korean War, for example, in the first Indochina war in which President Eisenhower wisely refused to intervene in 1954, and in the Cuban missile crisis of 1962. And it has had absolutely nothing to do with the gradual relaxation of tensions associated with the test ban treaty and the subsequent improvement of relations with the Soviet Union. I am reminded of "Mr. Dooley's" words about the observance of Thanksgiving: " 'Twas founded by th' Puritans to give thanks f'r bein' presarved fr'm th' Indyans, an' . . . we keep it to give thanks we are presarved fr'm th' Puritans."[2]

The crusading puritan spirit has had a great deal to do with some of the regrettable and tragic events of American history. It led us into needless and costly adventures and victories that crumbled in our hands.

The Civil War is an example. Had the Abolitionists of the North and the hotheads of the South been less influential, the war might have been avoided and slavery would certainly have been abolished anyway, peacefully and probably within a generation after emancipation actually occurred. Had the peace been made by Lincoln rather than the Radical Republicans, it could have been a peace of reconciliation rather than the wrathful Reconstruction which deepened the division of the country, cruelly set back the cause of the Negro, and left a legacy of bitterness for which we are still paying a heavy price.

The puritan spirit was one of the important factors in the brief, unhappy adventure in imperialism that began with the war of 1898. Starting with stirring slogans about "manifest destiny" and a natural sense of moral outrage about atrocities in Cuba—which was fed by a spirited competition for circulation between the Hearst and Pulitzer newspapers—America forced on Spain a war that it was willing to pay almost any price short of complete humiliation to avoid. The war was undertaken to liberate the Cuban people and ended with Cuba being put under an American protectorate, which in turn inaugurated a half century of American intervention in Cuba's internal affairs. American interference was motivated, no doubt, by a sincere desire to bring freedom to the Cuban people but it ended, nonetheless, with their getting Batista and Castro instead.

The crusading spirit of America in its modern form, and the contrast between the crusading spirit and the spirit of tolerance and accommodation, are illustrated in two speeches made by Woodrow Wilson, one preceding, the other following, America's entry into World War I. In early 1917, with the United States still neutral, he declined to make a clear moral distinction between the belligerents, and called on them to compromise their differences and negotiate a "peace without victory." In the spring of 1918, when the United States had been at war for a year, Wilson perceived only one possible response to the challenge of Germany in the war: "Force, Force to the utmost, Force without stint or limit, the righteous and triumphant Force which shall make right the law of the world, and cast every selfish dominion down in the dust."[3]

Even Franklin Roosevelt, who was the most pragmatic of politicians, was not immune from the crusading spirit. So overcome was he, as were all Americans, by the treachery of the Japanese attack on Pearl Harbor that one of America's historic principles, the freedom of the seas, for which we had gone to war in 1812 and 1917, was now immediately forgotten, along with the explicit commitment under the London Naval Treaty of 1930 not to sink merchant vessels without first placing passengers, crews, and ships' papers in a place of safety. Within seven hours of the Japanese attack the order went out to all American ships and planes in the Pacific: "Execute unrestricted air and submarine warfare against Japan." Between 1941 and 1945 American submarines sank 1,750 Japanese merchant ships and took the lives of 105,000 Japanese civilians. So much for the "freedom of the seas."

In January 1943, while meeting with Churchill at Casablanca, President Roosevelt announced that the Allies would fight on until the "unconditional surrender" of their enemies. Roosevelt later said that the phrase just "popped into his mind" but I think it was dredged up from the depths of a puritan soul. Its premise was that our side was all virtue and our enemies were all evil who in justice could expect nothing after their fall but the righteous retribution of Virtue triumphant.

"Unconditional surrender" was an unwise doctrine. Aside from its negativism as a war aim and the fact that it may have prolonged the war, we did not really mean to carry out its implications. As soon as our enemies delivered themselves into our hands we began to treat them with kindness and moderation, and within a very few years we were treating them as valued friends and allies.

The West has won two "total victories" in this century and it has barely survived them. America, especially, fought the two world wars in the spirit of a righteous crusade. We acted as if we had come to the end of history, as if we had only to destroy our enemies and then the world would enter a golden age of peace and human happiness. Some of the problems that spawned the great wars were in fact solved by our victories; others were simply forgotten. But to our shock and dismay we found after 1945 that history had not come to an end, that our triumph had produced at least as many problems as it had solved, and that it was by no means clear that the new problems were preferable to the old ones.

I do not raise these events of the American past for purposes of national flagellation but to illustrate that the problem of excessive ideological zeal is our problem as well as the communists'. I think also that when we respond to communist dogmatism with a dogmatism of our own we are not merely responding by the necessity, as we are told, of "fighting fire with fire." I think we are responding in a way that is more natural and congenial to us than we care to admit.

The great challenge in our foreign relations is to make certain that the major strand in our heritage, the strand of humanism, tolerance, and accommodation, remains the dominant one. I do not accept the excuse, so often offered, that communist zealotry and intransigence justify our own. I do not accept the view that because they have engaged in subversion, intervention, and ideological warfare, so must we and to the same degree. There is far more promise in efforts to encourage communist imitation of our own more sensible attitudes than in ourselves imitating the least attractive forms of communist behavior. It is of course reasonable to ask why *we* must take the lead in conciliation; the answer is that we, being the most powerful of nations, can afford as no one else can to be magnanimous. Or, to put it another way, disposing as we do of the greater physical power, we are properly called upon to display the greater moral power as well.

The kind of foreign policy I have been talking about is, in the true sense of the term, a *conservative* policy. It is intended quite literally to conserve the world—a world whose civilizations can be destroyed at any time if either of the great powers should choose or feel driven to do so. It is an approach that accepts the world as it is, with all its existing nations and ideologies, with all its existing qualities and shortcomings. It is an approach that purports to change things in ways that are compatible with the continuity of history and within the limits imposed by a fragile human nature. I think that if the great conservatives of the past, such as Burke and Metternich and Castlereagh, were alive today, they would not be true believers or relentless crusaders against communism. They would wish to come to terms with the world as it is, not because our world would be pleasing to them—almost certainly it would not be—but because they believed in the preservation of indissoluble links between the past and the future, because they profoundly mistrusted abstract ideas, and because they did not think themselves or any other men qualified to play God.

The last, I think, is the central point. I believe that a man's principal business, in foreign policy as in domestic policy and in his daily life, is to keep his own house in order, to make life a little more civilized, a little more satisfying, and a little more serene in the brief time that is allotted him. I think that man is qualified to contemplate metaphysics but not to practice it. The practice of metaphysics is God's work.

An Idea Mankind Can Hold To

Favored as it is, by history, by wealth, and by the vitality and basic decency of its diverse population, it is conceivable, though hardly likely, that America will do something that no other great nation has ever tried to do—to effect a fundamental change in the nature of international relations. It has been my purpose in this book to suggest some ways in which we might proceed with this great work. All that I have proposed in these pages—that we make ourselves the friend of social revolution, that we make our own society an example of human happiness, that we go beyond simple reciprocity in the effort to reconcile hostile worlds—has been based on two major premises: first, that, at this moment in history at which the human race has become capable of destroying itself, it is not merely desirable but essential that the competitive instinct of nations be brought under control; and second, that America, as the most powerful nation, is the only nation equipped to lead the world in an effort to change the nature of its politics.

If we accept this leadership, we will have contributed to the world "an idea mankind can hold to." Perhaps that idea can be defined as the proposition that the nation performs its essential function not in its capacity as a *power*, but in its capacity as a *society*, or, to put it simply, that the primary business of the nation is not itself but its people.

Obviously, to bring about fundamental changes in the world we would have to take certain chances: we would have to take the chance that other countries could not so misinterpret a generous initiative on our part as to bring about a calamity; we would have to take a chance that later if not sooner, nations which have been hostile to us would respond to reason and decency with reason and decency. The risks involved are great but they are far less than the risks of traditional methods of international relations in the nuclear age.

If we are interested in bringing about fundamental changes in the world, we must start by resolving some critical questions of our foreign relations: Are we to be the friend or the enemy of the social revolutions of Asia, Africa, and Latin America? Are we to regard the communist countries as more or less normal states with whom we can have more or less normal relations, or are we to regard them indiscriminately as purveyors of an evil ideology with whom we can never reconcile? And finally, are we to regard ourselves as a friend, counselor, and example for those around the world who seek freedom and who also want our help, or are we to play the role of God's avenging angel, the appointed missionary of freedom in a benighted world?

The answers to these questions depend on which of the two Americas is speaking. There are no inevitable or predetermined answers because our past has prepared us to be either tolerant or puritanical, generous or selfish, sensible or romantic, humanly concerned or morally obsessed, in our relations with the outside world.

For my own part, I prefer the America of Lincoln and Adlai Stevenson. I prefer to have my country the friend rather than the enemy of demands for social justice; I prefer to have the communists treated as human beings, with all the human capacity for good and bad, for wisdom and folly, rather than as embodiments of an evil abstraction; and I prefer to see my country in the role of sympathetic friend to humanity rather than its stern and prideful schoolmaster.

There are many respects in which America, if she can bring herself to act with the magnanimity and the empathy which are appropriate to her size and power, can be an intelligent example to the world. We have the opportunity to set an example of generous understanding in our relations with China, of practical cooperation for peace in our relations with Russia, of reliable and respectful partnership in our relations with Western Europe, of material helpfulness without moral presumption in our relations with developing nations, of abstention from the temptations of hegemony in our relations with Latin America, and of the all-around advantages of minding one's own business in our relations with everybody. Most of all, we have the opportunity to serve as an example of democracy to the world by the way in which we run our own society. America, in the words of John Quincy Adams, should be "the well-wisher to the freedom and independence of all" but "the champion and vindicator only of her own."[4]

If we can bring ourselves so to act, we will have overcome the dangers of the arrogance of power. It would involve, no doubt, the loss of certain glories, but that seems a price worth paying for the probable rewards, which are the happiness of America and the peace of the world.

NOTES

Introduction

1. Aldous Huxley, "The Politics of Ecology" (Santa Barbara: Center for the Study of Democratic Institutions, 1963), p. 6.

2. Quoted in Samuel Flagg Bemis, *A Diplomatic History of the United States* (New York: Henry Holt, 1955), p. 472.

3. Quoted in Barbara Tuchman, *The Proud Tower* (New York: Macmillan, 1966), p. 153.

4. Brock Chisholm, *Prescription for Survival* (New York: Columbia University Press, 1957), p. 54.

5. *Ibid.,* p. 9

6. Mark Twain, *The Innocents Abroad* (New York: The Thistle Press, 1962), p. 494.

7. Alan Moorehead, *The Fatal Impact* (New York: Harper & Row, 1966), pp. 61, 80–81.

8. Chisholm, *op. cit.,* pp. 55–56.

9. Neil Sheehan, "Anti-Americanism Grows in Vietnam," *The New York Times,* April 24, 1966, p. 3.

10. George Bernard Shaw, *Cashel Byron's Profession* (1886), Chapter 5.

11. George F. Kennan, "Supplemental Foreign Assistance Fiscal Year 1966—Vietnam," *Hearings Before the Committee on Foreign Relations,* United States Senate, 89th Congress, 2nd Session on S. 2793, Part I (Washington: U.S. Government Printing Office, 1966), p. 335.

12. George Bernard Shaw, *Getting Married* (1911).

13. *The New York Times Magazine,* July 11, 1965.

14. Edmund Burke, "On a Regicide Peace" (1796).

Chapter 1

1. Albert Camus, "Letters to a German Friend," Second Letter, December 1943, in *Resistance, Rebellion, and Death* (New York: Random House, 1960), p. 10.

2. First Letter, July 1943, *ibid.*, p. 4.

3. Michel Guillaume Jean de Crèvecoeur, "What Is an American," Letter III (1782) of *Letters from an American Farmer*.

4. A. T. Bartholomew, ed., *Further Extracts from the Notebooks of Samuel Butler* (London: Jonathan Cape, 1934), p. 120.

5. Louis Hartz, *The Liberal Tradition in America* (New York: Harcourt, Brace & World, 1955).

6. Alexis de Tocqueville, *Democracy in America*, (two vols., New York: Alfred A. Knopf, 1945), I, pp. 263, 265.

7. "Mission Over, a Controversial Visitor Departs," *The National Catholic Reporter*, August 18, 1965, p. 6.

8. *Ibid.*

9. Mark Twain, *Pudd'nhead Wilson and Those Extraordinary Twins* (New York: Harper and Brothers, 1899), p. 164.

10. Mark Twain, *Following the Equator* (two vols., Hartford: The American Publishing Company, 1899), I, p. 125.

11. Winston Churchill, "The International Situation," Speech in the House of Commons, December 14, 1950, in Randolph S. Churchill, ed., *In the Balance, Speeches 1949 and 1950 by Winston Churchill* (London: Cassell, 1951), p. 453.

12. Mark Twain, *The Mysterious Stranger* (New York: Harper and Brothers, 1922), pp. 119–120.

13. *The Collected Works of Abraham Lincoln* (nine vols., New Brunswick: Rutgers University Press, 1953), I, p. 432.

14. "The New Radicals," *The Johns Hopkins Magazine*, October 1965, pp. 10–11.

15. Quoted in "Protests in Perspective," *The New York Times*, October 24, 1965, p. 10E.

16. Archibald MacLeish, Address to the Congress of International Publishers Association, May 31, 1965.

Chapter 2

1. John Stuart Mill, *Considerations on Representative Government* (New York: Harper and Brothers, 1867), p. 116.

Notes

2. Theodore Sorensen, *Kennedy* (New York: Harper & Row, 1965), p. 702.

3. Speech to American Alumni Council at West Sulphur Springs, West Virginia, July 12, 1966.

4. William S. White, "Asian Doctrine," *The Washington Post,* July 19, 1966.

5. Thomas Jefferson, Letter to William Charles Jarvis, September 28, 1820.

6. "Comments on the Dominican Republic," *Congressional Record,* October 22, 1965, p. 27465.

7. Albert Camus, Second Letter, *loc. cit.*

Chapter 3

1. Letter to William Stevens Smith, November 13, 1787.

2. Crane Brinton, *The Anatomy of Revolution* (New York: Vintage, 1965).

3. Eric Hoffer, *The True Believer* (New York: Harper & Row, 1951).

4. Brinton, *op. cit.,* p. 146.

5. *Ibid.,* p. 234.

6. *Ibid.,* p. 157.

7. John C. Bennett, "From Supporter of War in 1941 to Critic in 1966," *Christianity and Crisis,* February 21, 1966, p. 14.

Chapter 4

1. Alberto Lleras Camargo, "The Price for the Intervention," *Vision,* June 24, 1966.

2. "Crisis Under the Palms," *The Washington Post,* June 27, 1965, p. E3.

3. C. K. McClatchy, "Cuban Dignity Has Soared," *The Washington Post,* September 26, 1965, p. E4.

4. Herbert L. Matthews, "Return to Cuba," *Hispanic-American Report* (Stanford University), p. 11.

5. Tad Szulc, *Latin America* (New York: Atheneum, 1966), p. 41.

Chapter 5

1. Bernard Fall, *The Two Vietnams* (revised edition; New York: Frederick A. Praeger, 1964), p. 90.

2. Hans Kohn, *The Idea of Nationalism. A Study in Its Origins and Background* (New York: Macmillan, 1944), p. 16.

3. Fall, *op. cit.*, p. 403.

4. Department of State, *Foreign Relations of the United States, 1944* (seven vols., Washington: U.S. Government Printing Office, 1965), 3, p. 773.

5. General Matthew B. Ridgway, U.S.A. (Ret.), *Soldier: The Memoirs of Matthew B. Ridgway* (New York: Harper & Brothers, 1956), p. 277.

6. Robert S. McNamara, *Hearings on Military Posture and HR 9637 To Authorize Appropriations During Fiscal Year 1965 Before the Committee on Armed Services*, House of Representatives, 88th Congress, 2nd Session (Washington: U.S. Government Printing Office), p. 6905.

Chapter 6

1. Quoted by Max Frankel, in "U.S. Ties Abroad Strained by War," *The New York Times*, August 11, 1966.

2. See Chapter 2, pp. 62–63.

3. Richard Lowenthal, "America's Asian Commitment," *Encounter*, October 1965, p. 58.

4. "Heavy Raids Mounted Against North Vietnam," *The Washington Post*, March 9, 1966, p. A14.

5. Mark Twain, *Europe and Elsewhere* (New York: Harper and Brothers, 1923), p. 398.

Chapter 7

1. Quoted in Han Suyin, *The Crippled Tree* (New York: Putnam's, 1965), p. 148.

2. Quoted in Ssu-Yu Teng and John K. Fairbank, eds., *China's Response to the West: A Documentary Survey, 1839–1923* (New York: Atheneum, 1965), p. 19.

3. John K. Fairbank, "U.S. Policy with Respect to Mainland China," in *Hearings, op. cit.*, p. 102.

4. Quoted in Teng and Fairbank, *op. cit.*, p. 25.

5. Han Suyin, *op. cit.*, p. 280.

6. *Ibid.*, p. 159.

7. Benjamin I. Schwartz, "U.S. Policy with Respect to Mainland China," in *Hearings, op. cit.*, pp. 184–185.

8. C. P. Fitzgerald, *The Chinese View of Their Place in the*

Notes

World (London: Oxford University Press, 1964), pp. 71–72.

9. John M. H. Lindbeck, "U.S. Policy with Respect to Mainland China," in *Hearings, op. cit.,* pp. 186–187.

10. Morton H. Halperin, *Ibid.,* p. 287.

11. "Debate in British House of Lords on Subject of China," reprinted in *Congressional Record,* March 8, 1966, p. 5046.

12. Edmund Burke, Second Speech on Conciliation with America.

Chapter 8

1. Gordon W. Allport, "The Role of Expectancy," in Hadley Cantril, ed., *Tensions That Cause Wars* (Urbana: University of Illinois Press, 1950), pp. 43, 48.

2. Muzafer Sherif *et al., Intergroup Conflict and Cooperation: The Robbers Cave Experiment* (Norman: University of Oklahoma Press, 1961).

3. Chisholm, *op. cit.,* p. 76.

4. Transcript of Press Conference of Secretary-General U Thant, held at United Nations Headquarters on January 20, 1966.

5. John K. Fairbank, "How to Deal with the Chinese Revolution," *New York Review of Books,* February 17, 1966, p. 14.

6. A. Doak Barnett, "U.S. Policy with Respect to Mainland China," in *Hearings, op. cit.,* pp. 4–5.

7. Fairbank, "How to Deal with the Chinese Revolution," *loc. cit.,* p. 16.

8. Erich Fromm, *The Art of Loving* (New York: Harper & Row, 1956), p. 20.

9. General Douglas MacArthur, "Can We Outlaw War?" *Reader's Digest,* May 1955, pp. 40–41.

Chapter 9

1. Donald S. Zagoria, "China's Crisis of Foreign Policy," *The New York Times Magazine,* May 1, 1966, p. 39.

2. Walter Lippmann, "Well, What Can He Do?" *The Washington Post,* January 25, 1966.

3. *The New York Times,* August 31, 1966.

4. *The New York Times,* September 2, 1966.

Chapter 10

1. J. W. Fulbright, *Old Myths and New Realities* (New York: Random House, 1964), p. 24.

2. Isaiah Frank, "East-West Trade," in *Hearings, op. cit.,* Part II, p. 135.

3. Raymond Aron, "The Spread of Nuclear Weapons," *Atlantic,* January 1965, p. 50.

4. John Kenneth Galbraith, "Foreign Policy and Passing Generations," speech at the Southeastern Pennsylvania Roosevelt Day Dinner of the Americans for Democratic Action, Philadelphia, Pennsylvania, January 30, 1965.

5. Address at Johns Hopkins University, September 1876.

Chapter 11

1. Norodom Sihanouk, "The Failure of the United States in the 'Third World'—Seen Through the Lesson of Cambodia," reprinted in *Congressional Record,* September 28, 1965, p. 24413.

2. Quoted by Harrison E. Salisbury in "Burma Chief Explains Neutrality," *The New York Times,* June 20, 1966, p. 1.

3. Quoted in *The New York Times,* September 3, 1965, p. 2.

4. John Duncan Powell, "Military Assistance and Militarism in Latin America," *Western Political Quarterly,* June 1965, pp. 382–392.

5. *Romeo and Juliet,* Act III, Scene 1.

6. Dean Rusk, "Supplemental Foreign Assistance Fiscal Year 1966—Vietnam," *Hearings, op. cit.,* p. 8.

7. Address by Secretary of State Dean Rusk, National Convention of National Rural Electric Cooperative Association, Las Vegas, Nevada, February 16, 1966.

8. Joseph Alsop, "Dividends on Vietnam Policy," *The Washington Post,* September 9, 1966, p. A23.

9. For a thoughtful discussion of possibilities for the development of an international fiscal system, see Dudley Seers, "International Aid: the Next Steps," *The Journal of Modern African Studies,* December 1964, pp. 471–489.

Conclusion

1. Archibald MacLeish, Address to the Congress of the International Publishers Association, May 31, 1965.

2. Finley Peter Dunne, *Mr. Dooley's Opinions* (1900), Thanksgiving.

3. Speech at Baltimore, Maryland, April 6, 1918.

4. John Quincy Adams, July 4, 1821, Washington, D.C. Reported in *The National Intelligencer,* July 11, 1821.

About the Author

J. WILLIAM FULBRIGHT, Democratic Senator from Arkansas, is Chairman of the Senate Foreign Relations Committee. He was first elected to Congress in 1942 and became a member of the House Foreign Affairs Committee, where he introduced the "Fulbright Resolution," calling for the participation by the United States in an international organization to maintain peace and generally considered the forerunner to the establishment of the United Nations.

Senator Fulbright is now serving his fourth term in the Senate. In 1946 he sponsored the international educational exchange program that bears his name. In 1954 Senator Fulbright was the one member of the Senate to vote against additional funds for the Special Investigating Subcommittee headed by the late Senator Joseph McCarthy, and was a co-sponsor of the censure resolution passed by the Senate against Senator McCarthy. During the same year he was appointed by the President as a member of the United States Delegation to the General Assembly of the United Nations.

In 1966, in addition to its normal legislative functions, the Senate Foreign Relations Committee conducted an extensive inquiry into American policy in Vietnam, America's relations with China, and America's relations with her North Atlantic allies.

In the spring of 1966 Senator Fulbright delivered the Christian A. Herter Lectures at the Johns Hopkins University School of Advanced International Studies. Many of the ideas and proposals developed in this book were first put forth by Senator Fulbright in those lectures.

Senator Fulbright's home is in Fayetteville, Arkansas. He is married to the former Elizabeth Kramer Williams.

CPSIA information can be obtained at www.ICGtesting.com
Printed in the USA
241511LV00001B/198/A